I0166811

PETER CLOTHIER

DEAR HARRY

Letters to My Father

Copyright © 2022 by Peter Clothier
All rights reserved.

No part of this publication may be reproduced in whole or in
part, or stored in a retrieval system, or transmitted in any form or
by any means, electronic, mechanical, photocopying, recording,
or otherwise, without written permission of the author, except
for the inclusion of brief quotations in a review.
For information regarding permission, please write to:
info@barringerpublishing.com

Barringer Publishing, Naples, Florida
www.barringerpublishing.com

Design and layout by Linda S. Duider

ISBN: 978-1-954396-29-6
Library of Congress Cataloging-in-Publication Data
Dear Harry: Letters to My Father / Peter Clothier

Printed in U.S.A.

For my grandchildren,
Harry's great-grandchildren,
Alice, Georgia, Joe & Luka

In memory of

The Rev. Canon Harry L. Clothier

With love.

PREFACE

This is the book I have been trying to write for my whole life. I have attempted it several times before. It's there, in a nutshell, in *Aspley Guise*, the first book of poems I published more than fifty years ago. It's there in a "novel" I wrote and titled simply *M*—and never published. It's there in a memoir I called *Sticks & Stones*. It's there, in part, in a memoir I did publish, *While I Am Not Afraid*.

But every one of these efforts left me feeling that much of what I'd wanted to say was left unsaid. They felt too personal, somehow, to be shared. I was always looking for a way to say these things, and never found it to my satisfaction until I stumbled into the idea of writing it all in the form of "letters to my father." The medium allowed me to be as intimate as I wanted to be, but with my father serving as a kind of buffer between writer and reader.

I started out with the idea that I wanted to know my father, who had always seemed to be beyond my reach—ironically until after he was dead. But it was not long before I came to understand that what I also wanted was for *him* to know *me*.

Dear Harry exists as a book because I think I share this longing with almost everyone who ever had a father. I have worked for many years with men and know that many of them, countless really, have suffered in their lives because of absent fathers, fathers addicted to drink, or work, or women, fathers who died young, fathers unable or unwilling to show the love they might have felt. Even those well-intentioned fathers who simply seemed distant or remote to children who needed nothing more than a word of approval or a hug.

I say "men" because I have worked most intimately with them. But I believe it is no different for women with their fathers. And I do believe that there's a cultural shift taking place that suggests that men are changing. They are becoming more easily attuned to their own feelings and therefore better fathers, more able to deal with the intimacy that good fatherhood requires.

My hope is that *Dear Harry* will be more than a memoir, more than a matter of one man's experience, one man's search; that it will invite fathers and children both to search more deeply in their hearts and become still better fathers to their children and still better children to their fathers.

Which would make, perhaps, for a better world at a time when that better world is sorely needed by us all.

Peter Clothier

1 July 2021

Dear Harry,

I have decided to call you by your first name, even though I'll admit it still feels awkward to me. I would never have presumed to do so while you were still alive. But now that I am approaching the age that you were when you left this world, I'd like to think I have earned that right and hope to be forgiven if you disagree.

For most of my early life, of course, I called you Daddy. We did not abbreviate the word to "Dad" when I was growing up, as is commonly the case over here in America. It was always Daddy. My mother, "Mummy," Peggy, an inveterate hoarder of family memorabilia, saved some of the letters I had to write to you from school (I say "had to" because they used to sit us down every Sunday morning and require us to fulfill this filial obligation). All those letters start out, in big, uneven, childish letters, with the words "Dear Mummy and Daddy." Most of them, those from my younger years, continue with stock phrases like "I am well. How are you?"

I think I was uncomfortable with "Daddy" even as a teenager, but certainly by the time I was a young adult and university student, I was embarrassed by the childish sound of it. Still, it was a while before I managed to make the transition to the more formal—too formal?—"Father," which I always found easier to write than to use in person. I also wanted to distinguish myself from the many people, especially among your high church friends and congregants who called you "Father" because that was your profession. I have a distant memory, too, that you liked "Padre" from at least one senior military officer, in the war years . . .

But now it's Harry. It will be Harry from here on. That puts us on a more equal footing, and at my age I think I've earned the right.

Anyway, I have been feeling the desire for reconnection, or rather a connection that we never quite had. It distresses me to feel that I never knew you properly, my own father, and I'm hoping now—so late in life!—to get to know you better by picking through old clues that in my self-absorption as a child and a young man I never bothered to register or recognize—clues that might have helped me know you for the man you were.

So, consider this the start.

With fond regards from your son,
Peter

2 July 2021

Dear Harry,

It also has to do with love.

If memory serves me well, this word was not much used in our family. Well, never, really. "My father never told me that he loved me." I heard this complaint from many wounded, maladjusted men in my later years—more of this in good time—and have to say that for a long time, I judged those words to be a bit of a whine. Alright, a major whine. But I've come to understand that they are in fact important to both say and hear.

We may have thought it superfluous to say them out loud, that it sufficed among our family members to take the fact for granted. We all loved each other, didn't we? Daddy and Mummy and my sister Flora and myself? We may have surrendered to old English inhibitions and conventional embarrassment, in the belief that matters of the heart were of little importance and better left unspoken. That, at least, was my impression.

But did we, Harry? Did we love each other? Really? Did you love me? Did I love you? These are questions to which I long to know the answer.

Your son,
Peter

3 July 2021

Dear Harry,

You are all gone now, my whole family—you and Peggy nearly thirty years ago—and not far apart. Flora, too, though her death was more recent. She died too soon, at eighty. You did not live to mourn her death. Which is just as well, because we all knew that she was the proverbial "apple of your eye"— ever since she was a little girl. It was something she found hard to believe; and when she did, all too often felt oppressed by it.

Once she grew up, you and Flora had a problematic, sometimes painful relationship. No one could hurt her as deeply as you could. I know because she told me so, and when the time feels right I'll pass along the context. Similarly, no one could hurt you as deeply as she could.

I was more on the other side, my mother's boy—blue eyes, like hers. Flora's were brown, like yours.

But that's how it often is, isn't it? Fathers and daughters, mothers and sons.

And now, for a growing number of years, I am the sole survivor of the four of us. I do miss you, really. Now more than ever. Miss you all . . .

Your son,
Peter

4 July 2021
Independence Day!

Dear Harry,

The truth is you were a mystery to me. An enigma. Who were you? Where did you come from?

I know this much: your father, my grandfather, H. W. Clothier, was a prominent electrical engineer in the early days of electricity. Among his other notable achievements, he invented something called oil immersion switchgear—don't ask!—allowing manufacturers to safely harness high voltage power for industrial purposes. A handful of studio portraits and less formal snapshots in the great tome Peggy called the "family album" show a thoughtful, elegant gentleman with a bushy, neatly-trimmed mustache and dark, twinkling eyes. I think to see a benign sense of humor in the soft gleam of those eyes and the gentle curve of his lips.

Your mother, my biological grandmother and your father's first wife, died when you were only thirteen or fourteen years old. It was around the time of the last great global pandemic, the 1918 Spanish flu, and I wonder if that disease might be what took her life at so young an age? I read that 22 percent of Newcastle's population were infected, and that over a thousand of the city's residents died. The rest of the Clothier family survived: your father, your older sister, Nancy, your younger brothers, Donald and Neil and you yourself, of course. But I'd be curious to know if you have memories of that time of mortal danger. Did you wear masks, as we have learned to do today, with our new pandemic? Observe social distancing?

We never spoke about your mother's death, but it must have left a deep wound in your heart. I did come to understand—did my own mother tell me this?—that your father's grief left you in some way responsible, along with your older sister, Nancy, for the care of your two younger brothers. The grandmother I knew, Granny Murcott, became a part of the family when your father remarried after a respectable period of mourning.

Then your father himself died young. He died of a heart attack I believe, on a business trip to New Zealand, when I was just one and a half years old. The way I calculate it—my mother was thirty years older to the day than I, and you were a year older than she—you would have been thirty-two or thirty-three years old. Which is still a young age to lose your father. I was nearly sixty when you died . . . Though Granny Murcott lived on for a while in Aspley Guise, the village where we lived when I was very young, I believe you were never really close with your stepmother. She died when I was about five years old.

From what I know about the loss of parents at an early age, I'm sure that this history must have affected you in ways I would have wanted to know, but never did. You never talked about it, at least not with your children. Perhaps you thought it inappropriate. Still, thinking back on it today, it would surely help me to unwrap the enigma to which your silence on the subject left me heir.

I think I might have been able to love you more, had I known more about the source of your vulnerabilities.

Affectionately, anyway, your son,
Peter

5 July 2021

Dear Harry,

Today, when I took our dog, Jake, out at seven o'clock this morning for his regular pee-and-poop walk, the air was still heavy with lingering smoke from last night's July Fourth extravaganza, and the smell of spent gunpowder was still pervasive in the misty light of the early California morning. Even at this hour, long after the celebrations, I could still hear the pop and fizz and boom of the occasional stray firework.

In the England of my childhood, as you will well recall, fireworks meant Guy Fawkes Day. *Remember, remember, the fifth of November, gunpowder, treason and plot . . .* went that old piece of doggerel. It was not "trick or treat" we children pleaded during the annual parading of the Guy Fawkes effigy, but "a penny for the Guy." Then, after dark, there was the lighting of the bonfire where he'd be burned at the stake each year in a revival of that old ritual. Amidst the sparks and smoke from the fire on those damp, misty November nights—it clung to our clothes for days—the fireworks were the crowning moment for the cheering crowds.

Sadly, Harry, this was not a celebration we could share, you and me. In November of course, at least from the age of seven, I was always away at school.

I wonder if you missed your son, back at home, on those nights of revelry.

These thoughts occurred to me as I gazed out over the city of Hollywood last night—Hollywood, imagine! I have lived here, improbably, for more than half my life, so far in time and space from the fireworks of my youth and with you gone already, these now nearly thirty years. And I found myself reflecting, not for the first time, how strange it seemed to have ended up so far from where I started.

July Fourth is the day when we Americans—yes, I am one now!—celebrate their independence from the country where you and I grew up. Is it my imagination that this year's celebration, now in the second decade of the 21st century, had an anxious, edgy, almost desperate feel to it? The rumble of exploding fireworks started earlier than usual, I thought, and continued longer—even, as I noted, until this morning. It also seemed more chaotic. While neighboring trees obscured our view to the south, where most of the action seemed to be taking place, the distant flashes and occasional nearby bursts of brilliant, multicolored lights were ubiquitous, ceaseless, relentless. It was as though the city were bent on asserting the freedom of Americans, come what may—and despite the current pandemic and the dire, unprecedented political threats against the very freedoms that were being celebrated.

Well, Harry, as I suggested, that's likely all in my own head. The truth is—I can share this with you, my own father, no? I no longer feel quite so at home in my adoptive country. I find myself longing for what I used to scorn: the social proprieties, the civility, the intimacy, and—yes, even during the war years—the safety of that English country village, the one where you were Rector and I, a small boy, was the Rector's son.

Affectionately,
Peter

6 July 2021

Dear Harry,

Did you feel it too? Did you regret it? That we were never close? Not really, were we? Would you, as I do, have wished it otherwise? Or was it just how things were "done"—to keep a safe distance between father and son?

(I have just started reading into a stack of letters from England, long buried away in storage here in Los Angeles and have begun to realize how much you felt the same regret . . .)

These thoughts occurred to me as I was writing in a previous letter about the early loss of your mother and trying to imagine how your father might have felt. You too, of course. I'm thinking that a mother's death left you with no one to model closeness. Perhaps the absence of that kind of closeness—the physical kind, the hugs, the kisses—was just the ethos of the English upper middle classes of your generation, a hangover from Victorian days with their strict, uptight adherence to propriety.

I well remember the first time I brought Ellie over to visit, that Christmas—this would have been in 1970 or 1971—and I gave you a big hug when you came to meet us at the train station. You made a point of saying, often, and telling your friends at the pub, how much it meant to you. Sadly, though, it was not from you I learned this simple act of intimacy but from Ellie's father, Michael, who first surprised me (even, at first, embarrassed me a little) with the big hug that I soon came to expect every time we got together. For Mike, it was a matter of course.

You and I, Harry, used to shake hands like proper Englishmen, grown man and boy, father and son! It's hard to believe it now, so long after learning to be comfortable with hugs from other men, but we would shake hands even when I was a little boy and you took me to the station and saw me onto the train that would take me off to school for months on end. And then when I got back home we would shake hands, hello, again . . .

Well, I promise I'd give you a big hug now, too, if that were possible. Maybe even a kiss on the cheek! How that would surprise you!

Your son,
Peter

7 July 2021

Good morning, Harry!

For some reason, I woke in the middle of the night last night thinking about your hands. They were fine hands, strong, supple, skillful, and they were prominent in so many of the daily actions of your life.

I think of your hands at the Rectory dining room, where you took such pride in your carving skills, reducing a beef or pork roast to precise, thin slices (this was wartime, there was meat rationing!) to be passed around the always crowded table or expertly separating the wings, legs and thighs of a bird— chicken, goose, or duck, or turkey, whatever the local butcher could provide at Christmas time during the war. As well, you sliced the breast on either side with same similar precision for an admiring audience of house guests. It was the kind of performance that you loved.

I think, too, of your right hand sketching the sign of the cross over the food as you intoned the words of our family grace: *Bless, O Lord, this food to our use and us to Thy service, for Christ's sake, Amen.*

I think of your hands in the workshop where you practiced the carpentry skills you had learned, at your father's insistence, as a pattern-maker's apprentice as a young man. Those hands could turn plain blocks of wood, like magic, into the toys you made for myself and Flora every Christmas: a big red train that was strong enough for me to actually sit astride and drive; an airfield, complete with hangers whose doors slid open, a miniature windsock, a fleet of Hurricanes and Spitfires, a walk-in doll's house for Flora and, when she was older, a kidney-shaped dressing table she could actually use. I used to watch in wonder as your hands created—not these things, because they were made in secret; the workshop was strictly out of bounds to us in the days before Christmas—but many other objects that we used around the house.

In your later years, you mastered the lathe and used the wood from a fallen walnut tree in the Vicarage garden to create bowls, vases, candlesticks, and salt- and pepper-mills. Your hands became the hands not merely of a craftsman, but an artist.

I think of your hands resting on the stick shift and the steering wheel of your car. Your favorite of them all, I think, was the long, sleek, elegant Armstrong Siddley coupé with its "pre-selection" gear system, an early forerunner of today's automatic. You were an expert driver, proud of that expertise—another "performance" now that I come to think of it. When you taught me to drive, remember—I was seventeen years old—you had me relax the tension in my own hands, white-knuckled, grasping the wheel too tightly in the ten-to, ten-past position you insisted on.

I think of your hands perhaps most vividly and with such profound resonance in church. I see them in the vestry as you robe, ready for the service, or disrobe afterwards at the altar—I was an altar boy—as I passed you the bread and wine for consecration; as you turned to the congregation and etched a blessing with that familiar, practiced sign of the cross; as you offered communicants, in turn, a white wafer from the silver paten and a sip of wine from the chalice at the altar rail. My mother would bring Flora and myself to the communion rail and you would pause along your way to give us, instead of the eucharist, your blessing.

Still today, I *feel* your hand on my head and, though I have forgotten them, hear the murmur of the words you spoke above me.

It was those moments that I remembered many years later when you lay dying in that bleak hospital ward in Cardigan, and I was moved to ask for your blessing—even though I had long since abandoned belief in your religion. I bowed my head at your bedside and took your frail hand in mine to bring it to rest on the top of my head, only to realize that I had overtaxed the recall power of your mind. I saw you searching for the lost words with a kind of desperation, eyes darting hopelessly this way and that, as though they might be written somewhere near; but no, you could no longer find them.

But I received your blessing anyway, without them.

> With loving memories from
> your son,
> Peter

8 July 2021

Dear Harry,

It is a bit irreverent, I know, to ask this—impertinent, even. But speaking of hands, I wonder if they were strong, and firm, and tender, when they touched my mother in the act of love? For all their skill, I do not myself remember them as loving hands. Not for me. I hope they were for her. I hope you treasured the touch of that smooth, warm skin I still recall beneath the silken transparency of her nightgown—should I even be saying this?—when I was allowed, as a very little boy, to clamber into the bed beside her in the morning?

And while we're on the subject, I recall your having said once, à propos of I know not what—because this still surprises me; why would you tell me such a thing?—that you were never interested in masturbation. So, Harry, truth: did you never touch yourself? Did you never experience the subtle pleasures of what your generation, judgmentally, disparaged as "self-abuse"?

As a boy, I recall being forbidden this delightfully sinful act. By you? I hope not! But indulging in it, sinfully, anyway. You might say obsessively. On every possible occasion.

You might say—I say, Harry!—that it's natural.

As a grandfather several times over myself now, I watch as even my newest grandson Luka, nine years old, is scarcely able to keep his hands away from that delightful toy. As a man in circles of mutually supportive men, I would watch in later life as almost every hand was raised when the question came up: how many of you jerk off? (I apologize for the crude language, Harry, Father, Padre, but these are the words we use . . .)

So, here's my question: were you being really honest when you said you never did? And why did you feel the need to tell me? Could it be that it was out of a sense of guilt? Come on, now, did your hand never stray between the black folds of your cassock—perhaps even at lonely moments in the vestry—or through the gap in your pajamas and seek out that irresistible source of masculine delight? Were your fingers really never curious enough to explore its size, its heft, the sense of urgency it generates? Did you really never pump away, as most men do, in the effort to reach that moment of quiet, solitary ecstasy?

They say the devil finds work . . .

But as I say, this is an impertinent question of a father from his son, so let's agree to leave it unasked. Or at least unanswered.

With due respect, your son,
Peter

9 July 2021

Dear Harry,

Yes! Hands! How could I have missed this?

You were a great believer in the "laying on of hands." You believed that hands had the capacity to heal disorders of all kinds, simply by being laid by the practitioner on the head of the person suffering, along with a prayer for recovery.

You were yourself a healer, you saw this as a part of your function as a minister of the gospel. The practice derives, surely, from the New Testament, with its numerous examples of Christ healing the sick.

You believed in miracles.

Well, you certainly believed in non-traditional forms of healing, witness the story of the warts. I was perhaps seven or eight years old. The first one, and eventually the largest, appeared on the heel of my left thumb. Then others started growing up the thumb, in descending order of size, towards the tip. Eventually there were, as I recall, about twelve or thirteen of them.

So, you took me to a wart charmer, the local blacksmith. The man had already managed to charm away a wart that was growing on the head of Hank, our border collie (we'll talk about him some more, one day soon). You drove me over to the smithy and we found the man in his scorched leather apron, busy at the bellows and the furnace, a red-hot horseshoe grasped in the long tongs. He was a huge man, swarthy, grimy, sweaty, and he towered over me. You placed a shilling in the hairy paw that was his hand, and he paused in his work for long enough to look at my thumb and reach down to run his finger over the hard little knots of growth.

"How many are there?" he asked. (Would you remember this?) I told him there were twelve. "Well, then," he said, "I expect they'll be gone in a couple of weeks."

They weren't. They were still there. Always one to expect your money's worth, you took me back to the smithy to complain. The blacksmith was puzzled, too. "How many, did you say?" he asked. I re-counted. There were thirteen, not twelve. Perhaps one had been hiding under the skin, ready to pop up to the surface like a knotty mushroom. "Ah, well," he said. "That's better. Now they'll be gone. You'll see."

And two weeks later, they were gone.

As miracles go, this was a minor one. The cures that you performed for your parishioners were long-term, and much less dramatic. They involved not just the hands—though these were always somehow instrumental—but your compassionate and always deepening understanding of human nature, backed up by what you had learned at university from your study of the new science expounded by Dr. Jung and Dr. Freud. You were fond of the term "psychosomatic," and resorted to it reliably every time we children—and everyone else, for that matter—had some physical complaint. You even had associative meanings for each finger on the hand. An injury to the thumb, I remember, implied a conflict with authority, the forefinger, guilt. And so on.

I do know that you helped people with all kinds of ailments, physical and psychological. The exception, if the echo of a distant memory serves me well, was a strange, young woman named Winnie. Pale, and with a stringy head of tangled, dark hair, Winnie was extraordinarily deft with her fingers. She used to make marvelous little dioramas for myself and Flora, magical landscapes with elfin figures fashioned out of tissue paper. No matter that you befriended this lonely soul and became her spiritual guide, you were unable to save her from the disease that left her visibly wasting away, becoming thinner and thinner, more and more emaciated, until she simply died. I don't know whether there was a name for the disease back then, or if you knew it. Today we call it anorexia.

Did she go to heaven? In those days, this is what you encouraged us children to believe would happen to good people when they died. I'm not convinced you managed to convince yourself. I do know—we'll talk about this later, Harry—how reluctant you were to leave this world when your time came.

There was one other exception to those you could do nothing to help: for all your empathy for those who suffered from illness or disease, for all your belief that the sick were not healed by medicine alone, you were never able to alleviate your own debility, the stomach pains from which you suffered so terribly throughout my childhood years. That old adage, "physician, heal thyself" could not have been more apposite. To my knowledge—and it could surely be deficient—you never interpreted that inner, physical turmoil in the same emotional terms you applied so readily to others.

Perhaps you did and I simply never knew. But it seems so obvious as I look back on it that the "ulcer" that tortured you and was so much a part of all our lives was a manifestation of your struggle with God, with faith, and the very real conflict between the persistent intellectual doubt of a fully human, humanistic man and the religious conviction that, as a minister, you were required to preach and model for those you asked to place their trust in you . . .

More on this later, though. Enough for this one day.

With love,
Peter

11 July 2021

Dear Harry,

About your ulcer, then. It's a painful story, one that colored most of my young years and left a consequential mark on the direction of my life.

You had persistent health problems throughout your life. It was at your doctor's insistence that our family originally moved south from Newcastle and the polluted air of the coal-mining city of my birth. Your first parish in the midlands was Aspley Guise, in Bedfordshire, not far from the county seat of Bedford. Except for the first year-and-a-half, we lived there for all my pre-teen years. Later, in the years leading up to and during your retirement, you suffered later from debilitating headaches, skin problems, bronchitis, and depression. By the end of your life, the pulmonary problems caused by a lifelong addiction to cigarettes had come back to haunt you.

But in Aspley Guise, it was the stomach pains that plagued you. We lived with them constantly as a family. We children, Flora and me, always knew to tiptoe around the pain, to do nothing, ever, that might upset you and make it worse. Our mother, Peggy, was forever on the alert.

You were always thin, skinny, emaciated almost. But you ate well. You ate heartily. Were you aware that your cigarettes contributed significantly to the acids that churned inside your belly? Even in those days they were jokingly called "coffin nails" by the men on the front lines who smoked them. But even if you knew the risks, you chose to remain in denial, as we say today, and made no serious effort to quit. It was only in your eighties, at the end of your life, living with my ailing mother in that small cottage in Wales, that you finally gave up the lifelong habit. Your beloved Peggy was suffering from chronic bronchial problems and the doctor put it to you unambiguously: the polluted air in the confined space was killing her. So, you quit. Cold turkey. Overnight. And never smoked another cigarette.

You did try everything to heal the stomach pains. You tried diets and pills of all kinds. You even resorted to psychotherapy with a practitioner who succeeded only in torturing you further. (Talk about practicing what you preached!) I remember you even went once on a long, expensive trip to Switzerland, where you'd heard of a Docteur Jeanneret who performed miracles with people suffering from precisely your kind of stomach problems. You took time away from your parish to make the pilgrimage to his consulting office and returned with boxes of enormous pills called—yes, I remember to this day—called *"les poudres de coq"* (literally, "cock powders"; the feathered kind, I hasten to add, for propriety's sake). I quite distinctly remember the image on the outside of the little red box, the silhouette of a raised hammer about to knock a wedge into a human head. The text read *"Enfoncez-vous ça dans la tête"*— ram *that* into your skull.

To the best of my recollection, even these monstrous pills had no effect.

On a more serious note, though, I have often wondered if it was not your pain that led to the decision to send me off away from home at such an early age. I have often told people, perhaps erroneously, that I was only six years old, but I think I was more likely seven when I was sent away to boarding school. We had a serious family talk and I was given a "choice" (I put the word in quotes because, in retrospect, it really wasn't one): I could either attend the nearest elementary school with all the local children (read, truthfully, lower social class); or, at great financial sacrifice on my parents' part, I could choose to go off to "prep school"—a private boarding school for younger boys and the start of a first-class educational path more suited, if you read between the lines, to young men of higher social standing.

So, I "chose" the latter. What else could I do?

As I told you later in life—and I remember how you expressed some hurt at my ingratitude—I was never happy at the schools you sent me to. And yes, truthfully, I have often wondered if it was really for the great educational opportunity you sent me there? Or was it rather, as I have suspected, to spare yourself the burden of having small children around the house, in addition to the pain you had to live with? (Flora, if I remember right, was spared for another couple of years; she, too, went off to boarding school at a very early age; and she, too, was a long, long time recovering from the experience. Perhaps—I have harbored this suspicion too—you were loath to share the attention you needed from our mother.

Well, Harry, as they say, that's water under the bridge. Right? I did receive an excellent education in all the right academic ways. But I also lost something that I needed as a child: that close connection with family, with warmth, with love. It was to be half a lifetime before I began to recognize the wound, let alone heal from its effects.

I'll be sure to tell you how that happened. In the meantime, though, I must add a few more thoughts about that pain of yours and promise to follow up in another letter. For now, let it be enough to assure you of my love and send sincere wishes for the healing that we need.

Your son,
Peter

12 July 2021

My dear Harry,

Yes, your pain. I promised more. There's another story.

This happened years later. In fact, it happened only after you died.

I've had this pain in the gut myself for many years. I remember first consulting a doctor about it back in the early 1970s, when I was still teaching in the Comparative Literature department at the University of Southern California. Perhaps 1972, 1973? Around then.

The pain is a sharp one, intermittent, but nasty when it happens. It occurs on the left side, toward the center, right beneath the lowest ribs. I can always feel it when I push my fingers in and up, applying pressure. I've sought medical opinion on numerous occasions, but have never received a convincing diagnosis, let alone relief. It still bothers me sometimes today, though I will say with less frequency than it used to. If I focus my attention on that particular spot, I can feel it there at almost any moment, but most of the time it just goes unnoticed.

Well, here's the story. I don't recall what took me to Ed Cohen's home clinic in the first place, but what he offered was a very deep tissue massage, something much like the rolfing that was pioneered at the Esalen Institute in its early days, releasing emotional and psychic as well as physical pain. Ed was good at it. He had strong, probing hands and knew how and where to use them to effect. Before coming to him, I had learned the benefits of what I would call trance work, for want of a better word—suspending normal brain activity in order to go deep inside and activate the unconscious mind. Knowing your fascination with the workings of the human mind, I'm sure this is something you would appreciate. Even though I suspect it was not something you ever experienced, Ed's work created an ideal space for this to happen. I know you would have relished the chance to spend time on his massage table.

So, there I was on this one occasion, stretched out face up on that table, having alerted Ed to that recurring pain beneath my ribs. He worked the spot intensely—and, yes, painfully!—his voice inviting me to experience the pain to the fullest and allow it to "speak" to me directly. And as he continued to apply pressure I heard the words materializing from my own throat, aloud, arising spontaneously, clearly, without my having formulated the idea in any conscious way: "This is not my pain," I said.

There followed a silence in which I listened to the resonance of those words.

"It's not your pain." I heard Ed's voice, repeating what I'd said. More silence, longer this time, while he continued with his work.

Then: "Whose pain is this, then?" he asked.

The answer came, again spontaneously: "My father's pain." I spoke the words with utter clarity. "This is my father's pain."

Odd, no, Harry? It made immediate, intuitive sense to me that I had been carrying your pain around with me for all those years. It seemed self-evident.

Was Ed's stimulation or the source of my pain a cure? For a while, I imagined that it might be, and for a while it seemed it was. The pain disappeared. But later it began to reassert itself, familiar as ever, and it still pokes at the inside of my ribs from time to time, reminding me that it has never completely gone away. In fact, right now, at this very moment, it is back with me as I write these words—perhaps because they have brought it back to consciousness. I have taken this same pain to other medical professionals since the experience with Ed. I have had hands-on physical examinations, x-rays, scans, but none of them has resulted in a diagnosis. There is no apparent cause for it, no medical problem doctors can identify. It remains a mystery.

I still think of it as "my father's pain": Harry—*your* pain. If that's what it is, the wound is very deep, impossible to root out. I think it will be with me until I follow you in death.

I'm sure you'll agree with both my diagnosis and prognosis. They would probably be yours, too, even given the passage of so many years. Psychosomatic, that's the word. And even so, Harry . . . It is odd. No?

So much for today, then.
With love,
Peter

13 July 2021

Dear Harry,

This one is hard to write. I have been giving further thought to the decision for me to go to boarding school—a decision that was, let's be honest, Harry, not really mine to make. I was seven years old, for God's sake. How could I be responsible for such a choice?

I can't believe that you didn't know how painful it was to be sent away from home at so young an age. I don't know if you were sent off to prep school at that age, like I was, because there's a years-long gap in my knowledge of your early history, before your mother's death. Were you spared that, at least? Did you remain at home with your parents and siblings until you went to Shrewsbury, one of the grand old English public— read "private"—schools up in Shropshire? You rarely spoke of your time there, but I well remember the pride with which you sported your old school tie. It was your favorite, with its broad diagonal stripes in gold, brown, and dark blue, and you almost always wore it with a tweed jacket or a blazer when you were in mufti, without your clerical dog collar and cassock.

And perhaps your experience at all-boys boarding school was different from mine. I believe you were already quite the sportsman and that would have helped. You rowed for your college eight at Cambridge; did you learn that sport at school?

A strong swimmer, you played water polo. In any event, the pride with which you wore that school tie suggests that your time at Shrewsbury was a memory you treasured, and in later life you certainly projected the social self-assurance of the public-school boy. Even your socialist views were informed by that hugely privileged education.

But here's what I really want to know, even though I realize that I never will: did you experience none of those adolescent agonies that I did, years later, at my own public school? Were you tougher skinned than I was, better able to absorb those slings and arrows? Did you ever realize how isolated I felt, how out of place? I was a total duffer at sports. I had trouble simply spotting the location of a ball in space. I became a passably good cross-country runner because running is a mug's game; anyone can do it with enough practice. I ran because it took less time than every other sport; I could be done with it quickly, in and out of the showers (I also suffered from intense body shame) before the other boys. Then I would wander off to some quiet corner behind a building or a hedge, where I could exercise my right to rebel by jerking off in solitude or smoking a forbidden cigarette.

In other respects, I was a fairly normal teenager—gawky, emotionally volatile and in need of reassurance as I struggled to understand and come to terms with those disturbing sexual urges that demanded response and preoccupied my adolescent mind. Like many others at this age, I struggled for years with acne. And I assume like every normal teenager, I fell in love. It happened that the only people around with whom I could fall in love were other boys, so as a younger boy, in my first years at

Lancing, I fell in love with older boys; as a senior, I fell in love with juniors. That's just how it was.

Did you know this? Would it have bothered you? Did you have no idea, when you sent me off, what boarding school had in store for me? And, Harry, did you experience none of this yourself? Was everyone around you at Shrewsbury immune to adolescent turmoil and sexual needs? That couldn't be!

One thing I know: I am not alone with the wounds I carried around with me for much of my adult life. Years later, I came across Boarding School Survivors, an organization dedicated to helping men and women to recover from the experience of childhood separation from the family. The need was obvious, Harry. I had learned by then to recognize the persistence of those early wounds. They play out not only in the inner life of individuals but also sometimes in the public arena, and at great cost. You can see their consequences in the actions of men of power and influence, in social and political, military, and corporate leaders, inheritors of the once world-dominant British Empire that crumbled so rapidly after the Second World War. I have only to look at England's current prime minister, the bullying, chest-puffing, bloviating Boris Johnson, an Old Etonian like so many of his predecessors in that office, to recognize the lasting effects of the British boys' boarding schools. These walking wounded take a long time to grow up, as I did. And many never do.

So that's how it is, Harry, Father, Daddy. This is what continues to perplex me as I look back to my childhood. How could you not have known? What really persuaded you to put your son (your daughter, too; ask Flora!) through twelve years of . . . well, hell is hardly too strong a word for it. I like to think that I'm past whining about all this now, at the age of eighty-five. But that's quite simply how it was.

Your son,
Peter

14 July 2021
(Le quatorze juillet)

Dear Harry,

Here's what I want: I want nothing more from you than to tell me who you are. I am writing the words, of course, but I do so, hoping they'll open a magic door and allow you finally to show yourself.

Think of these letters as an investigation of my childhood, a way for me to sift through the clues you left me. Then, perhaps you could not help but tell me exactly who you were in every gesture, every action, every word, every glance you cast in my direction. It was just that I didn't know enough as a child to catch what you were trying to tell me. I'm guessing that you didn't even know yourself. So, the task I've set myself is to go back over it all, as best I can, every tiny detail, in the attempt to recapture what I failed to grasp at the time.

I wrote an essay about this kind of thing once. I titled it "Tell Me Who You Are." The essay was an attempt to explain to myself, and convey to others, what it was I was looking for when I stepped into an art gallery in my professional capacity as a critic for national magazines. And this was the best I could come up with: Tell me who you are. Whatever talent I had as an art critic was perhaps also my greatest flaw. It was the wish to *listen* and *hear* what the artist had to tell me, specifically about himself, or herself. Substitute those words for *look* and *see* and you'll get a sense of what I mean. I tried to absorb the intensity of the personal communication in what I was looking at and give it words. I thought of myself as a translator rather than an opinion-maker. A "real" art critic, to my way of thinking, applied qualitative standards, judged what he saw and offered an evaluation—"good" or "bad" or anything in between—to share with others and to guide their views.

I have come to think this way about all creative work, including my own work as a writer. I see art—and writing—as a way to share with others the experience of being human among other human beings in the world, and a way to learn from others how to be fully human myself.

It's not necessarily "telling" in the usual sense of the word, though it can be that. The kind of telling I'm talking about is the telling that happens casually, continually, as though by accident, in a simple unthought gesture, a movement of the body, a word, or words, put out into the world without any intention.

So, I hope this will explain a little of what I'm trying to accomplish in these letters that I'm sending. There's no particular order, no chronology, no progression. There is just a growing understanding, an expanding consciousness, if you will, about the mystery of the man who gave me life.

Your son,
Peter

PS: I first signed this letter with a typo: "Your sin" rather than "Your son"! I can be sure you'd get a good chuckle out of the Freudian slip!

15 July 2021

Dear Harry,

The typo I caught in my last letter ("sin" for "son"!) reminds me of a couple of your own gaffes that caused us both to laugh out loud about when I was still a boy.

Can I remind you?

The first must have happened when I was about twelve years old—old enough to know something of your history and clever enough to be able to appreciate the subtleties involved. You had been reading from the Bible—perhaps the text was the Epistle of the day—in the chancel of St. Botolph's church in Aspley Guise where you were Rector. You were an impressive figure, standing behind the imposing golden lectern that carried the weight of that enormous book on the wings of an eagle about to take flight. The sonorous tenor of your voice, so much loved by your congregation, still echoes in my mind as I recall this occasion, when the actor you had once aspired to be popped up from ancient history and turned to the congregation, your "audience," instead of the altar, and bowed deeply to them, seemingly more in expectation of the applause you deserved for your performance than in reverence for the sacred words you had just read.

Do you remember this? Sitting in the Rector's pew beside my mother and my sister, I somehow caught your eye in one of those familiar moments of I-know-you-know-I know which degenerated, on my part, into barely suppressed giggles and, on yours, into a quick turn back to face the altar to conceal the realization on your face that I had caught you in an act of thespian vanity that slipped past those who knew nothing of your early love of theater.

The second occasion was also at St. Botolph's. This time it was in the vestry. I had been serving as altar boy at the early communion service and was disrobing from my cassock and surplice as you replaced your ceremonial robes on their hangers before taking a seat at the big oak table in the middle of the room to perform the final ritual of signing the registry. Unscrewing the cap of your fountain pen, you noted down the date in the appropriate column and next to it, in the adjacent, wider column, the name of the just-completed service: Holy Communion. But then, required to add your signature as the celebrant in the last column, you wrote it out with a great, unthinking flourish: not the usual Harry L. Clothier, no. I looked at the signature in disbelief. It read Holy L. Clothier. Holy Clothier. Remember how we laughed?

So, you see, it's these things I remember, the smallest things, the things that tell me precisely who you are. Or who you were. And, curiously, the most intimate of moments that we shared together, you and me.

Good memories, then. Your son,
Peter

16 July 2021

Dear Harry,

There are a few less pleasant memories from our years at Aspley Guise. You may not remember this one as clearly as I do. I hope not.

I would have been four years old or so. Maybe younger. Maybe terrible twos. Or threes. But I had done something bad. I had pulled Flora's hair, perhaps, or broken one of her dolls. The kind of bad thing a little boy does to his older sister, just to be mean. Or because she was being mean to me. The resulting screams of pain and rage must have brought you running up the stairs to the nursery, where you identified me immediately as the culprit. Reverting to some old school idea of punishment, you unstrapped the narrow black belt from where it cinched your cassock and yelled at me in a fury.

I ran.

Terrified, I ran from the nursery, out across the landing and down the corridor that led past the upstairs bathroom to the guest rooms, with you in hot pursuit, red-faced, shouting, that skinny leather belt of yours snaking out over your shoulder and poised to strike. Alerted by the uproar, my mother must have run upstairs herself and was now making our stampede down the corridor a threesome.

Reaching the dead end by the linen closet, I was cornered.

I made a desperate detour into the guest bedroom, with its twin beds. I remember every detail, down to the nubby texture of the striped counterpanes and their narrow pastel stripes, one yellow and orange, one dark and light green, and beige. But here I was, trapped against the nearest of the two beds. You towered above me in your flapping cassock, a giant black crow, your belt raised up behind your shoulder, ready for the first smarting blow.

"No, Harry, no! Please no!" It was my mother who intervened.

And you came to a sudden consciousness of what it was you were about to do. I saw it in your face. Your arm slackened, and with it, the belt. The rage subsided into something different. A sense of guilt? A realization of the imminent misuse of your physical strength and authority as a father?

I managed to relax a little as I watched you do the same. You fumbled with your belt and fastened it back around your waist. You said, "You're right. I'm sorry, Peter. I'm really sorry. I shouldn't have been so angry. And I promise—promise—that I'll never, ever try to hit you ever again."

And you kept your word, Harry. You never did.

I think you left my mother to restore peace and order in the family and made your way downstairs to resume the work in your study that I'd interrupted.

So that was that. I was spared.

But I was still afraid of you. And I could have used a hug.

With love. Your son,
Peter

17 July 2021

Dear Harry,

Spare the rod . . . ?

I'll grant you may have kept your word about never punishing me that way again—though you must have been sorely tempted when I tried your patience!—but you must have known that corporal punishment was the preferred means of punishment at both the schools you sent me to. It would have been the practice at Shrewsbury, too, your own boarding school, in those early years of your life. Were you never subjected to this painful and peculiar indignity? Perhaps—I can well imagine this—you were such a good citizen, always observant of the rules, that you never earned a caning.

The first time for me was when I was seven years old. This was at Windlesham House, my prep school, when the school was evacuated north from its home in the Sussex Downs to the Lake District, to be safe from the feared invasion by Hitler's armies. The big house we had taken over was not designed as a school so our dormitory rooms were small. There were three or four of us only to a bedroom, and our little group was caught talking during afternoon nap time when silence was the rule. The punishment that time was only three across the outstretched palm with a rubber strap—or a leather one, perhaps—but I know it smarted enough to make me cry.

The next time I was punished, I can't even remember what I'd done. This was after the school's post-war return to the big, brick building in Sussex. Whatever it was, the offense was obviously considered a serious one. I was summoned to Mr. Chris's study, the headmaster, and had to stand for many long minutes outside his big oak door, staring at its brass handle and trembling in fear until I was called upon to enter. The study was a big, serious room looking out over the front lawn, wood-paneled floor to ceiling and furnished with book-lined shelves on each of its walls and heavy, leather-bound chairs and sofas. It was redolent of the rich, sweet-smelling pipe tobacco that Mr. Chris would tamp down into the bowl of his pipes before lighting up in a hovering cloud of pungent, silver smoke.

Once called inside, still trembling with fear and anticipation, I was told to take my trousers down and bend forward over the arm of one of the leather chairs. The rumor was that you had to take your trousers down so you couldn't stuff your underpants with the pink blotting paper that was reputed to take the sting out of the blows.

That time it was six of the best with a cane, right across my bare behind.

I have wondered since if Mr. Chris could have derived some secret, salacious pleasure from this ceremony. Did the spectacle of little boys' buttocks cause him some peculiar delight, exposed as the deliciously unprotected target for his cane? I'll never know, but I'll admit I harbor my suspicions.

There was, too, a kind of pre-sexual excitement among us boys around corporal punishment. We used to do it to each other late at night, in the dormitory, just for fun. We'd choose a boy to be punished—it was often me—and have him take his pajama bottoms down and stick his bare bum up in the air while another boy would slap it fiercely with a bedroom slipper. A little precocious sadomasochism, Harry? I need to talk about this more . . .

As a teenager at Lancing, I was beaten twice. Again, bare ass—why did they insist on that? They would likely be arrested for it, these days, in America! Tiger Halsey, our housemaster, used a cane. Was it smoking I was called in for on the one occasion that he punished me? Then, later in my school career, the head prefect took his turn at caning me in a weirdly ceremonial event, myself bent over, holding my ankles, at the end of a standing gauntlet of his fellow prefects. I had been caught off-limits with another boy—I had been hoping, I'll admit it, Harry, to get into his pants, but more about this in a later letter—the two of us smoking and drinking in a billiards parlor.

I'm sure you never got up to such shenanigans. But I wonder, did you know about these punishments? Did the school communicate with parents to let them know their son was being beaten? Perhaps you simply felt that I deserved it? Accepted ritual punishment of this kind as a regular part of a sound education, to make a man of me?

I hope not. I hope it never happened to you. But to be honest there is still some small place in the back of my mind where I nurse a residue of anger that you allowed such things to happen to your son.

With love, though, as always,
Peter

19 July 2021

Dear Harry,

Here's a detail that just came back to me uninvited. I had a vivid image of the big, black, leather slip-on shoes you wore, protruding from beneath the hem of your black cassock. I remember the sheen of their soft, black leather, the wrinkles left on their surface by constant wear. They used to pick up a layer of dust on the path that led down past the chicken run and that great pine tree on the way from the Rectory to the church door. You had to shine them up again with a duster before the service. They had a big, silver buckle, like a pirate's shoe . . . I do remember them.

Your son,
    Peter

PS: That towering pine tree is gone now. Did you know this? Along with the Rectory itself, as I discovered to my grief when I visited Aspley Guise, many years ago, to show Ellie where I had grown up. Where the Rectory once stood, and the orchard behind with its grove of fruit trees—cooking and eating apples, Williams pears, Victoria plums—there was now a circle of small council houses with flapping clothes lines, children's toys and climbing frames, and little cars parked in front.

20 July 2021

Dear Harry,

One of the lasting images I have of you is the figure standing tall at the altar, your back to everyone but God, arms raised in reverence, face raised and catching light from the great stained-glass window at the east end of the church.

It was a point of pride for you to be a "high" churchman. You delighted in the robes, the rituals of the church, the solemnity of its ceremonies. You loved the candles, the decorative accoutrements, the flowers the church ladies would arrange on Saturdays in the tall vases standing on the altar and throughout the chancel. You would have used incense if your more conservative parishioners had not objected that it "smacked of Rome." Roman Catholicism (you insisted on the difference between Roman and Anglo-Catholicism) was still deeply suspect in the English countryside, with its burden of centuries of prejudice and fear—I guess since that dreadful Henry ruled the land and outlawed Papism!

You celebrated two communion services every Sunday: a simple, no-frills, half-hour Holy Communion early in the morning for the more conservative faithful; and at ten o'clock your favorite, Parish Mass (yes! You insisted on the Catholic word Mass) with all the bells and whistles. This was the communion service for families, the rest of us, and it included lots of hymns and chanted versions of the Introit, the Confession, the Kyrie, the Gloria ringing up to the rafters.

The Parish Mass included, too, your weekly sermon from the pulpit. How hard you worked at them! Even into the days of your retirement, when called upon to lead a service at your local church in Wales, you agonized! Reading your letters—and the letters, too, from Peggy—in your later years, I find recurrent references to what still amounted to a torture. As children, Flora and I had to tiptoe around your study, always sacrosanct, while you prepared them, writing them down in blue ink on special pads with your Parker fountain pen, in a scrawl that was unintelligible to anyone but yourself. You put heart and soul as well as every ounce of your sharp intelligence into every word—so much so that I came to believe, along with my mother I'm sure, that this work contributed enormously to the pain that devoured so much of your life.

It was from you I learned the love of words and the insistence that every one of them should count, every one of them should be used correctly. Like you, I agonized over them when called upon to deliver them in public—a lecture or a speech. But writing, even for publication, can be done in private, where foolishness and grammatical mistakes are readily correctible before they reach the eyes of readers. You could have been a writer, Harry, and a good one, and were, in private, in your letters and your caravan travel logs, but it never occurred to you to write for publication.

Yes, the pain. We have talked about this before. Forgive my mentioning it again, it was such an important factor in our lives . . . But back to our Sundays, when the Parish Mass was the main course in your weekly feast of services. If Holy Communion was the hors d'oeuvres, the dessert, at the end of the day, was Vespers, the Evening Service, with the solemnity of Gregorian chants as the congregation joined the choir in singing the psalms and, beyond the darkening stained-glass windows, the day turned quietly into night. No robes for Vespers. Just the black cassock, the white surplice, and the narrow white clerical dog collar, betokening your high church allegiance.

I wonder if you ever thought what it might mean to a very small boy, before I was even old enough to be an altar boy, sitting with his mother and sister in the Rector's pew, a few rows from the front, looking up through the chancel to where you stood with your arms raised, as I remember you, your presence haloed by that glow of multicolored light from that stained-glass window? What it meant to a small boy to look up to the pulpit and watch his father preach the word to an attentive congregation, or read from the Bible at that great eagle lectern? How small it could seem? How insignificant? How much in awe a little boy could be?

And then of course there were those times when I was just bored and wriggly, when Mr. Brown, the Verger, would take note of my discomfort and come forward quietly, seriously, to take me by the hand and lead me back to the great church porch and from there down the cold stone steps to the crypt below. Once there, he'd crank open the heavy iron door to the furnace, where the fuel burned hot and red, and have me help him stoke the flames with new shovelfuls of coal.

Respectfully,
Peter

21 July 2021

Dear Harry,

I'm glad you fell in love with that lovely girl from Swansea who would be my mother. The daughter of an Anglican minister herself (the Church of Wales in his case, but the same difference), she told me once that she always swore she'd never marry a clergyman. Until she did.

I must have known at some point the circumstances of your meeting. I have it in mind somewhere that it involved your Cambridge friend, Alan, the one who also took holy orders and married your sister, Nancy. Alan became a don at your old college, Gonville and Caius, which would later also be my own old college. You'd be happy to know that your great-granddaughter Georgia is there now, following in our footsteps. Alan stayed on at Cambridge for many years as professor in an arcane field, the study of Syriac and Aramaic, the long-dead languages of the Bible.

You "went down", as we say, in the mid-1920s and ventured out into the world. And I know that like myself a generation later you struggled to find your path in life. It was a time of great social turmoil, engulfing the entire country, the year the national Trades Union Council summoned workers everywhere to militate—finally!—for better wages, better working conditions, and called for what became known as the General Strike of 1926. It lasted for nine days. A good socialist already—a young man of conscience—you stepped up in support of the workers. Drove a bus . . .

What to do, though? Public (read "private") school and Cambridge! A great education! You had joined an amateur theater group at Cambridge and had relished your turn in the footlights. The stage tempted you, I know, but not eventually as a serious option. I suspect—no, I'm sure—you wanted to embark on something meaningful in your life, something in service to ideals greater than yourself. You had studied what was at that time the whole new science of psychology and your head was full of Freud and Jung. A generation later you might have gone into psychotherapy (you would have made a great therapist!) but back in the '20s professional opportunities in the field seemed likely limited to psychiatry, with a medical degree, or psychoanalysis. I could not see you sitting beside a couch and nodding wisely as you listened to the same patients investigate their dreams for week after week and month after month.

You met Peggy. And you were so scared (of commitment? Of the opposite sex?) that you went running off to a *monastery*! You thought seriously of becoming a *monk*? Really? That's the story, anyway.

I have no idea how Peggy managed to rescue you from that fate. I may have known how it happened at some point. If I did, I have forgotten now. But I'm glad you fell in love with her, and she with you. Glad she managed to overcome whatever fears you had. Glad the two of you got married and had Flora. Glad that in 1936, a year and a half later, you had me!

With love,
Peter

22 July 2021

Dear Harry,

Ever the actor, though! I remember how you used to ham it up on every possible occasion. You loved to be center stage, the object of everyone's attention, everyone's applause. You probably became a priest because that profession gave you a stage to perform on and an audience to give you the feedback that you craved. It offered your voice the opportunity, every Sunday, to play with the sound of words and give them sonorous expression. It allowed you to explore the subtlety of body language and convey the depth of your emotional experience to your fellow human beings.

This morning, as I woke from a deep sleep, my mind turned up the precise term for what you loved to be: the master of ceremonies. In church, of course. But also at home, where we always had a full house during the war: friends, family, billetees, the Bletchley girls . . . (More about them soon!) Also, over dinner, at social evenings in the drawing room, at village garden parties . . . That's it, exactly: you loved to act the master of ceremonies.

Remember Mike? With whom you shared that seder dinner in Los Angeles when you came to visit myself and Ellie and our daughter, Sarah, many years ago? Strange to think of him as your Jewish brother-in-law but isn't that what he'd be, as my father-in-law—though this was obviously a good deal later in life than the time we're talking about. You may be wondering why Mike comes to mind. The fact is that he, too, loved to act the master of ceremonies—it's one thing among many that the two of you had in common despite the vast differences in social background and geography, profession, religion . . . He was also, in the 1930s, a good socialist like yourself. But we'll come to all that later in this "narrative."

It was a joy to see the two of you getting along so well together, Anglican minister and Jewish paterfamilias, sharing the stage at that memorable "Last Supper."

Affectionately,
Peter

24 July 2021

Dear Harry,

(Another Freudian typo! I have corrected it, of course, but I first wrote: "Fear Harry"! The F is next to the D on the qwerty keyboard—you wouldn't know about that because Peggy always did the typing—and I have never learned to type with any accuracy. So, yes, a slip of the finger. "Fear Harry!" So apt! So very true!)

As an aside in this on-and-off chronological progression through the years, I need to pause here to thank you properly and sincerely for the name you chose for me: Peter. I am truly grateful for it, though I doubt you could have known just how apt and meaningful it would prove to be. I have always loved the name, loved all of its associations, loved all my namesakes—Peter Rabbit, Peter Pan, Peter the Great, Peter the Rock, Peter the Fisher of Men, and yes, even that slangy "peter" we men have slung between our legs! I love that I'm a Peter.

I have long known—and valued—the reason that you originally blessed me with the name: I was born on August 1st. In the Anglican calendar of saints this marks the Feast of St. Peter's Chains. Peter, of course, my namesake, Jesus's disciple, was thrown in jail and put in chains for the audacity of preaching the new Christian gospel in pagan Rome. The tale is that he was released from his chains by the intervention of an angel who appeared in Peter's cell to "burst them asunder."

That same Peter was confronted by his long-dead Savior once again as he was fleeing Rome at the urging of his followers who feared, justifiably, for his life. "*Quo vadis, Domine?*" Peter asked famously, in surprise and consternation: "Where are you going, Lord?" And when the Lord said he was returning to Rome to be crucified for a second time, Peter was shamed into turning around and hightailing it back into the city, where he was captured again and himself crucified. He denied himself the honor of dying in the same manner as his Lord, however, and insisted instead on being crucified upside down, as memorably recorded in that monumental painting that I love by Caravaggio.

I have told you in the past about the painful, deeply conflicted turmoil that descended out of nowhere to grip my life when I reached my middle years. No need to go back over it here. Enough to recall for you that great moment of epiphany when I came upon Peter's chains—or what purported to be those chains—in a reliquary in the crypt chapel of the church of San Pietro ad Vincoli in Rome. In the overwhelming, profoundly emotional revelation of that moment, I recognized in them my *own* chains, the ones I had allowed to weigh my life down with shame and guilt and fear, the ones I knew in that moment that I finally needed to cast off. That's when the meaning of my birthday came to me in a flash, there in the church of St. Peter in Chains, where I understood with blazing clarity the significance of my name and why you had given it to me so many years before.

I went back home to Los Angeles determined to find out how to change my life. I'm proud to be able to tell you I succeeded (even though that change eventually led along a very different spiritual path). But that's for another letter, later.

Such a complex character, then, that biblical Peter who became the first Bishop of Rome, the founder of the Roman Catholic church: the simple man whom Jesus met by the Sea of Galilee and chose to make his "fisher of men"; the one who cravenly denied his savior "before the cock crowed thrice"; the one who rediscovered his fortitude and courage and became the "rock" upon whom the Christian church was built. Did you know, Harry, when you gave me the name that I would "inherit" something of Peter's moral cowardice and something of his strength, something of his faithlessness, and something of his solid, rock-like reliability?

You gave me a name to live up to. I no longer imagine—if I ever did—that my namesake will be awaiting me with his keys to heaven's gate. But I have to wonder whether you found him waiting for you. I'll be reminding you in another letter, later, of how reluctant you were to leave this world. Was that because you, too, had doubts about that . . . well, let's call it by its name: that myth?

Your doubting son,
Peter

25 July 2021

Dear Harry,

Back to our story! It's time to talk about the Bletchley girls!

I have written about them in the past, because those extraordinary, smart, young women were an important presence in my childhood, Fiona, Vivian, and Peggy's sister, Gay. Not long ago, on a trip back home to England, I found their names inscribed in the book at what is now a Bletchley Park museum and visitor center. Now that the contribution of the men and women who worked there during World War II is widely known about through books, films, and television programs, the place has become a tourist attraction open to the world. Back then, during the war and for many years thereafter, their success in unlocking the secrets of the captured Enigma machine to break Nazi military codes was ultra "hush-hush"; and the girls who came to live in our house, an easy bike ride from Bletchley, were sworn to secrecy.

To me, a little boy, these women were mysterious, exotic, glamorous creatures. Their perfumed, powdered feminine presence loomed far above me, alluring in ways I was not yet able to understand. I remember the powerful sensual appeal of Fiona, a young woman whose body aroused in me what must have been, unrecognized, my very first sexual desires. She would have been no more than twenty-one or twenty-two at the time, I suppose, full of fun and bursting with erotic energy.

But I was just a child. For you, Harry, a virile and physically-aware man in his mid-thirties, a man in need of adulation, she must have been temptation in the flesh. It was Peggy who told me later in life that there were perilous moments in your relationship. Perhaps this was one of them. I have sometimes stopped to wonder if you ever succumbed to those carnal temptations about which you might warn others in your sermons. If anyone, I bet, this was one young woman whose attractions could have lured you into her all-too conveniently located bed, just a short corridor away from yours

But listen, Harry, there is a still darker and more disturbing side to your history with the Bletchley girls. I learned about it only after you were gone, much to my dismay—and quite by accident—in researching the Bletchley story, when I chanced upon a book called *The Hidden History of Bletchley Park: A Social and Organizational History*, by one C. Smith. I wonder if you ever knew about it. And if so, if you ever read this passage?

> [W]hile most residents appear to have been incurious, there were some locals, intrigued by the arrival of a military installation in their town, who attempted to discover what was going on. One such example was reported to CG&CS's (Government Code and Cypher School) security staff, who recorded the incident in some detail:

There is a parson in this neighborhood whose name is the Rev. Harry L. Clothier, The Rectory, Aspley Guise. We have had a number of people billeted there from time to time and as a host he is very kind. He has, however, apparently acquired a good deal of information about Bletchley Park, some of which gets rather close to the knuckle. The four girls who are billeted there now are getting a good deal disturbed about him because he not only seems to try and catch them out with the idea of obtaining a little more information, but he repeats what he knows to everyone that comes to the house and seems to take a quite unchristian delight in getting the girls into an awkward position when introducing strangers.

Well, Harry, to say I was gob smacked when I read this is a vast understatement. I was shocked that the Bletchley girls (Smith reports four of them; I remember only three) were "getting a good deal disturbed" about you, that you were repeating what you knew to "everyone that comes into the house," that you took such "unchristian delight in getting the girls into an awkward position." "Unchristian"? You, Harry? All this was news to me. But I was perhaps especially shocked because the report seemed, well . . . so believable. So much in character. You yourself confessed to being a show-off. Smith continues:

. . . if the [security] agency was too heavy handed with offenders then that, in and of itself, would have been revealing. As a result, CG&CS appears to have taken a policy of trying to frighten offenders into silence as opposed to resorting to legal action. In the case of Reverend Clothier, it was decided that the best course of action was that he be 'officially warned to keep his mouth shut.' Rather ominously, the security official suggested that what the Reverend required was 'a thorough frightening.'

So, Harry, I can't imagine what it meant for a proud man like yourself to be "officially warned to keep your mouth shut." Do you recall having received that "thorough frightening" from the security agency? How did they frighten you? With threats? Were you chastened by the experience? Were you any less chummy with the girls, more circumspect in what you broadcast from then on?

You always were something of a jokester as well as a show-off and I'm sure you thought your intrusiveness with the Bletchley girls was a rather harmless piece of entertainment. That government security officials saw it as potential treachery is alarming. I wish I had learned about it in some way other than reading a history book written by some anonymous stranger.

As usual, too, I wish that I knew more.

Your ever questioning son,
Peter

27 July 2021

Dear Harry,

The war years were memorable ones, no? You were exempt from military service for health reasons, and it's my recollection that you were somewhat conscience-stricken for not being able to "do your bit." Your brother, Donald, was an army officer— one of those who were stranded, and then rescued from the beaches at Dunkirk. Your Cambridge pal, Alan, married to your sister, Nancy, enlisted as an army chaplain. Even that path was closed to you.

In part to compensate for being unfit to sign up for active duty, you and Peggy opened up the Rectory as living quarters for military people of all kinds, in addition to the Bletchley girls. There was Edward, an officer in the Royal Navy, whose ship was sunk in the Atlantic by German torpedoes, and Miss Thom, a WREN—the women's branch of the navy—who I remember particularly for her smart, navy-blue uniform and her smart, round, navy-blue cap. At one point, for reasons I no longer recall, Miss Thom took over as the teacher at our Rectory nursery school (which deserves a letter of its own).

Then there was Frank, with his bristly, ginger mustache, an airman who was posted for a good long while at the RAF airfield down the hill at Cranfield. He was an artist, a painter, who returned to landscape painting when the war was over.

His friend, Woody, was a portrait artist, whose full-length portrait of you in your dog-collar and cassock was for many years a presence on the walls of our family homes. I wonder what became of it? Last time I knew, it was in Flora's home, before she died. I don't know if she'd have remembered this, but she and I would ride our bikes down past the railway crossing and the bluebells woods to watch Spitfires take off and land—I would not have known it then but I suppose it must have been while the Battle of Britain was raging over the midlands and the south. The planes would sometimes land dangerously, teetering on landing carriage damaged by enemy fire, or with flames bursting from their engines. The airfield at Cranfield was probably too small and the runaway too short for RAF bombers, because I don't remember seeing any there.

We did see them in the sky, though, and cheer the squadrons of British bombers setting out for Germany. Earlier in the war, we used to watch the ragged end of a formation of German bombers, stragglers limping back to their point of origin after opening their bomb bays over London, some sixty miles to the south. From our upstairs windows, looking south, we could even see the orange glow of the city burning. To the east, toward Bedford, across the valley, above the silhouettes of the tall smokestacks of the brickworks, the bulbous, flatulent bellies of dozens of barrage balloons were lit up from beneath by the roaming stalks of searchlight beams as they sought out their prey—the silver glint of fleeing German bombers—for the artillery batteries that launched round after ear-shattering round in the attempt to bring them down.

It was on nights such as this that—despite our mother's alarm—you would slip out through the back door of the Rectory, careful not to transgress the blackout rules, and pace the perimeter of our home—as though that ritual might somehow deter enemy attack. The worst that ever happened was the harmless explosion of a handful of jettison bombs in a meadow not far from our house, a quarter mile or so, as the bombers lightened their load to speed their return to Germany over the North Sea.

Would you remember this, Harry? I'm sure that you weren't with us when we went out on another adventure, this time in daylight, to clamber up on the wings of a Messerschmidt 109 that crash-landed and got stuck in the mud of a farmer's field not half a mile from our house. We gazed in through the splintered cockpit and wondered what could have happened to the German who had sat there in the pilot's seat. Perhaps, we fantasized as kids, to scare ourselves, the enemy had parachuted to earth, and was still lurking in the nearby woods . . .

It must have been different for you, of course—not to mention for those millions whose lives were directly threatened and too often cruelly taken from them in this conflict—but my memories of those days, as a boy of five, six, seven, are more of adventure than of risk, more of curiosity than danger, more of a house full of good, loving and mutually supportive people than of enemies.

As I'm sure you'll readily agree, Peggy deserves much of the credit for our relatively easy passage through the war years at the Rectory. She welcomed all, found beds for everyone, and saw to it that we all ate well. I can see her at the kitchen table with a pair of scissors, carefully clipping coupons from her collection of ration books, piling them up to take with her to the butcher's, the greengrocer's, or the grocery shop. There were even coupons for the sweet shop. With the help of a woman who came in from the village, she shopped and cooked for everyone. Somewhere amongst the family memorabilia there is still a letter addressed to her personally from King George himself, thanking her for her service to the country. It was a tribute that she well deserved.

But her first task, as everyone at the Rectory knew, was to take care of her husband. You were more than fortunate to have such a woman by your side, Harry, supporting you through all your illnesses and periods of self-doubt and uncertainty. I don't know what you would have done without her.

> With tender memories of Peggy,
> then, your son,
> Peter

30 July 2021

Dear Harry,

We had the billetees at the Rectory, yes, but then there were the refugees—a different bunch entirely.

They arrived from London by the bus or trainload, spilling out onto the village square by the horse trough with a chaos of baggage and a babel of accents that were nearly impossible to understand. These were all East Enders, Cockneys, bombed out of their homes. Most of them had never left the city before and here they were far from home in a country village with barely anything but the clothes they wore; mothers, mostly, and unruly children, along with a few dads and grandparents, all terrified by what they had experienced, the fire and fury they were fleeing. Their terror was palpable, infectious. Even as children we could feel it.

From their transport, they were distributed by volunteer organizers around the village, to anyone who had a place where they could sleep. We had no more beds but you offered our coal cellar, and these people were grateful for the shelter, any safe haven from the bombs.

It was dark down there. The only lighting was from a single bare bulb suspended from the ceiling. It smelled of stored apples, cookers, and eaters, Bramleys and Cox's Orange Pippins and other species from the big orchard up behind the house, all laid out on racks on top of beds of newspaper. Potatoes, too. And the coal that came rattling down from a chute into the coal bin when it arrived in the delivery lorry. No palace, it provided these frightened people with a temporary refuge on their way to some other, more permanent place for them to escape the German Luftwaffe. One family, I know, the Turners, stayed on and made their home in Aspley Guise, forever grateful to you for your kindness.

Even here in our small village, however, the wail of air raid sirens was inescapable. It penetrated the cellar door and the flight of wooden steps that led down to where the refugees were trying to grab some sleep on the hard brick floor, and that too-familiar sound brought back their terror. It was you, Harry, who went down there and spoke with them to calm them, while we children were sent down to huddle amongst them for our own safety for the duration of the warning, waiting for the relief of the all-clear siren that signaled the departure of the bombers eastwards over the horizon.

We thought you very brave. We were proud to have you as our father, a rock of sanity and calm whenever the storm raged. We were glad to have your strong, grown-up presence for protection, and learned to share you with whoever came to stay.

Do you remember all this as well as I do?

With love,
Peter

31 July 2021

Dear Harry,

I don't know what led you and Peggy to start the Rectory
nursery school. Perhaps the local schools were suffering from a
lack of funds, some of them even closed during the war years.
But you got together with a handful of like-minded parents
and proposed the Rectory drawing room as a classroom for a
P.N.E.U. home school.

I remember that acronym. (Odd, isn't it, the meaningless
little things that get stuck in your mind? I still remember for
example, eighty years later, the license plate of your first car,
the Austin 10 that brought us down from Newcastle to Aspley
Guise before the war: it was GTN209. The TN, you liked to
remind us, were the letters particularly assigned to Newcastle-
on-Tyne, TN being short for the river Tyne. You were always
proud of being a Geordie, a born Tyne-sider, and you'll be
pleased to know that I inherited that pride. I, too, am still
happy to tell anyone who might be interested that I'm a
Geordie, even though I haven't seen the Tyne or visited the city
in years. Well, decades. It's like being a Cockney, something no
one can ever take away from you).

Aside from Flora and myself in the nursery school, there
were Charles and Caroline Allen, whose father was later
knighted Sir Kenneth for his services to industry. (Many years

later, as a reasonably eligible young Englishman, I was to appear with Caroline in white tie and tails on the front cover of the high society magazine, *The Tatler*—a distinction of which Peggy was particularly proud!) There was Elizabeth Brown, whose father was an Air Vice Marshall in the RAF, and Hillary (I forget her last name) who lived with her mother down behind The Bell. And there was Robert John, who for reasons unknown pushed me off a six-foot wall at Aspley House and left me nauseous and concussed on the street below. You and Peggy were hovering anxiously over me in the drawing room when I came to. Robert John's father was the Chief Inspector of the Woburn police, the nearest town of any size, so I have often wondered if he was ever punished for his misdeed. I will never know

There were surely other children at the school, whose names and faces have been lost to time.

Your contribution to the enterprise emerged from your woodshop, in the form of beautifully crafted wooden boxes, big enough to store our pens and pencils, our colors and our exercise books, everything we needed for the school day; they doubled as stools that we would sit on for our classes. Each one had the name of its owner stenciled in large letters on the side, so there could be no confusion as to which box belonged to whom. They were beautifully painted, too, in bold enamel paint, some blue, some yellow, and they could be conveniently stacked at the side of the room when more space was needed— say, for a dance lesson.

We had a series of teachers. Aside from the Miss Thom I mentioned earlier, I remember only one, the unforgettable

Mrs. Smith, a tiny woman who wore tweedy suits and was never seen without a hat, fastened to her graying hair with a shiny hatpin to keep it from flying off in the wind. What I remember best about Mrs. Smith is that she would take us out on nature walks, rain or shine—in rain, with mackintoshes and Wellington boots—in the fields and woods around the house. Unfortunately, she was a kleptomaniac. People living at the Rectory began to notice things were missing, nothing of great significance to begin with—a piece of costume jewelry here, a bottle of bathroom scent or *eau de cologne* there. It was only when Grandfather's gold watch disappeared that the hue and cry went up. A little detective work soon revealed the culprit: the mousy, innocent-seeming, otherwise innocuous Mrs. Smith.

You had to fire her, and I remember this caused you great distress. You understood quite well—and explained to us at the time—that this poor woman was not truly a thief, but that she suffered from a genuine illness. Still there was no other option in a house full of guests. She had to go. Perhaps that was when Miss Thom was persuaded to step in. We all loved Miss Thom. In fact, I suspect I was a little bit in love with her. She was a lovely person.

Maybe you were, too?

More to come,
Peter

1 August 2021

Dear Harry,

My birthday! Peggy's birthday! There can't be many of us, mother and son, who share a birthday. You used to joke that I was her 30th birthday present. Were she alive today, she would be one hundred and fifteen years old.

I miss her, miss the birthdays that we spent together. She was the best cake-maker, whether for birthday, Christmas, or Easter. Weddings. Dark, rich fruitcakes, quite delicious. And they kept for, what? Weeks? And red cherry sponge cakes, equally delicious. They did not last so long. No one could resist them.

Anyway, here we are. The Feast of St. Peter's Chains. I already thanked you in an earlier letter for the name, and what it has meant to me. But it never hurts to be thanked again, does it?

People call me Peter, never Pete. The only one who ever called me Pete was . . . Peggy!

Sending good thoughts, then. We are back down at our cottage in Laguna Beach, not Glenview, but paid for mostly by the proceeds from the sale of Glenview following your death, and Peggy's. We have no plans, other than to have a few friends over for dinner. Ellie has not yet told me who they are, nor what time they are coming. It's a surprise.

With love,
Peter

2 August 2021

Dear Harry,

Is this not a strange coincidence? Just yesterday was my birthday and that mention of dance classes in my letter of a couple of days ago triggered the memory of what you told me about the first one ever. The first birthday. The actual one. And with it, the reminder that you were capable of remarkable, penetrating insights into the mysteries of the human mind. I have told this story before in another context, but it certainly belongs here, too, in these letters that I'm writing. It tells so much about you.

So here it is. Remember how you used to send us off to dance class every week in Bedford, Flora and me? It was something expected of children of a certain class in those days, more about social poise and posture, I suspect, than dance but there you are. We walked around with books on our heads.

Which was all fine, except that little Peter began to show an embarrassing aversion to the skipping rope, a simple prop that was regularly used in dance class. I began to howl whenever the dreaded rope was produced—a matter of some concern to you, my parents, and a distraction to everyone in the class.

What to do? Drawing on the knowledge of psychology you gained in your Cambridge days, you called me into your study one day for one of those serious father-son talks that surely shaped my life. On this occasion, I found you in your black cassock, sitting in the armchair by the fire with a skipping rope laid across your knees.

Reassuring me from my immediate recoil and the initial jolt of fear, you calmly began to tell me the story of my birth: how I was a blue baby, born with the umbilical cord tangled around my neck, and how I could have died at birth, but for the swift action of Mrs. Gates, the midwife, who seized a pair of scissors and cut through the cord in time to let me gasp for my first breath.

And crucially, as you were telling me this story, you took the skipping rope and looped it around my neck, tightening it gently from both ends until I felt the squeeze; and showed me that there was nothing more to fear, that what had happened, happened long ago, that I was saved—and that I had no need to cry when I saw a skipping rope in class.

You see? You would have made a great psychotherapist! I think back to that connection you were able to make and, particularly, to your action. As a therapy, it was far in advance of its time. Remarkable that you were bold enough to take the risk and had the confidence to know that this was exactly the right thing to do.

And you *were* right, of course. I never felt the need to cry when I saw a skipping rope again. But you'll be interested to know that the story of your fine-tuned intuition, Harry, returned vividly to my mind many, many years later. I was having a debilitating case of what is known as "writer's block" and was persuaded to join the kind of group training session that I normally despised. Challenged by my inability to name "the big lie" (oh! please!) that was supposedly holding me back, the group facilitator was inspired to ask what I remembered about the moment of my birth. The story of the skipping rope jumped back into my mind and I heard what sounded almost like an alien, though strangely familiar voice bring out the words: *I have no right to be here.* And there I was suddenly, laughing hysterically and crying at the same time as I walked around the room (this was the protocol), introducing myself to other members of the group by my big lie: "Hi, I'm Peter Clothier," I repeated to each one of them in turn. "I have no right to be here." Because . . . well, I should by rights have died at birth. I had no right to be here.

So, Harry, father, wise man, thank you for the insight.

Ever your admiring son,
Peter

5 August 2021

Dear Harry,

There's more to tell you about Windlesham, the boys' "prep" school that you sent me to. I keep thinking I was six but I must have been seven when I went there first. Which is when it was evacuated from its real home in the Sussex Downs up north to the Lake District. Ambleside. I mentioned this before. But as I say, there's more.

We moved back south after the war ended, so it must have been 1945. I would have been eight or nine years old, and I was beginning to understand that there were two Peters in me. One was Peter the good little boy. The other one was really, really wicked. These days, now nearly eighty years later and with all I have learned about being human, being a boy and, later, trying to become a man, I understand more about the dark side and the light, the animus and the anima, the masculine and the feminine, the yin and the yang. Back then, I did not understand any of these things, but I did know there were two Peters in me and one was very, very good and the other was very, very bad. (Remember that old rhyme about the little girl "who had a little curl/right in the middle of her forehead./ And when she was good she was very, very good,/ and when she was bad she was horrid." It was like that . . .)

The light side of Peter was a sweet, round-faced, blue-eyed, chubby little boy with charming freckles. I still have pictures of him, studio portraits taken with his pretty little sister, Flora. At school, he always did what he was told—even sometimes when he knew that it was not what he wanted. There was the time when he was sitting at the French table in the dining room where Mrs. Smith, the French teacher presided. She was the sternest but still the best of all my teachers and it was because of her, I know, that I became a language student, then a language teacher. We boys had to take turns serving and I was served this plate of stew and mine tased of vomit. I complained about this as best I could in French—you couldn't use English at the French table—but she wouldn't understand, or couldn't, and made me eat it all—every last bite. And then afterwards, I was told that it really was vomit, that some other boy had thrown up in the bowl before it was brought to me, And I'd eaten it. I'm sorry, Harry, I know this is really stomach-turning but I must tell you just to show you how I always did what I was told.

So maybe that's a bad start for the light side. But there's the little Peter who loved to go out hunting butterflies with his butterfly net, who went out one glorious, sunny afternoon and found a bush with literally dozens of fritillaries, all kinds, big and little species, all glorious gold and brown. He couldn't stop catching them, all kinds, and putting them in his ether jar, so many, so rare, so many different kinds of them. But then, maybe it was just a dream because somewhere along the lane as he hurried back to school, thrilled to be able to tell this story to the other boys, somewhere along that lane he lost the jar. So maybe it really was just a little boy's dream.

And then there was the sunny little boy who had his own garden, in the patch of gardens near the school were boys were allowed to grow their own flowers and vegetables. I loved that little garden, Harry. It was my own place. I grew cornflowers there, from seed, and when they bloomed they were the same deep cornflower blue as Flora's school uniform. I grew carrots and onions. But the best thing was my vegetable marrow. We call them zucchinis over here in America, and we never let them grow to the size of a vegetable marrow like we did in England. Peggy used to slice those big ones in half, remember, and stuff them with sausage meat and bake them in the oven before serving them up with a delicious white sauce. Yum!

Well, I discovered how to grow a marrow really big! When it's still just small, you thread a length of wool through the stem and put the other end of the wool in a jar filled with sugar water. You could almost watch the marrow grow from day to day, until it's literally huge! I don't remember what I did with mine when it was big. Perhaps I brought it home for Peggy to cook, but I doubt that, because it was in the middle of a term.

There were other memories, too, nature walks through the woods and, a few times, if we were lucky, all the way across the main road and up to Chanctonbury Ring, the best known of those ancient rings of trees they say were planted by the Druids for ritual purposes. Sometimes, we collected beech nuts, or chestnuts, or horse chestnuts, the ones you couldn't eat but you could use for "conkers"—a game where you tried to break the other player's conker at the end of a string. The one that lasted longest was the champion.

There were times when we all got to swim in the swimming pool, down below the assembly hall, all of us naked, dozens of us, little boys, jumping in, watched over by one of Mr. and Mrs. Chris's daughters, the witchy one. I forget her name. It was the other one, Anthea, the nice one, who chose me to be Snow White. I'll tell you about that when I write again, Harry. Meantime, the best moments ever, at Windlesham, were when you and Peggy drove down for a weekend in the middle of the term to "take me out." You can't imagine the excitement, knowing you were going to come and watching for your car to arrive at the end of the long, long drive, and the long, long time it seemed to take for you to get from the gate to the front door to pick me up.

Then, it was the drive to Washington, the nearest village, and the hotel where you were staying. With luck, the weather would be fine and we could sit outdoors in the sunshine and you and Peggy you would order tea and sandwiches and for me . . . strawberries and cream! You can't imagine how delicious that treat tasted!

Good memories, then. Your son,
Peter

6 August 2021

Dear Harry,

Snow White. It was, well, yes, a bit exciting as well as really, really embarrassing. I was in my last year at Windlesham, so I would have been twelve. I must have been a sweet-looking little boy with my round face and freckles, because Miss Anthea chose me from all the seniors to be Snow White in the juniors' play.

I had been in school plays before, and you and Peggy had come down to see our theatrical productions. I think you liked to see me act because it reminded you of the ambition you once had. But maybe not. Anyway, you came down to see me in HMS Pinafore. I was a junior at the other time, and all the other boys were seniors. I was Tom Tucker, the Midshipmite. I only had a couple of words to say—I think it was "thank you" when "poor little Buttercup" was supposed to hand me a stick of that pink seaside rock we used to get in England, with letters spelling the name of the town going all the way down through the white middle of the stick. The one she gave me was just pretend candy, a wooden stick wrapped in pink blotting paper—such a disappointment. Anyway, as Tom Tucker, I learned how real sailors walk down steps, sideways, for better balance in the high seas.

For Snow White they dressed me up like a girl in a long, white skirt that reached to the ground and a little black jacket. They painted my lips bright red. I was much taller than the seven dwarfs, of course, because I was a senior and they were all juniors, and I had a good soprano voice because I was in the choir at school, so I remember having to sing Snow White's solo, "One Day My Prince Will Come," and feeling really, really embarrassed by the whole thing. But I must have done well because everyone applauded. I think you were in the audience that time but I couldn't be sure. Do you remember?

Bowing out for now, your son,
Peter

7 August 2021

Dear Harry,

So, yes, there was the dark side too. I mean that part of me that I knew was really wicked. But I couldn't help it. I would not have dared to tell you any of this at the time. I would not have dared tell anyone. It was knowing these things were wicked and doing them anyway and being so alone with them, knowing they were so wicked, I could not tell anyone. Not ever.

Some of them were just thoughts—truly wicked thoughts. And some of them were deeds.

The wicked thoughts were mostly about pain. They were mostly about causing pain, sometimes on others, sometimes on myself. About torture. I knew about torture because I knew about the Nazis. I knew about the Gestapo, and how they tortured people. I didn't know much, didn't know the details, but I understood the concept—whipping people, beating people, giving people electric shocks, hanging them up by their hands and ripping out their fingernails and toenails. I had read about these things or heard of them. I knew about medieval torture, too, the racks, the red-hot irons, those things. And somehow I had them in my head. I was only ten years old, only eleven or twelve, and I had these things in my head.

It was mostly after lights out, Harry, when I was alone in bed. Sometimes, rarely, it was with other boys, acting out bare-bum beatings with bedroom slippers, sometimes them, sometimes me, and I have to say it gave me the greatest secret pleasure when it was me. I knew it was wicked and I was terribly ashamed, but the more ashamed I felt, the more I seemed to like it. Sticking my bare bum in the air and feeling the hard, painful slap as the slipper made contact. The thrill of waiting, waiting for the next . . .

So, there was that. But there was worse. There was more wicked still. Later. When all the others were asleep and I lay waiting, with those thoughts in my head. I don't know, I may have touched myself, my penis, I don't know. It may have been hard, may have called out to be touched. But that's not what I remember. What I remember is slipping out of bed when everyone was asleep and tiptoeing out of the dormitory and down the darkened corridor to the loo. It was a kind of attic room, with a sloping roof, and rafters. I remember that. It had a window that looked out over the dark lawn below to the masters' house, where there might still be a light burning in a window. And I'd let down my pajama bottoms and sit down on the loo and think—yes, Harry, this is true—I'd think truly wicked, horrible thoughts about Hitler and Himmler, Goebbels, Goering. About SS men in black with whips and big leather boots. I'd think about torture. And thinking about torture I'd take a finger and shove it up my bum as far I could make it go. All the way till it hurt. It's true.

Today, perhaps, it would take a psychotherapist to work this out. A parent, if he or she knew about such thoughts and deeds would send their son to a therapist to work it out. There was never a thought of therapists in those days. If there had been, I would never have told. It was a private agony, Harry. A private wickedness. It belonged in the dark. I would never have told anyone. But I knew that it was wicked.

There. I've told you. I got it off my chest. I'm glad you know about it, finally, because I never would have told you then.

With love,
Peter

9 August 2021

Dear Harry,

I neither knew this at the time, nor would I have been old enough to understand, I think, but I later learned that another member of our household in those war years came over to England from Europe on the now well-known Kindertransport. The story of the trains filled with children that left German and Austrian cities between 1938 and 1940 has been told in literature and film, on television too. I would not have understood this at the time but the children were mostly Jewish, sent off from home and family by desperate parents so that the little ones, at least, might find shelter from the rapidly approaching Nazi maelstrom.

You would know better than I, Harry, but I imagine Ernst would have been twelve or thirteen when he arrived in England—older than Flora and myself by a few years. He seemed to us a strange, lonely boy who lived up to his name—earnest. A part of that strangeness was the heavy accent with which he struggled, initially, with the English language. He retained a good part of that accent until his recent death this year, more than seventy years later, in his adopted city of Chicago. Reunited with his parents in America in Omaha, Nebraska, after the war, he lived with them there for many years; I can only imagine how hard it would have been for this family of Viennese Jewish refugees—no matter that they were now converted to Christianity—to adapt to a city deep in the American Midwest.

For several years after the war, in gratitude for our family's hospitality and care, we would receive regular care packages from the Schnabls. Those gifts were more than welcome at a time when food was scarce in post-war England and ration books still required for basic needs. Amongst the many delicacies in these exotic packages arriving from that fabled, unimaginable land of plenty far across the ocean, there were two that stand out forever in my memory: huge cans of salty, memorably delicious ham and jars of peanut butter. Peanut butter! This was something hitherto unknown in England, at least by us, a mouthwatering treat that Peggy packed into my tuck box to take back to school, where it became the envy of my classmates.

Until the day he died, already in his nineties, Ernst remained whole-heartedly devoted to you, Harry, and to Peggy, as well as to Flora and me. He did not, he told me toward the end of his life, have a good relationship with his own father, and I suspect that you had become a kind of surrogate. For a while, indeed, he was a part of our family, never quite a brother to Flora and me, but always a presence in our midst. He went to school in Bedford, where he received a good start in his education. And after his resettlement in the United States, he remained in close touch with you throughout his life in transatlantic correspondence and occasional visits. He would be genuinely pleased to know how often he is mentioned in your letters.

Importantly, with your guidance—though surely without your insistence?—he found in Christianity a refuge from the confusion of his own cultural roots. He remained deeply appreciative of your mentorship. A devout Christian throughout his adult life, he married a church organist and was devastated, in later years, by her loss. He was, though, a stubborn traditionalist, resistant to change—perhaps a consequence of the disruption in his early life. He was outraged, for example, when his daughter Emily, brought up by himself in the Episcopal tradition, decided to take Holy Orders—given his disapproval of women priests. Happily, father and daughter were reconciled in due course.

I was in touch with Ernst a number of times by telephone and US mail—not email! Not for Ernst!—in the years before his death. He was a gentle soul, loyal to a fault, and his gratitude to you personally and to our family was touching. This was one person, among many I'm sure, whose life you helped to change with your own special wisdom and compassion.

> With respectful thoughts, then,
> your son,
> Peter

10 August 2021

Dear Harry,

I'm trying to recall when I was first aware of Jews as a people somehow "different" from us Christians. Did I know, for example, that Ernst was originally Jewish? Did you ever make us aware of that—you must of course have known—and did it matter to you? There were no Jews in our little English country village. Indeed, I had scarcely any history with Jews until I married one when I was already in my thirties!

What did I even know, back then? What did you tell me about the Holocaust? I was eight years old at the time the camps were liberated, and you may have considered me too young to know about such horrors. I suspect you'd have wanted to protect me from that terrible, heart-rending truth about the depravities of our fellow man. I believe that I learned about it only later from my history lessons.

And yet . . . and yet . . . There is this: when Flora and I were still quite little, our mother, Peggy, used to read us bedtime stories from a pair of books called *Six O'clock Saints* and *More Saints for Six O'clock*. One of the stories was titled "Little Saint Hugh." It was about a boy who lived in the dark back alleys in the town of Lincoln (I always had the impression that it was an Eastern European ghetto, but no, this was in my own country, England, in the Middle Ages) and was supposedly sacrificed by Jews in what I now know to be the infamous "blood libel" myth that continues, even today, to be propagated among rabid anti-Semites.

It was a truly hideous, deeply anti-Semitic story, yet Peggy calmly included it without judgment or explanation with all the other saints' stories she read, apparently unfazed by sharing its disgraceful slander with her children. Did she believe in this calumny? Surely not! I prefer to think that her anti-Semitism was not malicious—I fail to see a shred of malice in her—but rather pure, unquestioned ignorance, reflecting more on benighted, ancient, shameful Christian lore than on her character.

Still—I need to say this, Harry—there was a grievously intuitive and unexamined part of Peggy's otherwise kind, generous personality (witness her welcoming of all and sundry into her home in the war years and her caring mothering of them all!) that bespoke prejudice, and not only of Jews but of people of other heritages and skin colors. She was, she herself would readily admit, a snob, and her class-consciousness was sometimes an embarrassment.

It pains me to mention this, but Ellie was sensitive to what she first experienced as Peggy's—let me avoid the term anti-Semitism, which mischaracterizes her—but her initial hesitation, a coolness before opening her heart to people with backgrounds different from her own. Born in the early years of the 20th century and brought up as one of seven siblings by a Christian minister father, mild-mannered to a fault, and a mother who could be severe and bossy, even acerbic, she had what was surely a protected childhood in the then remote city of Swansea on the southern coast of Wales. Not much exposure, then, in her young days, to the global upheavals and seismic social and cultural shifts of the post-Victorian, post-Edwardian world. But I do believe that Peggy was the first to make a genuine effort to recognize and overcome the prejudices that were not so much in her nature but were rather nurtured into her character. She was at heart a generous, kind, and loving person.

Do you see what I mean? Am I mischaracterizing her in any way? Am I doing her an injustice? Because I'm trying to explain to myself how it was that she could read that story to her children. I had a further thought about this the other day when I came upon a letter from her in the shoebox of old letters that has become my treasure trove. She was writing to Ellie and me about the books she was saving up for Sarah when she was still a little girl. She wanted a list of those Beatrix Potter's Peter Rabbit books we already had—also books she loved to read to her own children—and wanted to know if I remembered *Little Black Sambo*, the story of the little Black boy who foiled a ring of fierce tigers, as I recall, by churning them into butter. She had been told, she wrote, that the book might no longer be considered suitable for American children. What did I think?

It's difficult. Ellie has her own *Little Black Sambo* story. Her first teaching experience as a very young woman was in a predominantly Black elementary school in south central Los Angeles, where she was reprimanded—this was in the 1960s—for her insensitivity in bringing this little children's book to class. Today, years later and perhaps none too soon, we have begun to understand more about the subtle ways in which prejudice inserts itself into our ways of being together as mutually respectful human beings. I remember, truthfully, loving that little book. Did that make me a racist? I hope not.

As for you and Peggy, I'm sure you understood her foibles, as she did yours. You lived together and loved each other "for better, for worse, for richer, for poorer, in sickness and health" for more than sixty years.

Fond memories, then, of
both of you,
Peter

13 August 2021

Good morning again, Harry!

We did have fun, though, didn't we, with the Bletchley girls? They were especially kind to us children. Adoring, even.

There was that time at Christmas. It was a tradition in our family—one that was surely originally your idea—to celebrate the arrival of Father Christmas (we call him Santa over here in the US) with great fun and games, rather than make it a furtive, middle of the night, down-the-chimney affair whose only trace was the stuffed stockings left to be ripped apart in the morning. No, for us, Father Christmas came with fanfare and much clanging of cowbells or car horns and loud "ho-ho-hos" reverberating through the upstairs of the house. One time he was a giant, arriving on stilts—not your skill, Harry, but one of your guests; another time it was an alternating pair of bristly mustachioed twins from the RAF base at Cranfield down the hill ("I know what you think, you think I'm Frank. Well, I'm not, I'm Dougie!")

And then there was the time when Father Christmas arrived with great hullabaloo, driving a sleigh, an ancient perambulator (baby carriage, here) rescued from the attic and hauled along the top corridor by two harnessed "reindeer", Vivian and Fiona wearing fur coats, on all fours. I suspect it might have taken a few good gin and tonics to kindle their cooperation, but there they were, good sports, the whole party laughing wildly.

It was Fiona, too, who starred in another Rectory extravaganza inspired by your old love of theater. I don't recall the occasion—but perhaps you would? The title of the play was "Murder at the Rectory." Did you write the script? I'm guessing so. You did love your mysteries: Agatha Christie, Ngaio Marsh, Dorothy Sayers, Margery Allingham. You devoured them endlessly, Penguin paperbacks. There was always one or more on your bedside table. Your play was obviously inspired by them.

You staged it in the drawing room—the large, formal room with great windows looking out to the rhododendron bushes that marked the boundaries of the garden, the room where tea was served on special occasions with finger sandwiches and biscuits (okay, cookies here) and cake set out on the best art deco Burlington china tea service. For this occasion, you rigged a curtain across one end of the room and arranged chairs for your audience at the other. Of the play, I remember only the heart-chilling scream that came from Fiona's throat as the murder victim and the slash of bright red lipstick across her cheek where the "blood" poured out. I was terrified, clutching at my mother's hand for reassurance.

I believe that you, Harry, were yourself the murderous assailant. If memory serves . . .

So . . . be honest now. Scout's honor, Rector. Did you lust after this young woman secretly, this seductive Fiona, just as I did, a child still, unable yet to know what lust was all about?

Oh, Harry, I'd give anything to know!

Lost in these memories,
Peter

15 August 2021

Dear Harry,

We all knew that Hank was your dog. He was devoted to you. A Northumbrian, like yourself, he was a farm-bred border collie. Handsome, always eager, with soft brown eyes and remarkable intelligence, he came with the family when we left Newcastle in 1938 and headed south to your new incumbency in Aspley Guise.

If I close my eyes and feel it with my fingers, I can still recall the touch of Hank's thick, silky coat, mostly black but highlighted with white. I see you, black and white yourself in your long cassock and dog collar, striding along with black and white Hank "to heel" beside you, like the good dog he was. The pair of you!

The first "memory" I have of Hank—a "memory" in quotation marks because it comes from a photograph in the family album—is of him lying peaceably on a blanket laid out on the lawn in Holywell, your first parish, before Newcastle, where Flora was born. Hank is pretending to be lazing in the sun but anyone looking at that photograph will know that he's awake and fully attentive to his job, watching over the little baby in the pram beside him.

Border collies absolutely need to have a job, don't they? You taught me that. It's in their blood. They're herders. Up north, in the mountains of Northumberland, the shepherds send them off with a sharp whistle into the hills to gather the widely scattered flocks and bring them back down the mountainside to be sheared. With baby-sitting no longer needed, Hank was given a new job when we got to Aspley Guise, sent off through the village streets all the way to Granny Murcott's house up by the woods, a good mile from the Rectory, where she'd attach a little bag of sweets (candies, that is) to his collar for him to bring back to her grandchildren.

But his main job was to make sure we didn't get into mischief when we were little and see that we never strayed too far from his watchful gaze.

Flora and I were both away at school when Hank left us. He died of old age. We were in the back seat of the car when you broke the news, Harry, on the way back home from fetching us at the train station. You must have been devastated by his death yourself, but you had to put a good face on it. No man, no father was allowed to give in to grief in front of his children in those days.

Did we cry in the car? I don't remember. I suspect that even by that young age—I would have been, what? Seven? Eight?—I had learned to keep my feelings to myself. But I know that I'll never forget that terrible sense of loss, that emptiness, with Hank gone. We'd had deaths in the family before, but none that I'd understood with this same intimacy. The universe had shifted on its axis.

To relieve the gloomy silence in the back seat behind you as you drove, you told us you had a surprise for us when we got home. That was fine. The surprise turned out to be Benjy, an adorable little Cocker Spaniel puppy, who jumped all over us, as excited to meet us as we to discover that we had a brand-new pet.

We loved Benjy, of course. And Siân (Welsh for Jane, the "gift of God"), the snappy, little Pembrokeshire Corgi who was Benjy's successor after he died. But we all knew, secretly, the whole family, that neither of them could ever live up to Hank. Because Hank was the gentlest, kindest, smartest dog we ever had. Well, that ever lived. I know you loved him, Harry, though you would never have dreamed of saying so. In your universe, human beings didn't "love" dogs. Nor, especially, were human beings their dog's "mommy" and "daddy." You had nothing but scorn for such sentimentality when it came to animals. Now that you're no longer around to object, I can safely say that I know that you loved Hank and Hank loved you. He was the family's dog, yes, of course. But there was never the slightest doubt about whose dog he really was.

So yes, I see this wonderful creature walking obediently at your heel, ears perked, tail held high, beside the flapping black folds of your cassock. Your faithful dog.

Nothing but good memories today.

Your son,
Peter

17 August 2021

Dear Harry,

Not all memories are so good. I need to share a difficult one about Flora while we're still in Aspley Guise. Now that she too has been gone from our home planet these seven years, and you for many more, I feel the story of this trauma can be told. It was, for a little girl, the kind of wound that can last a lifetime.

How do I know about this? Was it you who told me? Or she? I'm pretty sure I knew the story at an early age, young enough to not fully understand its meaning.

She might have been twelve years old at the time, perhaps a year or two more, and came rushing home in tears one day from a walk on the heath, up behind the Rectory, beyond the end of the path with the blackberry bushes and past the sandpit—a quarry cut deep into the hillside a century earlier. We used to take tin trays up there from the kitchen, for the scary thrill of sliding on them down its steep, treacherous slopes, top to bottom. We took glass vials there too, from time to time, filling them with layers of different colored sands, red and green, yellow, orange, black, and corking them up securely to bring back home as gifts.

Further, past the sandpit, was a wild area of heath with waist-high gorse bushes, prickly, dark green with seasonal bright yellow blossoms, small but plentiful. It was here that Flora had come upon a stranger with his fly unbuttoned, cock in hand—though she had no idea what that strange thing might be—scaring her as it squirted "white stuff," so she said, all over the ground in front of him.

She was terrified. She knew it was something she was not meant to see. But she had seen it, and she ran back home in terror.

Did she just happen upon the man by chance, I have since wondered, his dismal, solitary act already in progress? Or did he see this pretty little girl and choose the moment to unbutton his fly and expose himself? Was he one of those broken men who get their kicks this way?

I have no answer to these questions and I suspect that you did not, either. But it fell on you to find the words to reassure your daughter, and comfort her, and calm her down. How could you possibly have explained what this man was doing?

As we well know, you resorted most frequently to Freud or Jung to guide you in such situations, so perhaps these luminaries helped. I know you were aware of what could be the lasting emotional repercussions from experiences such as this. In the long view, I wonder how this childhood episode might have affected your later efforts to understand your daughter and her problems when she grew to be a woman—and to offer her sometimes unsolicited advice about her relationship with men.

You may or may not know this, Harry, but she—your daughter, Flora—found something dark and disturbing about your efforts to intervene in this aspect of her life, no matter how well-intentioned.

Anyway, please forgive the honesty about this obviously distressing subject. It did not even happen to me, it happened to my sister and it happened many years ago. But for some reason the story continues, stubbornly, to haunt my memory.

> I am, as always, the son who
> wants to know,
> Peter

18 August 2021

Dear Harry,

We're about to leave Aspley Guise now, but let's take a moment to revisit a place of special interest.

The Bell was the pub at one corner of the (actually triangular) village "square." The Post Office occupied one side of the triangle with Aspley House across from it, on the opposite side. On the third side of the triangle were the shops: the butcher's, the grocer's and the greengrocer's and, sandwiched in between them somewhere, the tiny newsagent where you bought your copy of *The Times* and the shredded Golden Virginia tobacco for your home-rolled cigarettes. Occasionally, on a splurge, you'd indulge in a packet of Players or Senior Service.

Oh, and in the middle of the square, let's not forget, were the bus shelter and the horse trough.

But The Bell. You often used to stop there for a drink or two, mostly before lunch. In a way, I think you did your business there, or some of it, because as in every English village worth its name, the pub was the center of social life. All the local news was readily available here, so any news you wanted to put out into the community could be spread rapidly from this point out. It was here, too, that you could expect to meet many of your parishioners, particularly the male ones, and particularly those who might need a timely reminder that it was time to show their faces back in church on Sunday morning.

The pub was also an important place for you to maintain your credentials as a man of the people, not just a man of the cloth; a man who could be trusted to understand and share their problems, a man with his feet on the ground along with everybody else, a man you could share a cigarette and a pint with, or a game of darts. Not some hoity-toity snob who thought himself a cut above. It was only in the pub that everyone could call you Harry and know you'd have a laugh if they poked a bit of fun in your direction.

So that was The Bell in Aspley Guise. In Braughing, there was The Brown Bear, where you were given the goose eggs that hatched out as Susan and Sarah. In Sharnbrook, The Swan with Two Nicks; in Aberporth, where you retired, The Ship. These were your haunts—mostly, as I say, in the middle of the day but sometimes also before supper in the evening. Your usual was a bottle of Guinness.

I don't think I ever saw you visibly intoxicated but you were, fess up, a bit of a boozer, no? Aside from your lunchtime Guinness at the pub, there would likely be another one before dinner, carefully poured to produce exactly the right head of foam. You were fussy about that. Then the ritual glass of sherry, dry or medium dry and, with dinner, a glass or two of "plonk"— your wine of choice, always red, the cheapest you could find, though you did enjoy a glass of the finer stuff if someone else was treating. And even after all that alcohol consumption, you would usually want to complete the evening with a snifter of brandy or one of those tiny glasses of liqueur—Grand Marnier, Cointreau, Benedictine . . . Your favorite was Chartreuse, with a preference for the more expensive, finer-tasting green over the yellow. You swore you could taste every one of the forty-seven—or however many—herbs that went into the making. (Irish priest: " 'Twas made by the monks in France, you know?" And Paddy: "Sure, and it must have been the Protestants made the glasses.")

Anyway, yes, The Bell. Even when we were little children you would take us there when you finished your morning rounds, stopping by at the homes of your parishioners who needed a visit from the clergy, whether in sickness, social, or emotional distress. Children were not allowed to set foot in pubs under any circumstance in those days, so you would leave us in the car by the back door and come out with a glass of lemonade and a package of Smith's Potato Crisps ("chips", in the American vernacular) to keep us happy. Inside the package with the crisps came a tiny twist of azure blue paper containing just a pinch of salt, enough to season those delicious crisps to taste.

These are the things I recall most clearly, the everyday, unimportant, shining moments that seem to me now as intimate as any that we shared. These are the things that find a lasting place in some obscure corner of the mind, the memories I treasure most.

Nostalgically, then, your son,
Peter

21 August 2021

Dear Harry,

Aside from Hank and the usual succession of household pets—the cats and dogs that shared our homes with us— you had an odd, rather touching relationship with animals. I remember especially the mini farm at the Vicarage in Braughing, the parish we moved to when we left Aspley Guise.

It must have been in the year or two immediately after the war. The Vicarage came with a large property surrounding an elegant, if somewhat deteriorating, Queen Anne house. There was an expanse of green lawn out front, including an area that had been leveled out to make a rather lumpy tennis court that was, as I'm sure you'll remember, hardly ever used. Beyond it, the grass grew long and wild, requiring only the occasional trimming with a motorized mowing machine. At the bottom of the garden, downhill, to the right, was what could best be described as a large pond or a small lake, so completely choked with reeds and algae that the water was no longer visible; and up the hill from there, to the left of the tennis court, was a stand of beech trees large enough to warrant designation as a copse. Propped up against the house, on one side, a precarious greenhouse was home to a valiant old vine that did, in fact and surprisingly for our English climate, produce grapes.

Behind the house was a full-sized barn with stables that were no longer used for horses—not in your realm of interest, Harry!—and a cluster of outhouses of undetermined use. And two pigsties. Which called out for occupants, particularly in those immediate post-war years while rationing was still in effect and meat was in short supply. They inspired some previously hidden talent for animal husbandry on your part, as well to contribute to the national recovery.

Martha was the first arrival. She was a big, old sow who gave birth to a succession of litters of piglets, all of which, or most of which, were sent off to the market once they reached an appropriate age, though one of them, Mary, was kept on as a second breeding sow. Another, one of the runt pigs, the littlest of the litter, was spared the fate of his siblings, I think because you found a soft spot in your heart for the little guy and decided he should stay on at the Vicarage.

His name was Harry. You were tickled by the namesake, of course, but he got his name mostly because in that part of the countryside the runt of the litter is always called "the harry pig."

I don't recall what became of Harry, but he lived with us for quite a while and became something of a family pet. You didn't have the heart to send him off for slaughter. As for big Martha, she was the boss-lady and felt free to roam wherever she damn well pleased—even, on at least one occasion, into the house through the back door and through the dining room into the kitchen, where we caught her eyeing our dinner. She was quite indignant to be unceremoniously chased out, with the aid of broom from the cleaning closet.

And then there were Susan and Sarah. I have mentioned their names before. These two came to us originally as eggs—goose eggs, a gift to the Vicar from the innkeeper at The Brown Bear and intended for your breakfast enjoyment. There were three of them, actually, three eggs, and Flora and I begged you not to eat them but put them, instead, under a broody hen to see if they would hatch.

Unpredictably, they did. At least two of the three. And, not knowing how to determine the sex of those tiny balls of yellow fluff, we named them Susan and Sarah. Sarah, it turned out, was not a goose at all. He was a gander—big, haughty, unafraid of anything, and fierce. Susan, on the other hand, lived up to her name: she was a goose. She was white, subservient to her gander, sweet enough in her own way, but definitely aloof. We soon discovered that geese are imperious creatures, and none too friendly to their human benefactors; this couple soon took over the run of the property, strutting around as though they owned the place—which undoubtedly they thought they did. There was a game of dare I played with friends who came to visit, running out full tilt through the back door to see if we could make it all the way back into the house through the front door without being chased, pinned down and savaged by Sarah's hard beak.

And then one day, we discovered that Susan had begun laying eggs of her own in a straw nest at the back of one of the small outhouses. In time, we counted eight of them—and we were thrilled.

News got around in the pubs, as was to be expected, and you came home with the sage consensus of the local farmers:

never allow a goose to sit on her own eggs. She's too lazy, too self-involved, too easily distracted. She'll never stay with them. Put those eggs under a hen, if you ever want to see the goslings hatch.

You wouldn't hear of it. The philosophy you embraced, as always, was to let nature take her course. I'm not sure whether God had anything to do with it. Perhaps not. But you insisted that Susan be allowed to sit on her own eggs.

Improbably, she proved you right. Every one of those eight eggs hatched. All eight of the little birds survived and were soon strutting around the garden behind the proud father, all in line, Susan following after Sarah—we never changed his name—who stalked ahead with the eight goslings strung out behind them. They did not regard their territory as limited to the garden, feeling perfectly entitled to stroll through the Vicarage, in through the back door and out through the front, where visiting parishioners would sometimes be startled to encounter this pompous, proprietary avian procession emerging from the house to greet them.

We soon came to regard these birds as members of the family. Unfortunately, proud, and independent as they were, they rapidly became a nuisance. They pooped everywhere. On the tennis lawn. On the gravel driveway outside the front door. In the greenhouse. And ten of these large birds can produce an alarming amount of poop, especially once the goslings grew up into something more resembling adult geese.

Worse, Susan and Sarah and their flock became dissatisfied with what the Vicarage grounds could offer in the way of forage and found their way across the little trout stream that marked one of our boundaries and into the cultivated field beyond. In no time, they were wreaking havoc with the farmer's cabbage crop. He complained. Loudly. In public. In the pub. And you, good pastor, could not afford to alienate your parishioners.

What became of the rest of the flock I don't recall, but I do know what happened to Sarah. He was given to the farmer who wrung his neck and had him plucked and trussed up to be given away as a whist drive prize (we do Bingo in America today). The person required to publicly award the prize was none other than yourself, Harry, Father, Vicar of the parish. And you came home from the event as close to tears as I can ever remember.

It was a different matter once with that belligerent rooster. Do you remember him? This was in Aspley Guise, before Braughing. It was my job to feed the chickens—I was maybe eight or nine years old—and this creature started to attack me every time I opened the gate to the chicken run. You didn't believe me, though, and scoffed at my cowardice. So, you set out one morning to feed the fowl yourself, to demonstrate that it was ridiculously easy. Surprise! That vicious bird had the gall to attack you, the Vicar, beak and talons flying. He was the not unwelcome precursor of Sarah's fate, ending up on the dining table. This time the table was our own. And you had no compunction carving that bird up, as I recall.

> Remembering all this nonsense,
> with much love,
> Peter

22 August 2021

Dear Harry,

Is Braughing a good moment for us to talk about money? Because Peggy later told me, when I was old enough to understand about such things, that you took a hefty cut in your annual stipend to make the move from Aspley Guise. She herself was none too pleased with the choice, but apparently you felt called by God—and of course she went along.

God would have a hard time explaining to my satisfaction why Braughing needed you more than Aspley Guise. It was a smaller village. The Church was St. Mary the Virgin and the main pub, as I mentioned earlier, was The Brown Bear. The main street was The Street. You could not put that more plainly, could you, Harry? There were two fords for cars (carriages? wagons? hay carts?) to cross the little stream that flowed through the center of the village. No way to ford it, though, when, it was in spate. Once or twice a year, perhaps, the little stream became a riotous river for a day or two, sometimes leaving exposed in its muddy banks the relics of an ancient Roman encampment, dating back to the time when Braughing was a stop along the arrow-straight road that led from Londinium to the barbarian north. Your annual salary was a handsome 250 pounds sterling. You managed to eke out a few more precious pounds by also taking on the nearby parish of Westmill, just the other side of the A10, the highway that led from Puckeridge, the nearest small town, to Buntingford. Peggy told me this because she thought I should know what a huge financial sacrifice it had been for you to send both Flora and me to private boarding schools. True, both schools offered discounts to the clergy, but even so it was clearly a financial stretch for you.

Anyway, whether God wanted it or not, we made the move. You simply felt that after ten or twelve years you had completed the work He had given to do at Aspley Guise. As we say in our vernacular over here, I can relate.

I think it's true to say that money never meant much to you. As Peggy always said—and she warned Ellie about this, because she saw the same in me—if you had it, you spent it. And, Lord, you loved to spend! Your delight in sometimes quite reckless indulgence was visible, almost palpable, and you managed to be quite profligate insofar as your trifling stipend would allow. I think you believed in all sincerity that God would provide. Well, He did provide free housing for your family throughout your years working in His service. The rectories and vicarages were a part of your remuneration package. But you were not impressed by people simply because they had money, and you had endless sympathy for those who had none, or little.

It was only much later in life that I learned to my surprise that you'd had access to other resources than your salary. Your father had left you and your siblings shares in A. Reyrolle & Co., the electrical switchgear company that developed and marketed one of his inventions, and it appears those shares increased substantially in value over time. It was this resource that enabled you to send us to school and eventually, too, to buy the little cottage in Aberporth where you and Peggy spent the years of your retirement. Before your move to Braughing, too, Miss Stone, a lovely old spinster living down the hill from the Aspley Guise Rectory with her caregiver (a Mrs. Bridger, if I recall? There was a Bridge in there somewhere) left you a nice little sum as an inheritance when she died, I assume in gratitude for your friendship toward her and your pastoral visits. She also left you a silver christening mug etched with the initials of her family name; I wonder what became of it? We children were invited over to her cottage from time to time. The gentle, silver-haloed Miss Stone seemed to take a special delight in having us for tea—wheeled into her spotless, if rather musty drawing room on a trolley by the solicitous Mrs. B and served in elegant china cups and saucers, with scones and cake on tiny matching plates. Those visits required a special effort at politeness and special attention to good manners.

You yourself, Harry, were scrupulously, meticulously honest when it came to money and were outraged when others did not meet your standards. We'll talk more in due course about my friend, Barry Evans, an exuberantly bohemian artist who lived in a tiny cottage on subsistence earnings with his unruly family up the hill from the Vicarage in Braughing; enough, for now, to note that one of the reasons he became your nemesis was your loan of sixty pounds to tide his family over a tight spot—a loan he never bothered to return.

I should note finally, while we're on this topic, that when you died, and Peggy shortly after you, you left behind an estate worth more than I thought possible. There was little remaining in the way of actual money, but you owned Glenview free and clear, that beautifully located seaside cottage on the Cardigan coast. The proceeds from its sale, even when shared equally with Flora, allowed me and Ellie to reinvest the money in the purchase of another cottage, this one half a world away on the Pacific coast, in Laguna Beach, California. It was a pleasingly appropriate exchange; I was tempted at first to call our cottage Glenview. But of course . . . no glen! And just a peekaboo view of the Pacific. But it has become our quiet retreat and we will always treasure it.

> With love and gratitude,
> Peter

23 August 2021

Dear Harry,

Tea-time, that hallowed English ritual. There were other genteel homes, aside from Miss Stone's, where Flora and I were invited regularly to tea by your parishioners.

Do you recall the single woman at the bottom of what we called Sandy Hill—was that its name?—in Aspley Guise? Just across the road from where the bombs fell? I remember little else about this kind old lady, not even how she looked, but I do remember very clearly the rowdy pink and grey parrot who was kept in a cage in her living room. His name was Algy—short for Algernon?—and she had taught him to dance. She would run her finger back and forth across the bars of his cage and urge him on: "Dance-y, Algy, dance-y, Algy" she would croon, and the bird would repeat the words she said in his strange little parrot voice as he hopped cheerfully from one claw to the other on his perch.

Then there were Mr. and Mrs. Gates, an elderly couple who lived at the end of a different, rather more socially proper sandy lane and were delighted when we would visit them for tea. They had a big armchair with a footrest that could be converted into a long, cushiony slope for us to slide down. Best of all, though, was the gazebo past the little rise of their rock garden, out in the middle of the trim, green lawn. It was built on a circle of steel rails and could be swiveled at any time of day to face the sun—if sun was to ever be found in Merrie Olde. But it also served as a jolly carnival ride. Poor old Mr. Gates, we would have him drag us around and around in circles on the noisy metal rail, faster and faster, until we were all dizzy and laughing in delight before Mrs. Gates would make him stop and call us in for tea.

And then, for tea-time too, there were Grace and Arthur Young, who lived in a small redbrick house halfway up the hill on the main road that led up and over the hill to Woburn Sands. Arthur was your churchwarden and they sat behind us every Sunday in the Rector's—not the People's—churchwarden's pew, each identified by its tall, brass-topped "wand" that stood by the center aisle. I most often went to the Youngs' alone, I don't know why, but this was my favorite place of all to go for tea for a special reason: Arthur was in the Home Guard and had a .22 rifle which he taught me how to shoot, setting up a row of clay flowerpots as targets in the back yard and showing me how to steady the butt of the rifle tight against my shoulder and aim down the sights. I got to be quite good at smashing pots.

There was tea at the Misses Tanqueray, off the main square and next door to the sweet shop. When we went there we played games of Concentration, with buttons and brooches and little silver thimbles and a dozen other tiny objects laid out in tidy order on a green felt-covered tray, to be memorized and recalled from memory, each in its exact location, when hidden by a tea towel.

And there was tea, of course, every day at the Vicarage or the Rectory, wherever we happened to be, with sandwiches and cake and crisp biscuits, ginger snaps, and chocolate-coated McVities, and mother pouring tea as mothers are supposed to do.

You did love your cup of tea, didn't you, Harry? Here's another thing we share; I still bring Ellie a cup of English tea in bed first thing every morning. Never fail, never miss. For fifty years! As for you, every time I drink a cuppa, I think of you, and think of Peggy. And think of England . . .

Cheers,
Peter

26 August 2021

Dear Harry,

England! Yes! I do still miss that England in which you brought me up. More than ever, to be honest. These are parlous times here in America and I sometimes think how good it might feel to return to the country of my birth and live there again in my old age, after more than sixty years away. But then, I remind myself of Brexit, and of Boris Johnson. Worse, I remind myself of the long, slow, everlasting drizzle of rain, the constant clouds, the miserable winters, and I return reluctantly to my senses. Ellie was born and raised under the clear, sunny skies of Southern California and the reliable, temperate warmth. The climate of the British Isles would soon overwhelm her with its peculiar, ineluctable gloom. Besides, Harry, are things any better over there than here?

This is not the America I came to in 1964. I fled a country in which I had become a marked man, identifiable— classifiable—by any of my fellow Brits as soon as I opened my mouth. My first words betrayed me as "public school and Oxbridge", well-educated, privileged, upper class-ish, perfectly acceptable at the highest levels of society. I was unmistakably a toff, welcomed as one of them by the fortunate few and scorned by many, not for who I was but for the stereotype I represented. When I first came to America, I delighted in the fact—I think now it was no more than an illusion—that no self-respecting gas station attendant would regard himself as in any way less of a man than any other because of his job and would not resent those who had done better than himself but instead be confident that with work and dedication he could do as well as anyone. I can't tell you, Harry, how refreshing this ethos seemed to me when I first arrived here.

It was my idealism, surely, that blinded me to the racism and other deep social discontents that were never far beneath the surface. There was, most obviously, the divisive war in Vietnam, which caused a rift between young and old, the educated and the less well-educated, the wealthy and the poor, and of course between people of different political persuasions. But then I thought it great that everyone felt free to go out there and make their opinions loudly known. The push-and-pull, the clamor of democracy at work seemed to me entirely beneficial, a healthy alternative to the angry, resentful politics of class that I had left behind.

But then the resentments started to turn ugly even here. The sometimes-violent response to the protests of a discontented underclass in American society appalled me. The aggressive fury of the Black Panthers opened my eyes to racism. But I think I first became aware of a seismic rightward shift with the tax rebellion in the early 1970s, shortly after my arrival in California. I discovered to my surprise that "socialism" was a dirty word, used as a weapon by the right wing against the left. Ronald Reagan oiled his way onto the political scene, first as governor of my new home state, then as president with what I despised as a poisonous agenda to benefit the rich and privileged at the cost of working people and the poor. I watched, at first with disappointment and then with increasing horror as America swung more and more wildly to the right, until even "Democratic" presidents were intimidated—and guided in their policies—by fear of powerful, monied conservatism. I kept thinking, well, the pendulum must begin to swing back, as it always does. And it didn't. It never has, not even at this moment. We ended up—logically, it seemed to me—with a self-important, self-serving man of great and probably ill-gotten wealth in the White House who was himself the very model of the money-grubbing, money-worshipping oligarch, a man so vile, in my judgment, so little concerned with the welfare of anyone but himself and his own kind, so transparent in his greed, nepotism and corruption that you would think Americans would soon reject such a creature from his position of power over them.

But no. Even after his deplorably narrow defeat at the polls, the man has refused to go away and threatens to return. The spectacle of an entire political party and a "base" of rabid, violence-prone supporters groveling before him leaves me appalled, in a constant state of disbelief. This is no longer the America I came to with such hopes for a democratic future, the America that led the rest of the world with its respect for human rights and its support for everything that might improve the lot of the human race. There are even vast numbers of people who call themselves Christian in America these days who make a mockery of every Christian value that you brought me up with: justice, mercy, care for the poor, the sick, the powerless. And the latent racism that has stained my adopted country's history has been unleashed by an ugly would-be emperor with no clothes.

Oh, Harry, good socialist, good Christian! I know that you would be just as appalled as I am by the direction that not only America but the world has been precipitously following in the few years since your death. You would find it hard to believe, I'm sure, that the insatiable greed of powerful oligarchical interests and their grip on compliant politicians are at this very moment working to enable the (yes! imminent!) actual destruction of the human species and the planet that is our only home.

It is monstrous, Harry. We are careening, seemingly unstoppably, toward a self-created, self-ordained apocalypse even as we squabble pathetically over a few crumbs. And England is complicit! What could you possibly have thought of Brexit, you who so loved your freedom to travel on the European continent?

And I must ask this, Harry: what about your all-seeing, all-knowing, all-powerful God? Is He a cynic? A black humorist? A sadist?

Or is He simply his nemesis, Satan, in disguise?

Your son,
Peter

28 August 2021

Dear Harry,

Forgive my cynicism! For God's sake let's change the subject after that jeremiad! Let's talk about something healthier, something that was close to your heart but impossible for us to talk about when you were still alive.

Let's talk about sex.

You liked to think of yourself as an open-minded, frank, not easily embarrassed man. You loved to engage in sexual innuendo, in your flirtations with the Bletchley girls at the Rectory . . . but all I really learned from you about sex was the blush of the English schoolboy. And oh, how I blushed! I blushed "like a girl"! The blood would come rushing to my cheeks at the slightest provocation. I continued to blush uncontrollably for an embarrassing number of years past normal blushing age. Even as a doctoral student at Iowa, I recall, in a class about the poetry of John Donne, Robert Herrick, and the English Metaphysicals, I blushed like a teenager at the mere mention of a breast. I blushed at my own blushing, desperate in my vain attempts to conceal my horrible embarrassment.

How's that for a would-be Romeo?

So, I would have been, what—twelve or thirteen—when I was summoned to your study for the obligatory sex talk at the Vicarage in Braughing. It was a tiny room, off the front hall, hardly big enough for your blond oak desk and matching chair and, as I recall, one comfortable leather easy chair.

On this occasion, when you called me in, you had a black chalkboard set up on an easel. It was time to initiate your son into the mysteries of sex, and if you were embarrassed, it was not half as much as I was.

Obviously, with the chalkboard, you wanted to make your lesson as objective as possible. All science and medicine. No mess or joy. You sketched the outlines of the operative parts, male and female, with a piece of white chalk and explained (roughly) how they could be brought together in an act designed (by the good Lord, surely!) to create new baby human beings. You explained about eggs and fertilization, about incubation and birth. You did your best to say what you thought needed to be said.

I did my own best to listen attentively as I knew I should. But in actual fact—I tell you this now, so many years later, and after you are long gone from this world!—your explanations were superfluous, at least their theoretical intent: by what accident or providence I no longer recall, I had a copy of Gray's Anatomy on the bookshelf in my bedroom and had scoured its pages—and the accompanying illustrations—often enough in search of this same information, trying to put it all together with the mysterious physiological effect that manifested in a region of my body I knew I was supposed to refrain from touching.

On multiple occasions, too, I had proved to myself that the required restraint was more than a boy could reasonably practice. The temptation to touch was too great, the mysterious pleasure too hard to resist. But I was not yet well enough developed to take things further than that exploratory touch.

No matter how well intended, I'm afraid to say your explanations did little more than add to my confusion. And soon, there was another of those major, life-changing events that I knew must somehow be related to all this but was unable to fit in to the confusing picture. You heard about it later, didn't you, not from me but from another source? But that deserves a letter all its own and I'll write more tomorrow.

Meantime, Harry, I do know that you struggled with this. I can't imagine how much harder it must have been for you to have this talk with Flora. But perhaps you left that task to Peggy? I'm curious but must acknowledge that this is just one other thing that I will never know.

Your son,
Peter

29 August 2021

Dear Harry,

Okay, this one is hard to write. It's time for us to talk about Mr. Ellis.

We spoke about this only once, not long after it happened, and you never mentioned it again. Which is odd, because you always insisted that trauma needed to be remembered, not buried, and forgotten. I remember, for example, the time that my son, Matthew, your oldest grandson, was run over by a station wagon at the age of four—literally, the driver didn't see him and the vehicle backed right over him—and you told me I should help him keep the incident in mind and not let it sink back into the unconscious, where it might do lasting damage. You worried that he might end up a race car driver! (He didn't. Thanks!)

Your advice was assuredly based in a sound understanding of the workings of the human mind, which is why I find it odd that you neglected your advice yourself.

Here are the facts as I remember them. I was about twelve years old. I can't be sure, quite honestly, whether it came before or after that chalkboard talk that I reminded you about when I last wrote. Enough to know that I was still largely ignorant about sex. Mr. Ellis was the math teacher at the first boys' boarding school you sent me to, and he had inherited from his uncle a property far from the school but not far from where we lived—in Braughing, at the time. He let you know he would be happy to have me come for an overnight stay if ever it was convenient and it so happened you were due to attend a weekend ruri-decanal conference (I remember that term!) and thought it would be nice (I'm assuming, here) to take Peggy with you for the event.

So, you dropped me off at Mr. Ellis's, grateful for his kindness.

I'm surprised you could be so trusting. Or were you just so keen on the idea of having a quiet weekend away with Peggy that you chose not to speculate about Mr. Ellis's motivations? We never had that conversation. And you never knew, never chose to ask about what actually happened.

I don't know why, but it feels important even at this late date that I tell you.

After you dropped me off, Mr. Ellis was all charm and affection for his twelve-year-old guest. He took me around his small farm, the chicken run, the duck pond, the pig sties. We ended up in a big barn with all kinds of interesting old stuff—lanterns and horse harnesses, antique pitchforks and gardening tools, a fully stocked shelf of ancient oilcans, bottles of turpentine and other more mysterious liquids.

But the real treasure amongst all these treasures was the biggest of them, right in the middle of the barn: an antique motor car, a survivor from the days when cars had brass lanterns instead of headlights and horns you had to squeeze to produce a delightful farting sound. Mr. Ellis let me climb into the driver's seat and pretend-drive this fantastical machine with its big wooden steering wheel and its knubby gear shift. For a boy of my age, this was an undreamed-of adventure.

Dusk was falling by the time we were done, and it was dinner time. Inside the house, the lights were dim, the furniture was sparse, and it smelled of long-neglected wood, as though no one had cared for the place for many years. Mr. Ellis made us a simple dinner, meat and potatoes and peas, and we ate together at the kitchen table. It was soon time for bed.

I was already beginning to be unnerved by the strangeness of the house, not to mention the strange solicitude of the person I knew only from my math classes at school. Mr. Ellis was a short man with thinning grey, wavy hair and a friendly smile, and clear blue eyes that matched the friendliness behind his rimless glasses. Even today, I can see his pink, smiling face. He led the way upstairs and showed me the narrow bed that was made up for me in the bedroom we were to share and took me to the bathroom to be sure I washed my face and cleaned my teeth. Then helped me into my striped pajamas and perhaps even had me say my prayers before tucking me up in bed.

How do I describe the feelings and sensations as I lay there, still awake and listening to Mr. Ellis's own preparations for the night? There was the feeling of suspense, of something yet to come, of something like danger, even . . . There was the feeling of being very alone, without you and my mother nearby, because this was the first night I can remember that I spent away from home—except, of course, for the school dormitory. But then there were all the other boys. There I was that night, alone with myself in that little bed, and I could hear my teacher coughing, running water, even, I thought, peeing in the loo.

And it was cold. It was a big, old, drafty house, and there was no heating anywhere, still less in the bedroom. So yes, I lay there shivering as I listened to Mr. Ellis in the bathroom, getting ready to go to bed himself. Heard the quiet sound of clothes being shed and draped somewhere, the back of a chair, perhaps. Heard the creak of floorboards as he crossed the room and the squeak of springs as he climbed into the bigger bed, across the room from mine. Heard the strange sighs he made as he prepared, I thought, to sleep.

Then his voice: "Peter? Are you cold?"

Yes, I was. I was cold.

"Why don't you come over here and we can keep each other warm?"

It felt more like an order from my teacher than an invitation. I was scared, yes, but I had been taught to do what I was told. I climbed out of my own bed and padded across the cold, wooden floorboards to where he held the bedcovers open to welcome me in his. "There," he said, "That's better, isn't it?"

I was terrified. My heart was beating wildly with the strangeness of it all. The strangeness of my teacher's body in bed next to my own. The strangeness of his breathing.

He was doing something. He was doing something down there, groping, feeling for that thing I loved to touch myself, but I still had no idea what he was after. I held my breath.

Then his head went down beneath the covers. He slid down, down further, to the level of my crotch. I felt his fingers find a way through the slit in my pajamas and pretty soon I felt his lips close around that strange, wonderful, irresistible part of me that I had often touched but only used, until then, to pee. And that strange, wonderful, irresistible part of me was responding in a strange and wonderful way, stiffening up impressively between his lips. I knew this was wicked. I knew that you, daddy, would never have approved. I was terrified, yes, and at the same time, in a strange way, thrilled. Thrilled in a way I couldn't understand, in a way I knew was wicked, and I shouldn't.

Mr. Ellis sucked and sucked and sucked until I knew that something was supposed to happen, I was about to burst, but I didn't dare. It felt like I was about to pee at any moment in Mr. Ellis's mouth, so I held it back desperately, held on, refusing to let go. It seemed like forever until finally my teacher stopped. He came back up from under the covers and lay beside me, breathless, breathing strangely, and then suddenly I felt something strange and hot and hard against me, down there, where he'd been, something I had never, ever felt before, it was so strange where it was pressed against me. And I knew that something strange was happening down there, something intense and urgent, but I didn't know what it was.

Next thing I knew, Mr. Ellis breathed what sounded like a great sigh of relief, and he lay there a few moments longer, as if almost unaware that I was there. Then he turned to me and told me that I'd better go back to my own bed.

I did what I was told. I must have gone to sleep, finally. I must have awakened in the morning, fearful that Mr. Ellis would be angry with me for the night before. That I'd done something wrong. But no, he was perfectly cheerful as he made me breakfast, as though nothing at all had happened. And then later, Harry, you arrived to pick me up, and told me I should say goodbye nicely, and thank you, Mr. Ellis. And chided me in the car, on the way home, because you thought I had not been nice enough.

That's it. I'll need to talk about this some more. But for now, it feels like it's enough to have told you what happened as exactly as it happened, more than seventy years later. Why do I need to tell you? Is it punishment? To make you feel bad? Guilty? Is it revenge of some kind, after all these years? I have talked about this, written about it even, several times before, but you and I never mentioned it, except for that one time when you asked me if I wanted to talk about it and I said, No.

But yes, I did need to talk to you about it. To you, specifically. And never did.

More about this when I next write. In the meantime, forgive my need to have shared this story with you. With, specifically, you.

Your son,
Peter

30 August 2021

Dear Harry,

So, about that one time, when we talked about what happened with Mr. Ellis . . .

It was several weeks, perhaps several months later. Not more. Not years. You knocked at the door of my bedroom in the Vicarage one morning when I was still in bed. The light was streaming in through the window that looked out over the front lawn, over the tennis court that no one ever used, over to the copse at the far end of the garden. It was a small room, but a nice one, my private space, sandwiched between two other bedrooms, my sister's and a guest room.

So, there you were. That in itself was a surprise. You hardly ever came into my bedroom; in fact, I can't remember a single other time. So, I knew this had to be important.

There was some awkwardness, perhaps on my part, because the occasion was so unusual, my father coming to my bedroom; perhaps on yours, because of what you had just learned, what you had to tell me, what you had to ask.

"It's about Mr. Ellis," you said. I think you sat down on the edge of the bed. There would have been nowhere else to sit. "I had a telephone call from Mr. Chris"—the headmaster at my boarding school. "He said there had been some trouble with Mr. Ellis, that they'd had complaints about him, um, interfering with other boys." You paused, to give me a moment to process this. Then you said, "So I have to ask you . . . That time when you went to stay at Mr. Ellis's house, did he . . . well, did he do anything he should not have done?"

I must have mumbled my confession that, yes, something had happened, because you said, "I suppose that was why you were not very nice to him, when I came to pick you up and drive you home?"

I remembered the occasion. I remembered you chiding me for not being polite enough when I said goodbye. I must again have mumbled my assent. I knew it was bad, what happened. But was it my fault? Were you angry with me? Would you punish me? I could never have expressed the feelings that I had in words. I could never have identified them even for myself because they were so confused. There was guilt, not just for having allowed something so bad to happen to me but worse, for the wicked thrill I'd felt, along with knowing I'd done something bad.

Something dirty. That was the word.

There was a long silence. Then you said, "Do you want to talk about it?"

And I said, "No."

And after a pause you said, "Alright then. I'm sorry, Peter. I should not have let that happen." And left the room.

That was the sum of it, as I recall. You left. I could be wrong but I'm pretty sure it was never mentioned, ever again, between us.

What I don't understand, you see, is how you could have left it there, like that. You of all people, who understood the mind. Who insisted that trauma should never be ignored and buried but remembered. Why you didn't gently lead me into what I so much needed at the time but did not know how to ask for because I was so terribly embarrassed. Because you understood these things. You understood that people, especially little children, need to talk about the things that hurt them. Need to be heard, even if they themselves don't know it. Need to be forgiven. Need to be consoled.

Surely you knew that, Harry?

I know it's too late now to ask it, but there's something in me that still wants you to understand, and still believes that somehow just the act of writing a letter like this one can fulfill that need.

Silly me, that it still hurts, now that I'm an old man, older than any of us were back then. And I hope a lot wiser. But strangely, yes, it does.

In any case, this was another occasion when I could have used a hug.

Your son,
Peter

31 August 2021

Dear Harry,

While we're on the subject I have another confession to make, but this one is not quite so bad.

I'm not sure at what age exactly I stopped enjoying your favorite summertime activity, but by my teenage years I'm pretty sure I hated it. Well, hate is probably too strong a word, but I was no longer sharing your enjoyment of the nomadic life.

I'm talking about the caravan. In the years immediately following the war (when petrol once again became more readily available), our caravan trips consumed most of the family time away from school during the summer holidays. As a little boy, I'm sure I went along with it unquestioningly. It was what we did. As I grew older, I began to hate (that word again!) the hours spent in the back seat of your car with Flora; the daily search in the Caravan Club handbook for the next site where we could pull in and "put the legs down"; the arguments over the best routes between you and Peggy in the front seat; and the perfection you insisted on in leveling the caravan by cranking each of the four corner legs to your exacting requirements. I hated the smell of the Elsan tent (was that invented by you? Your brother Donald?) a tall, narrow tent with squatting room for one on the portable loo, supported by a brace at one corner of the caravan. I was lazy. I wanted to spend my summer lounging around, escaping all the rules and impositions of school life. I was reaching an age where boys begin to sense the possibilities of freedom, and the last thing I needed was more constraints.

The one thing I did like was my little pup tent. It was easy enough to put up, a short way from the caravan, and it was my little private space. I loved the beat of rain on the canvas sides, and the still greater sense of splendid untouchability. The tent was meant for one, but it could sleep two people at a pinch, and it was here I was initiated into the much-needed understanding of that thing between my legs whose purpose you had attempted to explain to me and which Mr. Ellis had inexplicably attempted to devour. Aside from its mundane application in the loo, however, (or, when camping, behind the nearest hedge) its more interesting behaviors continued to mystify me.

Do you remember Philippe, Harry? The French boy who came over to stay that summer when Flora first went to stay with his parents in France? We took him caravanning with us, and every time we passed a Citroën on the road he would point and shout, delightedly, "Ah, zee car of my fazza!" That seemed to be the sum of his interest in the lovely English countryside.

Philippe was Flora's age—a year and a half older than me; so, fourteen going on fifteen—and compared to myself he was already a physically strong, muscular, well-developed young man. He was proud of his body in the tiny bikini bathing suit he wore and liked to show off his muscles. And he shared my pup tent . . .

We each had a sleeping bag and slept side by side, and one evening, shortly after bedtime, I could sense that something other than sleep was going on beside me. Philippe, when he spoke, seemed a little breathless, husky. " 'ave you done eet yet?" he asked.

Done what? I had no idea what his question meant.

"You know," he said—but I didn't—"done eet, veez a girl?"

Of course, I hadn't, but I had by now exposed the full extent of my ignorance. Philippe quickly understood that it was time to educate me. He reached over and slid his hand down in my sleeping bag to perform a manual investigation of my penis, hard already, but as yet quite small and skinny. "Ah," he said sympathetically, " 'ees still too leetle, you see? 'ere," he added: "feel zees."

He took my hand and led it down inside his own sleeping bag. I was amazed, first, by the contact of my fingers with the mat of wiry hairs—I mentioned, didn't I, that Philippe was well-developed for his age? I had only a soft down, as yet—and still more when he wrapped my fingers around his erection. It was not long, but fat, hard, throbbing and, well, exciting to the touch. Philippe was quite clearly very proud of it. He said, "You see, one day 'ee grow beeg, like zees.'"

So that was settled. He took care of his own need right there in the pup tent as he continued to tell me the (perhaps fictional?) story of how he had already lost his virginity—"you poot eet up inside 'er", he explained—having been seduced by an older woman, the mother of a friend, and how he planned to resume their intimacy once he got back to France.

So, Harry, the caravanning holiday that year served an unexpected and for me revelatory purpose. What Philippe had to show me was soon, as I matured just a little further, to open the door to a pleasure that accompanied me through adolescence and beyond—the pleasure that you claimed once to have denied yourself. The pleasure that you and your generation disparagingly called "self-abuse."

Your sinful son,
Peter

1 September 2021

Dear Harry,

There is a pleasant postscript to the Philippe story. The year after the exchange with Flora that brought him to England for the summer and her (miserably!) to France with his parents, you decided it was my turn to go. It was my first time there. Philippe and his father, Monsieur, came to pick me up at the airport, and I was hugely impressed, on arriving at their house in Maisons-Lafitte, just north of Paris, by his father's genial ease with what, in our home, would surely have been an awkward source of embarrassment. They had just acquired a new kitten and it was busy taking care of business for the first time in its poop box when we arrived. Monsieur was delighted. "Eh, *chérie*," he called up to his wife. "*Viens voir la merde du chat.*" Come see the cat's shit. I knew I was in exactly the right place, a place where freedom from convention and all the old English inhibitions reigned.

I was disappointed by one thing, though, that first night in France. I had been looking forward, secretly, excitedly in fact, to the opportunity to further pursue my sexual education with the expert guidance of my experienced friend. I had gained some confidence all alone in the intervening months and was expecting to be able to play more sophisticated games this time around. Alas, Philippe showed not the slightest interest—not even the hint of a memory of what had been, for me, an unforgettable encounter the previous year. He had his own room, I had mine. He seemed even older, even more aloof. No more touching, no more stories. I felt quite bereft.

But—Harry, you'll be relieved to know this—I did fall in love that summer in France. For the very first time with a girl.

Her name was Nicole. Her soft skin was a lovely sandy brown. She had always curious, challenging dark eyes, brown hair that glistened almost gold in the sunlight, and the irresistible energy of a thirteen-year-old. She wore orange jeans and white blouses open at the neck, allowing tantalizing glimpses of what promised to be gloriously feminine breasts, and she had a beguiling smile that infatuated me the first moment that I saw her. Her brother was Philippe's best friend, Jean-Claude. I used to tag along with Philippe and Jean-Claude, whose favorite occupation now was making pipe bombs and exploding them on a vacant lot, and the advantage of their age and life experience left me feeling like the useless third wheel on a bicycle. But then one day Jean-Claude's father called on his son to help with the annual harvest of the green plums ripening on the tree in their backyard, ready to be stuffed into a barrel to ferment for a few days before they could be distilled into his home-brewed brandy.

Philippe and I were pressed into service to join the work gang.

Picture now, Harry, this deeply diffident, horribly self-conscious and now hopelessly infatuated early teenage boy and the amorous urges he felt, standing there in such close proximity to the girl of his impossible desires. I would have been too clumsy, too shy to even begin to approach the object of my adoration in other circumstances—but here we were, fingers touching aching fingers as together we stuffed ripe plums into the dark bunghole of that barrel . . .

As you can tell, Harry, I'm still in love. That memory is still as fresh, as intense, and as maddeningly erotic as it was back then.

Your amorous son,
Peter

2 September 2021

Dear Harry,

Dark days ahead. Fair warning.

Did you really believe in sin? Okay, sin, yes, I understand. I no longer believe in it myself, not in the same way, but that's for another letter. But what about evil? You believed in the existence of evil in the world—how could you not, after the unadulterated wickedness of Adolf Hitler and the willful massacre of six million innocent human beings in his concentration camps, not to mention those innumerable other atrocities he and his henchman unleashed on humankind in World War II. And let's be honest, the atrocities were not limited to "the other side." I was too young to realize the full immensity of that horror, but what did you feel, Harry, when you heard news of Dresden? Berlin? Hiroshima? Nagasaki?

Evil? Yes. For sure. But hell? Eternal damnation? Redemption? There are hints in your letters to suggest how deeply you struggled with all that. Your mind was shaped not only by the long history of Christianity, but by the skepticism of post-Enlightenment and modern times. The supposedly civilized western world had been shaken to its core by the first world war. And now the second?

But sin. I wish you were still around to tell me what your own sins were. I could be your confessor, Harry! Which would be okay, wouldn't it, now that we're no longer bound by the old father-son conventions? Pride, for sure. You may have tried to disguise it with your modest "simple country priest" act—which served, to those of us who knew you well—only to hide a raging ego! Doubt? Is that a sin? Quarrels with your God? I do wonder what other sins you might have had to confess if you still went to confession in your later years.

But anyway, *à propos*, could you not have found some other, well, less onerous gift on my Confirmation than that copy of St. Swithun's prayer book? I lost it many years ago. It never really felt like mine. It was your book. If I'd had the nerve I would have given it back to you.

I will say that it was a beautiful little volume, bound in soft, pliable maroon leather with gilt edges all around. It was nice to hold, to touch, and the pages required a careful hand to turn, crisp and new and wafer-thin. But—surely you'd recognize this now?—inside the book was a booby trap in the form of what in today's jargon we would call a heavy guilt trip, a burden of conscience for a boy who knew his first obligation was to live up to his father's expectations. No ordinary *Book of Common Prayer*, St. Swithun's was a special version of that compendium of catholic liturgy, with an enlarged text that included, at the end, a complete user's guide to the sacrament of Confession. These final pages categorized in exhaustive detail every transgression in thought, word or deed committed by man or woman, from peccadillo to cardinal sin. If you wanted to know what kind of sin you had committed, you could do no better than consult St. Swithun.

Welcome to the Christian religion! This was my confirmation gift from you, Harry. My Father. Padre.

Guilt.

You yourself had prepared a handful of us children for the ritual. We had dutifully learned the catechism of the Anglo-Catholic church (we were not, you always insisted, Roman Catholics, but neither were we Protestants!), the basic rules and conventions of church dogma. Then Michael, Bishop of St. Albans came on the big day, arrayed in his purple cassock and his bishop's ring. He laid his hands on our lowered heads, admitting us officially into the arms of the church—and permitting us to eat a thin wafer at the altar rail and take a sip of wine. Afterwards, there was tea at the Vicarage.

(Forgive the levity, Harry. It does seem quaint, in retrospect).

I took my prayer book back to school with me. As you'll recall, it was a very catholic Anglo-Catholic school, where attendance at chapel was a daily requirement. Holy Communion was an optional extra, but now confirmed and wanting to be a good son to my father—who was after all getting a discount on my attendance—I felt obliged to show up for the service, and in preparation, for confession with the school chaplain in the crypt chapel below. To ready myself for this encounter, I made a conscientious study of what St. Swithun had to say.

There were a good number of sins I could identify with: pride, envy, greed, and—what a great word!—concupiscence. But the most glaringly obvious and grievous of my sins, the one I knew I would be obliged to confess, was listed with appropriate circumlocution in the category of lust.

I can tell you now, Harry, what I could never have told you at the time; I was by then fully addicted to the sinful pleasures of the flesh, whether solo or sometimes, if I was lucky, with the collaboration of another boy. What I had learned to my delight from Philippe in that little pup tent had developed into a full-blown obsession, perhaps still more pleasurable because I was now quite sure it was a sin. In bed at night, daytimes in the Groves (the communal school loos) or out in nature behind bushes and trees, I was at it as often as opportunity allowed. I even worked an ingenious hole in my trousers pocket so that I could offer myself at least a little promissory note of pleasure to come in the classroom or in chapel.

So here was something that needed to be confessed. Indeed, it stood out—if you'll forgive that way of putting it—as the one sin that was the most frequent and most culpable. But how to present it to the chaplain in such a way that would not cause him—or me!—embarrassment? Or dishonor you, the fellow priest whom he certainly knew to be my father?

The options presented by St. Swithun tiptoed delicately around the subject, but rather than come out and confess to the embarrassing truth, I settled on evasion, opting for the more general and unobjectionable "I have sinned in thought, word and deed." Evasive, true, but it had the benefit of honesty. And the Chaplain seemed more than ready to settle for my obfuscation. Serving at an all-boys boarding school, I'm sure he was perfectly prepared to read between the lines.

It's also possible that the good chaplain himself had a hand beneath his cassock in the confessional. I wouldn't put it past him.

With apologies, again, for the irreverence,

Your son,
Peter

(It would amuse you, BTW, to know that the saintly Swithun has something in common with an American groundhog named Punxsutawney Phil. His saint's day, 15 July, has the same place in English weather lore as 2 February, Groundhog Day, this side of the Atlantic. Thus goes the doggerel:

St. Swithun's day if thou dost rain
For forty days it will remain
St. Swithun's day if thou be fair
For forty days 'twill rain nae mare.

See? Except that Punxsutawney Phil predicts, not rain, but the end of winter . . .)

3 September,2021

Dear Harry,

Ha! Another Peter! Well, actually, two of them.

I found them as I was writing in my last letter about the catechism and Google-searched the word for further information.

Did you know that the very first catechism was written by a Peter?

This one was Saint Peter Canisius, who became a Jesuit under the aegis of yet another Peter, Peter Faber, one of the founders of the Society of Jesus in the mid-16th century.

(I worked for the Jesuits once later in life, as you might recall, at Loyola Marymount University).

Anyway, fascinating! These Peters keep cropping up all over.

I have found no connection, by the way, in my Internet research between St. Swithun and the prayerbook that bears his name. What gives?

In puzzlement, your son,
Peter

4 September 2021

Dear Harry,

Why do I need to burden you with the unhappiness of my school days so many years ago? Well, none of this is obviously going to burden you now that you have left us for another realm of being. Obviously, then, it's more about disburdening myself than burdening you.

You'll remember that my secondary school, Lancing College, was another Anglican institution, another all-boys' boarding school. It was—is, I suppose—best known to the outside world for its chapel, an impressively tall neo-Gothic building placed prominently on a foothill to the Sussex Downs and overlooking the gray expanse of the English Channel. To the east is Brighton, that mecca of the Regency; to the west, Worthing; and to the south, the small towns of Shoreham and Lancing. It was—is, I suppose—a cold place, with little protection from the chill winter winds that drive in from the sea. I shiver to this day when I recall the many times I huddled up against the cold as I hurried through the cloisters and across one of the two quads to get from our "house" to the dining room or chapel.

Tell me, did you never feel at Shrewsbury, your own boarding school, that dreadful, excruciating, all-consuming loneliness that I experienced, even surrounded by all those other boys? That sense of irremediable otherness? That I just didn't belong, and never would? Twelve years, this lasted. I'm not wanting to whine or pass blame. I just need to establish the fact of it, the not fitting in. By all accounts—which may or may not be based in historical fact—you took part in sports at school, particularly rowing. Water polo, too. You were on the team. I was always a dead loss when it came to anything that involved a ball. I was simply never able to work out where it was in space. I could not catch it, hit it, kick it, to the merriment—or scorn, or sometimes anger—of my teammates. My sport, since I was required to have one, eventually became cross-country running, a sport that suited me well enough because when you run, of course, you run alone.

Then there was body shame. In my first year or two at Lancing, I had not yet developed the ectomorphic frame I had throughout my adult years. I was a tubby, little boy at thirteen, and I was teased about my tub. Worse, my genitals were painfully slow in developing—in my judgment, anyway—in comparison with my peers. I was terrified of being seen naked in the shower and tried everything I could to avoid showering at the same time as others. Which gave me another good reason for cross-country running: it was done faster and finished sooner, when the changing rooms were still likely to be empty.

Do I sound ridiculous? Perhaps. I longed to be the proud possessor of one of those strong, hairy bodies that some of the older boys could boast. And I could not.

Behind all those crushes I had on big boys when I was a little one and on little boys as a senior, was in part the burning need to come to terms with my growing body. To know that it was not something to be ashamed of. That I was not deficient, not some kind of a freak. My longing to touch and be touched was focused on the forbidden body part that had always caused me the most anxiety, that most obsessed and mystified me. I needed the reassurance that others than myself found it acceptable, normal, even desirable. I was perhaps also looking for the trust that goes along with touch. And, though I would never have acknowledged it, not even to myself, I was looking for everything implied by that big word that, even though I yearned for it, I trusted least of all—love. I love you. Even knowing how important it is to be able to say and hear these words, for many years, I had trouble saying them aloud and hearing them, even with those I love and who I know love me, and long to hear those words. They just don't come easily and naturally to me and more's the pity. It's my belief—perhaps misguided or distorted by the years—you could argue with me about this, Harry—that little Peter missed out hearing those words, and being held and touched, perhaps even in infancy but certainly through his early years. I think that the expression of love was simply not a priority in our family. Physical contact, particularly, was deemed somehow unnecessary, superfluous, an invasion of personal privacy, even a bit embarrassing.

Am I right? Or am I imagining this? I wish I could have you here to help me understand this better than I do.

Your son,
Peter

5 September 2021

Dear Harry,

You'd have no way of knowing this I hope, but there were some seriously awful things that happened to me during those anxious teenage years at school.

Did you know, for example, that your son was gang-raped? In public? Maybe not technically, but I can promise you that's how it felt.

The scene: the junior dormitory, with its two, long rows of identical beds beneath the leaded windows, each covered with its identical bright red blanket, each separated from its neighbor by an identical wooden chest of drawers where we kept all our clothes. At the far end, the bathroom had symmetrical rows of tubs with no partitions in between. There would have been toilet stalls I suppose, but I only remember those outside, the ones we called the "Groves." After lights out at eight o'clock, silence was supposed to be imposed, but furtive, whispered conversations would persist long after dark. If you wanted to read a little longer, as I often did myself, there was always the option of a flashlight under the covers—so long as you didn't get caught.

That's where it happened.

The facts: there was a big bruiser of a boy named "Bunter" Scott, fifteen years old, just one year ahead of me at school.

He came back after one of our holidays boasting that he'd had sex with a girl. Of course, none of the other boys believed him, so he set out after lights-out in the dormitory one night to prove it. Whom should he choose to be his partner in this demonstration? They settled on me. It was a matter of common consent. I don't know why. Despite my protests they gathered around my bed with flashlights in their hands, pointing the beams at me and laughing and cheering him on as he climbed on top of me, pulled down his pajama bottoms and forced himself between my legs, plunging away to the noisy encouragement of his spectators.

Having proved his point, he took time to acknowledge the admiration that was now his due, tucked himself back in his pajamas, and returned to his own bed. I was left shamed and humiliated, obviously, but also with that desperate sense of loneliness, of being irremediably other than the rest of them, the ones in the know, the ones who belonged.

No one, to my knowledge, ever mentioned the incident again. I would not have dared to tell you about it at the time. The aftermath was mine alone to live with.

In all the anger and shame, I managed to blame myself. What was wrong with me?

We have grown smarter and more compassionate as a society about these things today. We know to dismiss self-blame as inappropriate. We have learned to encourage victims of such acts of molestation or sexual assault not to accept responsibility for it themselves but to hold the aggressor accountable for his act. But I knew no better at the time, and this was a question that I asked myself repeatedly. What had I done to make this happen? There was no one else to ask. And, of course, I had no answer.

I don't wish to punish you, Harry, for those twelve years at school. But that's no reason for not taking the opportunity to absolve myself.

Those words from the confessional come back to me, "Forgive me, Father, for I have sinned." False words. St. Swithun be damned, there was no sin in this on my part. Nor was there sin in my pursuit of lonely pleasure. Sin? Along with so many other aspects of the religion you embraced; I reject the very notion of it.

But maybe you can forgive me that!

Your son,
Peter

6 September 2021

Dear Harry,

Time for a laugh? I think so! Writing about the Bishop at the Vicarage tea on the day of our Confirmation reminded me of an old joke which you probably heard many times already, but it stands repeating. You were no prude. You could always get a little chuckle out of irreverence.

So . . .

The new curate has been very nervous about delivering his first sermon and asks the Vicar in the vestry afterwards if it went well. "Oh," says the Vicar, reassuringly, "it was very good—aside from a couple of tiny faux pas."

"Faux pas?" asks the curate, unsure what that means.

"Well," says the Vicar, "remember that time when the Bishop came for Confirmation? And we all came back to the Vicarage afterwards for tea, and he pricked his finger in the rose garden?"

"Yes," says the curate, he remembers this.

"And then afterwards, at tea, my wife asked, 'How's your prick?' and he said, 'Still throbbing,' and I said, 'Christ!' and you dropped the teapot?

"That," says the Vicar, "was a faux pas."

I can hear your chuckle, Harry. Ever the humorist.

Be well. Your naughty son,
Peter

PS: Regarding your sometimes risqué sense of humor. It was you who told me about the fundamentalist religious group at Cambridge during your days there. They called themselves the Cambridge University New Testament Society, you recalled with more than a hint of mirth, and spread word of their pious evangelical events with posters headlined by their acronym.

8 September 2021

Dear Harry,

We both realize, of course, that all my efforts to rescue you from the past and come to know you, perhaps even love you in a way I never could before, are just as much an effort to come to terms with myself—and perhaps be loved by you. Or perhaps even love myself.

In what ways am I like you? What would you recognize of yourself in your son? These questions are of interest to me because at one time I wanted so much to be *not* like you.

I have my mother's eyes, blue, not brown like yours. Flora had your eyes. She was also, like you, skinny. I have a tendency, as I age, to put on weight. Remember that "spare tire" around the belly that Peggy accumulated in her later years? I have that, too. You never did. At the age I have now reached, your hair was sparse, combed flat across your head, and barely concealed your scalp. Mine, though long since turned to grey, is still quite long and thick. Oh, and I still have most of the teeth that I was born with. I was scared years ago into the habit of nightly flossing by my fearsome Chinese American dentist; my mouth had begun to show the ravages of poor dentistry—worse, for sure, in Britain during the war—and the cavalier neglect of my youth. Most of yours had been replaced long since by the dentures you took out and left in a glass on the bathroom shelf each night.

Is my voice a little like yours? Perhaps. Sixty years this side of the Atlantic have worn the edges off the public school-Oxbridge accent I grew up with, but even after so long this side of the Atlantic, my fellow Americans immediately hear the remnant of my original British accent. They still look askance when I say the word "art," for instance, losing the "r" in favor of an "h": "aht." They seem to love the sound of my voice, however, so I might have inherited some of the mellifluous quality of your baritone—though I incline more to tenor.

I have none of your skill with hands. When it comes to anything handy I'm a hopeless klutz—a term you are likely not familiar with but will surely understand. You'd laugh. Put a hammer in my hand and I'll end up breaking something. With luck, it won't be my finger. The kind of things you took care of with ease—the home repairs, basic electrical and plumbing— are things I need a handyman to help me out with.

I inherited your love of mysteries, thrillers, suspense books of all kinds. I even wrote a couple of them myself, back in the 1980s. Their venue, of course, was the world of contemporary art—or "aht"! Did you ever read them? I can't remember anything you might have said about them—but then, I can't be sure I gave you them to read. But I did take the skill you had with words and turn myself into a reasonably worthy wordsmith.

There are other, more fundamental things that lead me to believe we have more in common than might appear at a cursory glance. When I sit in silence for my daily half-hour's morning meditation, for example, I often see you sitting in your straight-backed chair, silent, prayer book in hand, completing the "office" that was your unfailing commitment even in the years following your retirement. I came to my personal need to delve into the realm of the spirit only much later in my life. We'll be coming to this later.

I inherited your social conscience, your socialism, your left-wing political views, your commitment to social justice. I watched as you became more conservative toward the end of your life—you were never a Thatcherite, I hope!—but by the time you came to the broader perspective of advancing years, the England of your youth was barely recognizable. Such is my impression, anyway, from where I sit half a world away and after more than half a century's exile. By the time you reached old age, social programs like the National Health and National Insurance had long been institutionalized in Britain. The Labour Party had become less about the welfare of the working classes, it seemed to me, than the advancement of the nouveau middle class. There was Tony Blair, a halfway Tory. Mass immigration from India, Pakistan, the West Indies, Africa, and the Middle East had changed the racial demographic of old England and introduced racial tensions little known in the early years of the twentieth century. It was all about class, not racial struggle back then, in "our day". And with the construction of the Chunnel between Dover and Calais, the age-old insularity of the British was no longer assured by the island's physical isolation from the European Continent. Clinging to their treasured pound while other European countries adapted to the euro, the Brits finally had to yield to the metric system in their currency. No more twenty shillings to the pound, twelve pence to the shilling.

An inveterate traveler and explorer of the Continent in the caravan you towed everywhere behind you on your summer trips, you would have been mortified by Brexit and the xenophobia it betokened. You prided yourself on being tolerant, open to historical and demographic change, curious about the customs of your neighboring countries, especially their food and wine. You welcomed people from throughout the world into your home—Monu from India, Graeme from South Africa, that Japanese Anglican minister, a ping-pong wizard whose name I have forgotten, the black, African bishop with his dark, gleaming, always laughing eyes and startling gray eyebrows, handsome in his purple cassock—and relished both the cultural differences and the intellectual conversations with your guests. More gregarious than I have ever been, you embraced humanity and the joys of human interchange. While I suspect there must have been an introverted part of you, there was always that actor, too, the extrovert. Sometimes, as I know you readily admit, the shameless show-off.

Your Christian faith . . . I would love to have talked to you about this because, while I abandoned that faith long ago (shame on me for never having dared to tell you face-to-face for fear of hurting you), I do share your belief that there is more to human existence than the physical body and the material world it lives in. I had not yet opened my mind to Buddhism by the time of your death; for much of my life, indeed, I scoffed at it, as at all non-secular belief. I wish I'd had opportunity to talk about this too, however, because we would surely have found plenty to agree on. I admire not only the humanistic aspect of the Buddhist dharma and its dedication to principles of ethical behavior—essential, really, to a well-lived life—but also its embrace of values that transcend even death.

Oh yes, I would have loved that conversation, Harry, and I am sure you would have, too. Your Christianity was anything but exclusive; you were curious and informed about other faiths and eager to find common ground between them. In your last years, you became deeply involved in new ways of practicing the Christian faith and wrote to me about the several pilgrimages you made to the ecumenical community at Taizé, in France. I remember, too, the spirited exchange between yourself and Ellie's father, Michael, at the seder you attended when you and Peggy came to visit us in Los Angeles, exploring the similarities and differences between Christianity and Judaism, between the rite of Passover and that of the Last Supper. Was that not an occasion to be remembered and celebrated! I know Mike relished it and recalled it often. That you were unable to pursue that friendship was a matter only of the geographical distance that lay between you. Such a shame!

And finally, now that I think of it, there is one other thing we share—you were a tease. I am a tease. Just ask my grandson, your great-grandson, little Luka—who is a pretty good tease himself!

So, I'll sign off with a smile for now.

Your son,
Peter

9 September 2021

Dear Harry,

There is another, painful thing we shared: headaches.

Though Peggy mentioned migraines in her letters, I would not have known you suffered from the agonizing attacks known as cluster headaches until Flora surprised me with her mention of that diagnosis some time after your death. It was after I had myself been diagnosed with this peculiarly horrible affliction that manifests in series, producing blinding spasms that arrive at the exact same time each day and engulf the whole of one side of the head, eyes, teeth, and jaws, in excruciating pain. As I imagine you well know—did you experience them in the same way?—they are so regular in their daily recurrence, you can almost set your watch by their arrival. They are usually also of a fixed duration—mine, at the time I suffered from them most frequently, were mercifully brief, an hour or two at most—but incredibly intense; they say that clusters are worse by far than migraines. And, like the migraine in this respect, they leave behind them, every day, a shadow that hangs around inside your head for much longer than the pain itself, a premonition of the next one to come.

I wonder how you dealt with them. For me, the only relief I could find—and it was minimal—was physically rocking. I'd climb out of bed—they usually came late at night or early in the morning—and clamp my head tight between my hands and rock back and forth for as long as I could stand it. The repetitious movement seemed to help more than any medication could, though Peggy once mentioned in a letter that you took some pills whose side effects were almost as dire as the headaches. Perhaps they have since discovered a more effective drug.

Then finally, in my experience, after a few days or a couple of weeks, the series would end as suddenly and inexplicably as it started, and there would follow months without a trace of them.

This memory was evoked by their strange return after years of blessed absence, coinciding strangely with the start of these letters. As they say over here: go figure. This new series had thankfully been quite mild, a slightly different physical sensation than the worst of clusters. The pain, far less intense, is almost an exact replica of that brilliant, sparkling aura on the left side of the head; but—this puzzles me still more—instead of occurring at the same time every day like the usual clusters, they seem to be arriving, oddly, almost precisely one hour later each day than the day before.

Are they clusters? I don't know. I've also been unable to determine whether there's a genetic component to this strange affliction. Neither of my sons, your grandsons, has mentioned them to me—but they are now still only in their fifties, and I believe that clusters tend to strike in later years. The worst of mine occurred when I was already in my sixties. I'm happy to be able to report that it has been at least a decade since the last of them, so to say that I was surprised by this latest, mildest onset is an understatement. I wonder, could this be another instance of "my father's pain"? Genetic? Psychosomatic? I dread to think. I'm not sure at what age you were afflicted, or if or when they stopped. And sadly, Flora is not around to ask about them anymore.

Anyway, I thought I'd mention this strange common affliction. But you, now, are finally beyond pain . . .

With love,
Peter

10 September 2021

Dear Harry,

Let's see, where were we? Braughing, no? Did you know that this was where I fell in love for the second time. After Nicole.

It was quite innocent. For sex, in adolescence, there were only boys, the ones at school, but that was different. I've mentioned this. But yes, of course you knew about Mary—that was her name—because Peggy was in something of a panic; she was convinced I was going to run off and get married, or worse—at the age of fourteen!—and that silly fuss brought out the snob in her. Mary, as you'll recall, was the daughter of the local gas station (um, sorry, garage) owner; her best friend Brian's parents ran the post office next door. So . . . not a suitable match for the Vicar's son! (Yes, you used to be the Rector of Aspley Guise, but now you were the Vicar of Braughing. I never knew the difference if there was one).

If I'm to remind you about Mary, though, I'll need to start with your nemesis, Barry Evans. Yes, the artist. You know who I mean. I have come to think he represented everything you most missed and most feared within yourself. He personified the naughty Harry, the irresponsible little boy, the sensualist who longed to come out and play—the one the other Harry, the respectable Vicar, felt obliged to keep contained. Barry rejected anything that smacked of social convention. He lusted unashamedly after women and had no qualms about sleeping with them if he could; he was blatantly unfaithful to his wife, another Mary. As I recalled just recently, he borrowed money from you once and never bothered to return it. He was a man to whom histrionics came naturally, unrestrained by the propriety to which you were bound as much by nurture as by nature. Barry Evans was the wild man you kept carefully buried deep inside.

It was your love of theater that brought the two of you together. One of the more memorable events I recall from our Braughing days was your production of *A Christmas Carol* in the village hall. Was it genius or some wicked demon that led you to cast Barry in the role of Scrooge? He reveled in it. Even more than the pleasure of theatrics, I suspect, he relished the opportunity to get a rise out of the Vicar. No one could outclass you as a natural born ham better than Barry Evans. He was a brilliant, way over-the-top, and charmingly grotesque Scrooge. He was also a wildly undisciplined actor, happily improvising lines, and outlandish gestures, puffing out the white powder from his hair, for example, to get a laugh from the audience. He was hilarious and abominable all at once.

Offstage, he was also quite scandalously irreligious, indulging happily in the buffoonish, public exhibition of those doubts that tortured you so painfully and privately within.

So, there was Barry. Mary, meantime—my Mary, not his, not Barry's wife—was cast in the play as one of the Victorian street urchins. I was away at school during the early rehearsals of the play so I could not be included in the cast, but you brought me in as an assistant make-up artist to help backstage with the production when I came home for the holidays. One of my daily jobs before curtain time was to smear Mary's smooth legs with sooty make-up, to evoke the filth of Dickensian London streets. I was fourteen years old by this time, quite possibly fifteen, and the task was thrillingly erotic. The make-up reached only to the bottom hem of her knee-length skirt and my ignorance of such things prevented me from even imagining what might happen in the darkness that lay beyond, but I was fully aware of the desire awakened in the all-too excited flesh. I could hardly wait for each night's performance. Small wonder that I fell in love.

It happened that Barry also loved to play the Pandar. He and Mary—his Mary, not mine—had begun hosting weekly soirées for young people like myself, and they included my Mary, of course, and her friend Brian. It was an evening of cheese and cheap red wine from Spain, poetry (Dylan Thomas!), stories, modern art (Picasso! Braque!) and music (Poulenc, Satie, Stravinsky!) beside a roaring fire in the hearth, with Barry and Mary's young children running amok amongst the guests. It was an ideal circumstance in which to fan the flames of love.

Still, it took a while before I found the gumption to ask Mary to go out with me. In Braughing, "going out" at this time of year meant taking long, chilly walks along the wintery lanes and out into the countryside. The nearest cinema was many miles away and we were too young for pubs. I was intensely shy. Perhaps she was, too. I could only fantasize about the wicked things I would never have known how to do, and still less dare. Did we ever even kiss, along those shady country lanes? Perhaps. I do remember the tantalizing thrill of holding hands and how daring that seemed. Our friend, Barry, was positively itching to get us into bed together and would gladly have provided one, had we been ready.

But, of course we weren't. We were innocent village kids. Barry's untiring efforts notwithstanding, Peggy need not have worried.

I no longer recall how things ended with Mary, but it's clear they neither ended as my mother feared, nor as the lecherous Barry would have wished. The most obvious answer is that I just went back to school. Once there, I do remember mooning about for her for a good long while and gloomily engraving her initials, MM, on my desk in Latin class, where they mingled with a century's worth of similar, equally lovelorn inscriptions. For all I know, they could still be there. But then at school, there were other, more immediate sexual possibilities, far less challenging and complicated in their gratification, a quick one-off behind the hedge or in the Groves. So, I probably just forgot her.

Do you remember her, Harry? A shy girl, rather pale, with brown hair. A lovely English village girl—and I say that with respect. I think of her warmly to this day, as I do of every girl I ever loved. She was the second. Too bad that I, too, was so shy! Too bad I had to go back to school so soon after that Christmas.

With more than a pinch of nostalgia, then.

Your son,
Peter

11 September 2021

Dear Harry,

Indulge me. I need to take a detour, just for today, because I cannot let the occasion slip by without some comment. You would have no reason to know that September 11—it lives in infamy here as "9/11"—is a bleak and solemn day in American history. Had you survived a few years longer than you did, it would have been late afternoon, early evening in Wales when the atrocity began to happen. News time. I'm sure you would have been watching the television, as you did every night throughout your later life. Another ritual. You may have missed the first terrible event, as I did, here in Los Angeles. But your news channels would have switched to New York in time for you to watch in horror as a second jet airliner, with a full complement of passengers, slammed into the second of the two World Trade Center towers at the southern end of Manhattan. And soon after that, a third, flying fast and low to explode in the façade of the Pentagon in Washington, DC; and a fourth, diving to its shattering destruction in an open field in Pennsylvania.

I'm sure the hijackers of those doomed planes were praising their god as they met their fate, along with the nearly three thousand innocent human beings whose lives they took with them. Among the latter was the brilliant and promising young son of one of our oldest, closest friends.

You would have been horrified as I was, Harry, as was every other person of sound mind on the planet, by this proof that fanatical belief in any god could inspire men to commit such hateful, devastating acts. Blind adherence to religious belief—unhappily, paradoxically—has engendered as much evil in the world across the centuries as the good it seeks to promote in the hearts of men.

Unhappily, too, there was nothing but vengeance on the mind of the American President, the American Congress, the American people. I have to admit that it was on my mind too. It became the national obsession to kill—to kill the man soon known to be responsible, to kill his followers, and to kill all those who helped them.

Twenty years have passed since that terrible day. Twenty years of killing, of misguided warfare, leaving many thousands of our own as well as many thousands of our purported enemies dead. We have finally, as a nation, now twenty years later, come to a recognition of the futility of retribution for this one act of terror, even though our more widespread "war on terror" seems to persist in many forms, in many different parts of the world.

Our achievement, after twenty years of brutality in Afghanistan, the country that harbored 9/11 terrorists? Ironically, though we succeeded finally in killing the attack's chief architect, we have left that other target of our wrath, the Taliban, even stronger than the day we first attacked them.

Vengeance is mine, saith the Lord. That's your God, Harry. We would have left done better to leave it to Him. My own religious inspiration is the Buddha. He would, I'm sure, have counseled otherwise.

> In grief for humanity, today,
> your son,
>   Peter

13 September 2021

Oh, Harry! Daddy!

I do you such a grave injustice, making you out to be some kind of unloving ogre. Just yesterday, I returned once more to that cache of skinny blue air mail forms, letters written to me over the years by both yourself and Peggy. I had not previously read them well. Not well enough. I had skimmed through, paying more attention to the story than the tone. There are dozens of them. Reading, sometimes between the lines, I find them filled with such love, such compassion, such concern that I am humbled.

In one of those letters, written at the time when both Flora and I were having trouble in our relationships and when both our marriages were falling apart, you wrote these words (you write so well, I quote the short passage verbatim):

"I am convinced (between you & me) that a lot of the trouble is relationship adjustment (horrid phrase). The old 7-year itch. 7 to 12 yrs. seems to me the biggest test of a marriage. If you can 'make it' over that period, not just accepting, but winning through, then you achieve a wonderful fulfillment in each other. It's never easy-going."

Well, Harry, what you say is true. You would be proud of me and Ellie, who have sailed past your 12-year point many times over now. But then you continue in the next paragraph, with words that touch my heart: "My heart ached for you, reading your last letter, and all our thoughts will be often with you at Christmas." I'm not sure what I wrote to cause your heartache on the occasion, but mine ached when I read how you continued:

"As I am aware of both you and Flora now, I do often reflect on my own failings as a father. How much have I passed on to you my lack of self-confidence, apart from much self-centredness & I suppose irritation and frustration. This doesn't depress me now, but it does sadden me. You both have many creative gifts and yes, somehow, you both appear to have a tendency to destroy your own happiness, even perhaps your own success."

And you signed yourself "Your ever affectionate, Father."

Thank you for those words, Harry. Thank you for the insight, the compassion, and the self-awareness—something I have been struggling for these past twenty years and more. Thank you especially for the affection. If I have made too little of it in these letters, for that I ask forgiveness.

Your ever affectionate son,
Peter

14 September 2021

Dear Harry,

Let's go back to school! (Do we have to? Yes). To Lancing. There's more I need to tell you about my time there.

What I was learning or thought to have been learning about myself in the exclusive company of other boys was almost comically wrong. That's what years at boarding school will do for you. Well, rather what it did for me. I'm not sure about you, but I think not. By the time I left school, with inexpressible relief and gratitude for that final release at the age of seventeen—it was just a couple of days before my eighteenth birthday—I was pretty much convinced that I would forever only fall in love and have sex with boys and men. Yes, as you know, I had already "fallen in love" with two girls outside of school, but they were impossible fantasies. My only actual, real-life experience was with those who had a penis, like myself.

What I did not know then but realize now—indeed, I realized it immediately after leaving school—was that there was nothing remotely "gay" about those early sexual encounters. It was a perfectly normal need to experiment with my bodily equipment, and for the better part of my life thus far the only humans readily available for my tentative explorations were other boys. With Nicole and Mary, I was far too shy and insecure about my physical self to engage in even the most innocent of sexual play. But I could, and did, with boys. And at that time in my life, I felt obliged to think of these games as "love" to explain and justify them to myself.

You could have known none of this, for sure, but I was quite certain in my belief that you would have been deeply shocked, disgusted, even, by my adventures. St. Swithun left little room for doubt that sex, particularly with your own kind, was the worst of all possible sins—the kind that, when you die, gets you sent straight off to hell to burn for all eternity in Satan's furnaces. "Dirty" was the word that was generally used to describe anything to do with sex—as in "dirty jokes" and "don't be dirty." Still, Harry, you were not intolerant. There were tacitly acknowledged gay men in our social lives with whom you felt quite comfortable. Witness David, the flamboyant American interior designer and his architect partner who lived across the lane from your St. Mary's Church in Braughing. This unabashedly gay couple—we knew no better than to call them "queer" or "homo" on those days—had refurbished an old cottage with the kind of elegant perfection you find illustrated in the pages of contemporary architectural magazines. They entertained the somewhat bemused village gentry in their home with elaborate cocktails and canapés and tales of exotic Florida and eternal sunshine. No one in our world would be impolite enough to draw attention to their difference from any other couple.

You loved it that way! That was fine. I think it's true to say that you felt much more at ease with this couple than you did with the flamboyantly heterosexual Barry. And despite my wayward activity with boys at school, I think it's true to say that I never felt the slightest curiosity or interest in these men's sexual lives, still less did I feel inclined to join them. Well, there was the one occasion when David drove me in his huge convertible motor car to see another of the cottages they had worked on, where we went out back to take a pee in the garden and he swung around to show me, with some pride I have to say, what seemed to me to be an extraordinarily large dick. On the way back home, he regaled me with highly erotic, anatomically detailed stories of his (rather improbable) exploits with exotic women in Paris night clubs after the war. But that was just in fun.

You might have had some concern about me a few years later, in Sharnbrook—I was now a late teenager—when you called me into your study for one of our serious conversations. As a courtesy to the Vicar, the local police inspector had informed you I had been seen on several occasions visiting a nearby house that was under surveillance and was subject to an imminent police raid. (Homosexuality was still a crime in England in the 1950s, and punishable by prison sentences). I had been visiting people I considered to be friends without much thought that they might be gay, but simply charming, sophisticated people whom I respected and liked. We'd share a glass of wine, a few laughs, and the kind of intelligent conversation you'd not find in local pubs or the parties in the homes of more conventional village society. The inspector came with the friendly warning that this might be a good moment for your son to stop knocking on that particular door. Shamefully, as I see it now, I followed his advice. I never heard further about what might have happened to my friends—but it would shame me further, deeply, to know they ended up in jail.

In any event, as we'll see, the doubts that needlessly tortured me about my sexual identity did not outlast my time at boarding school. Not even by one minute.

How would the story of my teenage years have been different, I have often wondered, had you and Peggy sent me to a local state school, nearer to home, where boys and girls mixed naturally together, day by day? With everyday contact with the opposite sex and the opportunity for emotional development more in line with my natural proclivities, I like to believe it would have taken me far less time to leave boyhood behind me and become a man. As it was, I was destined to remain an emotional adolescent well into my adult life. I was burdened with both a chronic emotional and a physical timidity. I had learned to protect my distrusting self from a hostile world, to hold back, to never quite let myself embrace life and love—or the people that I loved—because I could not trust my heart.

By way of postscript to this admission, Harry, you may be as pleased as I to know that most formerly all-boys' boarding schools—including Lancing—have been admitting girls for several years now. Some things have changed for the better since our day. When I last visited Lancing, with Ellie, years ago, I was delighted to find a gaggle of giggling teenage girls enlivening that same dormitory where I once scarcely knew enough to even dream of them.

And even—can you believe this, Harry?—even your old college at Cambridge, once the exclusive domain of young males like you in the 1920s and like me in the 1950s, even your old Cambridge college now welcomes women undergraduates! As I already mentioned earlier, your own great-granddaughter, Georgia, is now enrolled there as a student in Linguistics. How proud you'd be!

    With love,
    Peter

16 September 2021

Dear Harry,

I'm amazed. Here in Southern California as I sit wondering what I might have to say to you this morning, I find myself looking out through the windows of our cottage into a slow, inexorable drizzle, a spectacle unheard of in September in this part of the world. Glistening on the big green leaves of ivy that hang over our fence, these raindrops have me re-envisioning the England of my youth . . .

A pleasant interlude!

With love,
Peter

17 September 2021

Dear Harry,

Back to your nemesis, Barry. Braughing. Your son is now sixteen, seventeen, back in his last year at school in a turmoil of anger, self-doubt, and confusion. There were two things that kept me sane that last year and, at times, brought me back from the edge of despair. I'll return to Barry later because he was one of them. The other was the one school term, that wonderful, blessed, liberating three months of the year that I was lucky enough to spend as an exchange student at a state school in Rendsburg, a small town situated halfway along the Kiel canal in Schleswig-Holstein, in the extreme north of Germany. My exchange partner was Manfred Eckhardt, and the Eckhardts proved to be the most fabulous of surrogate parents. For the first time in my life, I rejoiced in the experience of going home every day after school to spend the evening with my "family," of sleeping comfortably in my own bed, in my own room, and going off to school again the next day.

What bliss, Harry! You can hardly imagine what bliss that was!

I was "allowed" to smoke, in moderation. Herr Eckhardt himself enjoyed his Turkish cigarettes and his cigars. He invited me to join him on business trips in his chauffeur-driven Mercedes, puffing contentedly on a cigar on the back seat beside me. At dinner—usually an *"Eintopf"*, a rich stew that warmed both heart and belly at the end of a cold winter's day, or sometimes a delicious smorgasbord of cold cuts of meats and a variety of cheeses—I was poured a glass of wine as a matter of course, along with the adults. At seventeen, I was encouraged to feel like an adult in their circle of family and friends. You can scarcely imagine, Harry, how that felt!

It was January, though, and by God it was cold in Schleswig-Holstein. Most days, I walked along the iced-over canal with deep snow on the ground to get to school in the early morning, head down against a mercilessly biting wind, wrapped up in a heavy winter coat. No uniform! Just whatever I chose to wear! But coming from the moderate climate of our own country, Harry, I was not ready with one of those warm down parkas that my schoolmates wore. I just had that heavy English winter coat and thick woolen gloves and mufflers. It was the first time in my life that I had experienced the kind of cold that cuts straight through to the bone and leaves the body frigid. I learned—clumsily! At risk of broken limbs—to skate!

The compensation was to arrive at the Hochschule every day and make the transition through the big front doors from bitter cold into wonderful, all-embracing warmth and the dense smell of hundreds of teenage human bodies regaining body heat. And then to find myself sitting in the classroom, elbow-to-elbow with classmates of both sexes! The difference from everything I knew about school from the age of seven could not have been neither starker, nor more appealing. I fell in love (again!) from a distance (again!) with a girl named Anneliese, blond, and to my eyes totally captivating—and of course untouchable. Among the strange things my mind brings back with amazing clarity across the years is a moment in our classroom where Anneliese is batting at a bee that has improbably found its way into class and hovers insistently around her head. And as she does so, she cries out—I transcribe phonetically as best I can—not "ay-nie", "eine Biene," which would have been correct, but "eenie," "eenie beenie," a whimsical, rhyming mispronunciation that even so many years later I recall as utterly charming. And obviously memorable.

And, Harry, there is this: while I was happily fantasizing about being in love with Annaliese, I was actually more in love with someone completely different. Without knowing it. Stupid, no? But how could I have known? She was an older woman; I could not have imagined such a thing. Her name was Iris. She came from Cardiff so she was Welsh, a fellow *"Ausländer"* also in Germany on an exchange but in her case as a teacher. We often used to walk to and from school together, since she was staying not far from the Eckhardts, and when I had the car accident that was the unhappy conclusion to my stay in Germany, she was the constant visitor at my bedside. She was kind, understanding, caring, always ready to listen and offer the feminine warmth and sympathy I had missed throughout my school years. In short, she was everything my deeply confused and adolescent self so badly needed at time. I wish I'd been sufficiently aware to realize then how much she meant to me—and I perhaps to her—a fellow stranger in a strange land . . . Did she ever understand this as I came to understand it later, when I found to my surprise how much I sorely missed her?

Anyway, that accident. Remember? You must have been out of your minds with worry, both you and Peggy, when someone called to let you know. I could easily have died.

Did I tell you the story, Harry? I suppose I must have done. I had a friend at school, or maybe it was the friend of a friend, a year or two older than myself, who had been able to borrow his father's DKW for a jaunt to a neighboring town and invited me and a couple of other friends along for the ride. (DKW, by the way, is today's Audi, with the same linked circles in its company logo. The acronym DKW—*Deutsche Kraftwagen*—translated into a schoolboy joke: *Das Krankenhaus Wartet*, "the hospital awaits", which proved in my case to be uncomfortably true). We drank beer, all boys together, had a jolly time, and it was dark already by the time we got started on the return trip to Rendsburg. The road was icy. Our driver was probably traveling too fast. He may have had one beer too many. A set of oncoming headlights dazzled him and he braked too hard, sending us into a long, dizzying skid. It came to an emphatic, screeching stop when the car slammed head-on into a farm tractor parked at the side of the road.

We ended up in the ditch. I don't know how long I was unconscious but when I came to there was warm blood streaming down across my face. I could hear people screaming, "*Bist Du OK? Bist Du OK?*" Are you okay? I thought I was. The worst thing, it seemed to me, was that there was blood spattered on the cover of my copy of Dylan Thomas's *Collected Poems* which I happened to be holding on my lap. (I kept that book for years, with its bloodstained cover. I probably still have it somewhere, in one of the many boxes that I keep in storage).

They managed to free me from the wreck and struggled to prevent me from trying desperately, irrationally to remove my outer clothes, despite the freezing cold, because these, too, I noticed now, were getting stained with blood. The next thing I remember was being in piled into a stranger's car, still in a daze, and driven back to Rendsburg.

The Eckhardts were beside themselves. They took me straight to the nearest hospital where the doctor stitched up two deep cuts, one above the eye, one leading back across my skull. He reported a fracture, a splintering of the skull that was apparently not serious enough in his opinion to keep me in the hospital overnight. Besides, the Eckhardts were anxious to get me back home—a mistake perhaps, but a kind intention. In retrospect, back home in England, the doctor thought I should have received better treatment for concussion than the few days I spent in bed. But at least, I had constant, loving care from the good Frau Eckhardt—and those daily bedside visits from Iris that I shall not forget. Like so many good people from those days, I wish I were able to let her know today how much she meant to me. I'd love to be able to travel back in time and tell her.

But enough for one day, Harry. To be continued in my next.

With love,
Peter

19 September 2021

Dear Harry,

What could you have felt about this, you and **Peggy**, when your son came home looking pretty odd with half a head of hair (they shaved off the other half) and two rows of as yet unhealed Frankenstein stitches? Were you worried? I know that Ellie and I would have thrown a fit, had it been our daughter Sarah. But for you not so much; it seems that you were ready to pack me off for my last term at boarding school.

Grin and bear it? That was always your philosophy. Grin and bear it.

Back at Lancing, though, I began to suffer from persistent headaches. It may be that I exaggerated them for the attention that they brought me, along with the respite from the routine of daily life at school; I was quite happy to be sent off to "the san"—short for the sanitarium, the school's little hospital. Located up behind all the other buildings and halfway along the path that led out onto the Downs, it was the domain of a woman I remember only as Sister, a woman who covered her sweet, caring nature with a starched nurse's uniform and the pretense of strict adherence to professionalism.

Another "older woman," in that last year of school!

Lucky for me, I was Sister's only patient at the time, and she spared no effort in looking after me. She gave me a soothing magic pill to help me fall sleep at night; even today I recall that welcome, swift and dizzying descent into oblivion. Best of all, she allowed me at least one daily cigarette. I was already well-addicted by this time; I had started back in France with Philippe and Jean-Claude, at the age of fourteen, smoking those black, throat-ripping *Gauloises Bleues*, and had pursued the outlawed addiction furtively behind the bushes throughout my time at Lancing. In Germany, I had been smoking *Roth-Händlers*, as black as those *Gauloises*, with no objection from the Eckhardts. Now, with Sister, we would meet like conspirators in her little office and share furtively in the dark pleasures of our nicotine addiction. (Damn! There it is, Harry! Another thing we shared, you and me! Not that I'm blaming you . . .)

What would I have done without Sister and the refuge of the sanitarium that last term at school? She was my blessing, my guardian angel, showering me with the unspoken love and the understanding that I needed.

What else did I do? I worked toward my final exams, the "A" levels. I labored over an essay about Heinrich Heine that easily won me the school prize in German Literature. My success led ironically to the one final insult awaiting me at the end of my years at Lancing. It came in the form of a summons to the Headmaster's study on Prize Day, where I was subjected to a scathing reprimand for the book I had been invited to choose freely with my prize money: a handsome, hardcover edition of James Joyce's *Ulysses*.

Okay, Harry, I don't doubt that my choice was intended as a final, cocky, middle finger to the school, its religion, its rules, and regulations, and mostly its repression of my rebellious self. So how could I claim to be shocked when he, the headmaster himself, one Mr. Dancy, red-faced with anger, his black teacher's gown flapping furiously behind his desk, demanded that I remove "that filth" from the prize table. It was the Bishop himself who was to hand out the prizes, and in the presence of the entire school board! How dare I be the cause of such embarrassment to these dignitaries!

You were there that day, Harry! Did you know, when you came to pick me up that one last time, what was happening behind that carefully orchestrated pomp?

Perhaps not. I surely never told you.

Your wayward son,
Peter

21 September 2021

Dear Harry,

As promised, I can tell you now—as I would not have done back then because it would have cost you sleep at night— about the second thing that eased my bumpy passage through that last year of school. This was the reliable weekly flow of florid, wonderfully literate, and exuberantly salacious letters from the man whose influence on me you had come to worry about more than anything: Barry Evans.

I looked forward eagerly to their arrival. Our letters at school, when we received them, were distributed at the end of breakfast in the dining hall, and Barry's were instantly recognizable from his impeccably stylish art school italics. I have lost those letters and no longer recall the details of their content, but I do know they were filled with the kind of subtle, tongue-in-cheek sexual innuendo that typified our conversations when I visited him at home. In the letters I sent him in return, I can be sure that I mentioned none of the truth about my sexual escapades with other boys at Lancing; Barry was all about girls, the women he lusted after with his insatiable appetite and those about whom he endlessly fantasized. He was impatient for me to be finally out of school and into the real world, where he'd be able to supervise the loss of my virginity.

You can see that your son was lost in a profound, tormenting conflict, Harry. The fears provoked by actual experience led me to conclude that I would never dare touch a girl. And yet, there was some not yet fully-awakened part of me, the part that was easily seduced by Barry and his letters, that longed desperately to be initiated into the terrifying mysteries of the opposite sex. It was to take some time before that happened.

It was not only in this that I was timid. I had learned too well to tame the wild creature that lurked beguilingly within my soul. It was not for nothing that Barry took to signing off each letter, "Your Wicked Uncle." His presence was certainly a greater influence than yours at this time of my life. I longed to be the rebel that he was. And yet . . . I had been taught from my earliest days to be quite the opposite; to be the Good Boy, the Boy Scout, honest and loyal, truthful, obedient in all things, and obliging. I had learned this code of honor from you, Harry, and from the schools you sent me to. In my den of Cubs and from the Boy Scouts too—the option I had taken over the ROTC at Lancing. It proved a daunting challenge for that good boy to allow the Barry part of me to emerge from the deep place where I'd learned to hide, repress, and deny him.

Oh, I did make every effort to prove myself the rebel in that last year at school. Aside from Barry, I had a "friend"—I put him in quotation marks because I wished so much to be his friend; for his part, he did not need my friendship. He collected bebop records—Charlie Parker, Dizzie Gillespie—and played them loudly in the corridor of little studies we were allotted as seniors. He drank black coffee. He was remarkable for the extreme pallor of his face and his short, dark, curly hair. He wore his trousers ultra-tapered in the Teddy Boy fashion of the day. He openly, defiantly flouted the school rules, and got away with it. He smoked. He drank. He swore. I won't tell you some of the things he said, but I remember them. The very words.

His name was Chris. I ran a search for him online as I was writing this and found that he had died at the age of 69 in Tanzania, still a jazz afficionado and immersed throughout his life in African culture.

In my study across the corridor from his at Lancing, I longed to be as bold, as arrogant, as rebellious as Chris—the only boy at school I ever called by his first name. I played the artist, covered my study walls with two huge, clumsy murals, one a free-hand abstraction, the other an enlargement of one of those late blue cut-out figures by Matisse. I had my trousers tapered, but never managed to achieve the Teddy Boy look that Chris did. I visited the barbershop in nearby Brighton and got myself an American haircut. A Perry Como!

Perry Como! Hardly the bebop iconoclast, but at least an American.

None of it worked. I never got to be the bad boy Barry had in mind for me. The Good Boy prevailed, and I succeeded mostly in looking, I suppose, in the long view, more than a little bit ridiculous. And when I did get to be bad, just occasionally, I ended up feeling terrible for what I'd done.

So . . . still the Good Boy, Harry. Still the Good Boy, to this very day. You'd be proud of me.

Your son,
Peter

22 September 2021

Dear Harry,

Do I need to remind you of that other remarkable event on Prize Day? The one that placed a final, definitive full stop at the end of the story of my time at boarding school?

Remember? You brought salvation in the car with you on that last day when you and Peggy arrived at the school to pick me up—the same day I got so royally chewed out by the Headmaster (I'm surprised he managed to refrain from bringing out the cane for one last time and having me bend over!) You brought Jeannine. I opened the door to the back seat of your car and found her sitting there beside me. You had written to let me know to expect another exchange student from France but I had entirely forgotten that she had already arrived to stay with us. And there she was, beautiful in her spotless white blouse and tartan skirt, mysterious, infinitely tantalizing, French, feminine, and casting (so briefly!) in my direction what I came to know as her private, impenetrable feline smile.

Of course, I fell in love again at once.

Says your youthful son, who always fell in love too easily but never managed to love well.

With love,
Peter

23 September 2021

Dear Harry,

Timidity! It's the quality that goes along with being the good boy—something I would rather not have learned at school. Oh, I was otherwise pretty smart, Harry, after all that education! I was articulate, well-spoken, and I had learned to present myself with a certain natural—though some might think affected—English public schoolboy charm. I knew Latin! I was versed in English literature, as well as French and German. I could speak both languages fluently. I knew a lot of stuff. What I had not learned was how to leave behind my boyhood and become be a man.

There I was in Paris, Harry! Paris! With Jeannine, the new love of my life. It was autumn, just a couple of months after leaving school forever. The city was glorious, glowing, living up to its popular name, the City of Light. I was free, for the first time in my life! Free from all those rules and regulations. Free from you and Peggy! I was in love, and I'm pretty sure that Jeannine loved me in return.

And what did I do about it, Harry? Nada. Nothing. I could hardly summon the nerve to kiss the girl. Oh, we held hands a lot. We strolled along the boulevards as lovers are supposed to do in Paris. Lingered around the book stalls on the banks of the Seine. Talked books, carefully, because Jeannine had recently passed her baccalaureate and was ten times better read and smarter than I was myself. We went to the Louvre, where you could still see art up-close, because this was in the days long before the glass pyramid, before tourists from throughout the world were lining up with cell phones to take selfies with the Mona Lisa (consider yourself lucky, Harry, to have lived your whole long life without ever knowing about selfies!) The galleries could still echo with the lonely visitor's footsteps.

I was in lover's heaven, Harry, and could barely bring myself to touch the girl I so much wanted. I actually had only the vaguest idea what it was I wanted anyway, and still less the guts to make it known, or how to ask her if that was what she wanted, too.

What a klutz, Harry (again that word you probably never heard)! No wonder the French scoff at the English lack of *savoir-faire* in matters of the heart. More importantly, the bed. There I was, still an awkward English schoolboy, all *politesse* and no performance. As the French say, *merde*!

Your son,
Peter

26 September 2021

Dear Harry,

I hate to say this, but I was crippled with the same timidity when I went up to university. (You'll know what I mean when I say "went up" to Cambridge because that was the language in your day too. We also used to "read," not "study" what over here in America is called "your major." It's what we said).

You met Susan because I brought her home to the Vicarage on at least one occasion. Susan was the Girton girl I fell in love with the first time I sat down behind her in a French Romantic Poetry lecture class. Ever the romantic opportunist (um, the cad), I was quick to ditch Jeannine in favor of my new infatuation. After regaling her with her a blizzard of yearning love letters promising eternal devotion, I wrote one last time to announce, with only partially feigned regret, that our undying love was doomed by the regrettable existence of geography. Back on the ground, I eventually overcame my timidity enough to speak to Susan after one of our lecture sessions, and we soon became friends. It took a long time, though, to find nerve enough to invite her up to my college rooms for tea and I think I was taken by surprise and not a little panicked when she cheerfully accepted. This was the moment, I promised myself, when I could declare my love, kiss her, maybe even . . .

I scarcely dared to think.

Harry, were you like me, with girls? When the day came, I was beyond nervous. For hours before her visit, my heart was already beating wildly with anticipation. I arranged with my roommate, Jerry, to be out for the afternoon. As can happen with assigned college roommates, Jerry was my polar opposite. He was a sportsman, a rugby football player, and I had to hide his dirty wet socks and his smelly jock strap from where he'd left them out to dry in front of the gas fire in our communal sitting room. The jock strap particularly, with its in-your-face evocation of the male appendages, would have been acutely embarrassing. I bought chocolate-coated McVities to accompany the tea. Added a shilling to the meter to ensure the heater would hold out.

She arrived! I "sported the oak." You'll know about that too, Harry, closing the outer door to your college rooms to indicate the need for privacy. Made a pot of tea. Served the McVities on the best plate from our rudimentary kitchen. We made small talk.

Once the tea was done, there was nothing for it but to make my move. I took the seat beside her on the sofa, in front of the gas fire. Put a tentative arm around her, drew her closer, and noticed with growing panic that she did not resist. Seemed even to welcome it. Snuggled in. And raised her face to mine . . .

If only the magnitude of my desire could have been translated into that little bit of confidence and courage required to respond to what she obviously expected—and clearly did not object to. She was so close, so feminine, so utterly desirable. So . . . well, so available. Not in a bad sense, she was just plainly eager for a kiss. Maybe more than a kiss. Was I wrong in thinking that she mouthed the words, Come on?

And yet there I was, behaving once again like the English public schoolboy that I was, so lacking in self-confidence about my ability to even touch a woman in some acceptable, loving way that I was paralyzed. I loved this girl! I wanted her more badly, more immediately, more urgently than anything ever in my life. But I couldn't do it, couldn't even bring myself to kiss her. I did not know how. I was not man enough, no match for the woman in her, the woman she had already grown to be. Beside her, I was still a boy.

Not man enough.

I remember, those words, Harry, when your insight challenged me years later. "Are you man enough for her?" you asked me, at a moment of crisis, when my marriage was falling apart.

I was not.

But that's for another letter. Suffice it for now to remember, with some pain, some sadness, and not a little shame how emotionally stunted I was as I embarked upon my life as an adult. It is perhaps too easily self-exculpatory to attribute my immaturity to those protected years at school. But it's my suspicion that I was not too much unlike you, at that time in your life. Did you share that paralyzing physical, emotional and, yes, sexual timidity? Was your libido as fierce as mine, and your fear as deadening?

The upshot of these persistent doubts about my manhood was an inner rage that I kept buried in some deep place inside me for too long, a toxic rage that I refused steadfastly for years to recognize, let alone express.

And there's more of this still to be revealed, I fear. Meantime I am, as always,

Your undoubted son,
Peter

29 September 2021

Dear Harry,

It's Saturday in Laguna Beach, California. I'm looking forward to sitting out on our balcony this afternoon, with its view out over the Pacific Ocean, and lighting up my weekly cigar. La Gloria Cubana.

It's a treat that I allow myself. You'll be pleased to hear that I finally managed to give up smoking cigarettes in my fiftieth year—a few decades sooner than yourself. I had been trying for years. Had tried everything, from patches to nicotine chewing gum to hypnosis. Nothing worked. Until I listened to a friend who advised me to take a positive approach. To stop telling myself, No, I shouldn't, mustn't, can't and so. Instead, I tried giving myself permission to light up but choosing, instead the benefits that came with not smoking: the ability to climb a flight of stairs without panting for breath, for example, and having clothes that didn't stink of stale tobacco. I made a list, and the list was long. It didn't hurt, too, that Sarah, from her earliest years, kept nagging me insistently to stop.

Like you, I was addicted. But I managed to quit. I haven't smoked a cigarette since 1986.

A while ago, however, I gave myself permission to enjoy the occasional hit of nicotine with a cigar. Just for the pleasure of it. I don't believe I ever saw you smoking one of these. The cigarettes you smoked were mostly those you rolled yourself. I say "rolled," but you had all kinds of ways of making them, all kinds of intricate little machines. The making was as much a part of the fun for you as lighting up and smoking, but you were happy to kid yourself that the shredded tobacco you used was less harmful to your health than store-bought cigarettes. Still, I'm sure they did you no good. I'm glad you had the good sense it took, so late in life—and the love!—to quit the nasty habit when you understood that it was harming Peggy.

Knowing of my addiction, I ration myself to that one cigar a week—though sometimes, I'll admit, I manage to sneak in a second one if no one else is counting. No smoking in the house, of course, these days but the weather here in Southern California is rarely a deterrent. I slip out onto the balcony or the patio behind the cottage and enjoy my smoke as I complete a New York Times Sunday crossword. (That was never one of your addictions, was it? In that at least we differ . . .)

Am I addicted? Maybe. Just a little bit. Is that like being a little bit pregnant? Maybe. But I figure, well, at this stage of my life it won't be the occasional smoke that kills me.

See you out on the balcony, then.

Cheers,
Peter

2 October 2021

Dear Harry,

It took a patient, sweet, kind-hearted, and easily exploited girl—the girlfriend of a friend's girlfriend, to ease my awkward and self-doubting self out of my virginity. I was 19, nearly 20! From what I hear, that would seem laughably retarded to today's young people, who apparently "hook up" with random others with barely a second thought.

You would likely not remember my friend, Paul, from Venezuela, though I'm pretty sure you met him. Short in stature? Swarthy? Dark hair? Wavy? He was one of those friends I'd bring home with me because he had no family to go home to in England in the shorter holidays. A year behind me at Caius, he was far ahead in the kind of experience I lacked—and sorely needed. His pretty, cheerfully promiscuous girlfriend at the time was Mickey, and on more than one occasion he prevailed on me to help free up the flat she shared with her friend Debbie, to allow him to enjoy an afternoon of undisturbed libidinous pleasure with his lady friend.

So, I took Debbie out—to the cinema, perhaps—and we became friends ourselves. Sort of. I'm ashamed to say I may have considered myself a cut above this good young woman. May have? No, I did. Paul and I were university students, after all, and the girls were town girls, with jobs in local stores.

(I'm aware, of course, that attitudes of this kind do not speak well of the privileged young man I was). There came a time, however, when Paul—and Mickey too, I suspect—decided it was time for their friend Peter to grow up. They conspired to invite me over for a cup of tea one afternoon, and shortly afterwards announced that they had evening plans, leaving me and Debbie free run of the flat. It was obvious to both of us what was expected.

We sat on Debbie's bed. I took courage in both hands and began a fumbling exploration of her body. She seemed perfectly willing to allow it, unhitching her bra beneath her blouse and allowing me, too, to kiss her as I fumbled further. Breasts. Had I ever touched a woman's breasts before? Jeannine's? Would I have dared? The result of this delight was predictable in my nether regions, Harry, and Debbie's fingers proved skillful in further stimulating the arousal. Then, with much awkward wriggling and repositioning of bodies, she guided my fingers into the mysterious triangle of silken hair between her thighs and opened herself to my breathless digital exploration of that unknown territory.

By now a tangle of body parts and half-discarded clothes, we fell back on the bed and Debbie squirmed out of her panties, dumping them over the side of the bed as she spread her legs for me to lie between and slip myself into that now moist and beckoning interior. And I lost it. My recently rampant cock went suddenly limp as a great wave of self-doubt and insecurity surged up and disempowered me, along with a flood of shame. There she was, this patient, lovely girl, all ready and willing, eager, even, for me to enter her most private sanctum . . . and I couldn't do it.

"Sorry," I said. "Oh, my God, I'm sorry."

And Debbie said, "It doesn't matter. Honestly, it doesn't matter," she insisted. "It happens all the time."

Which was kind of her, but it did nothing to relieve the intensity of my embarrassment and shame. What mattered was that it had happened not to other men but to me. Incredibly, I had been so hot with desire, oozing, literally, with the urgency of that long imagined, long craved moment and then . . . nothing.

Well, Harry, as an old man now myself I can readily imagine that the same thing does happen to a great number of young men on their first attempt. I wonder even, since we're being totally honest here, if it might have happened to you?

Might as well say it here. I only ever saw your penis once, and that was by accident. You were standing naked in the caravan and I burst in unexpectedly. I was probably no more than eight or nine years old and I was shocked by the size of it, the dangle, the thicket of hair. The startling image froze inside my mind and stuck there, even though you covered yourself quickly with a towel. So, it was no more than a glimpse. But it is strange, isn't it, that I remember this moment so clearly even today?

Anyway, to get back to my story: I'm thankful to be able to report that the disaster with Debbie was quickly followed by recovery and triumph. Debbie's kindly ministrations proved exactly what was needed to regenerate what I'd lost, and she managed to guide me gently into that place I had so lusted after for so long. Virility restored, I buried myself joyfully inside that tunnel of love and ploughed away like a real man till I was done. Which was probably much too soon for Debbie—I'm sure I had as yet no idea that a woman, too, could have an orgasm. But I was relieved and grateful beyond words, as you can imagine, to have finally endowed her with my unwanted virginity. The door—if you'll forgive the rather crude image—was open. It would never close again.

Your ever priapic son,
Peter

3 October 2021

Dear Harry,

Phew! We can be happy to have finally passed that milepost.

Considering how kind she had been to me—and how kind she would continue to be, so long as I knew her—I was as shamefully cavalier in the way I treated Debbie as I had been with Jeannine. We did continue to go out together, sometimes for dinner at one of those inexpensive Indian restaurants where you could get a delicious, spicy, satisfying meal for no more than half-a-crown. I don't know what that would be in today's money, maybe something like a couple of dollars. Or we'd go to the flicks. Perhaps it was with Debbie that I saw *East of Eden*, the first time I saw James Dean, and the first movie that he made. After which and before he died in that car crash in his Porsche at a remote California crossroads, there were *Rebel Without a Cause* and *Giant*, the one about the Texas oil man in which the (for many, eternally) young actor aged, none too successfully, into a nasty, rich old drunk. I mention James Dean because like so many other young men at the time and at that age, I identified so keenly with both the actor and his roles; the easy, boyish surface charm that covered a hornet's nest of insecurities and anger; the lost, mumbling man-boy, so anxious to please the father for whom he was never good enough and earn the love of the mother who rejected him.

I *was* James Dean. Well, a self-conscious, reedy English public schoolboy version of the same.

How many of us James Deans were out there on the streets with our nervous tics, mumbling away and grinning quick, angst-filled grins, and brushing nervously at our hair? We were, as they say, legion.

You of all people, Harry, with your love of Freud, would doubtless spot the Oedipus lurking in our psyches. But then I can be sure you never saw any of those films I loved so much. You were never a serious movie-goer, as I recall, and in any case their whole ethos would have been "too American" for you and Peggy.

For what it's worth, my favorite line from a James Dean movie is this one: "Well then there now . . ."

Riddle me that, you wise old man.

Your son,
Peter

4 October 2021

Dear Harry,

I'll admit it. I squandered the enormous privilege of my three years as a student at Cambridge, one of the greatest universities in the world. Freed, finally, from the strictures of school life, I had too much growing up to do. There were girls. There were smoky pubs, and cigarettes, and beer. There was the freedom to do the work . . . or not. At the beginning of my last year at Caius, I made the requisite appearance in the college rooms of my Director of Studies, a wry, unsettlingly perceptive Scotsman with a wicked sense of humor. "Well, Clothier," he asked, puffing his pipe into action with a Swan's Vesta match as I settled back into his leather chair for our annual discussion. "How do you plan to spend your last year at this illustrious institution?"

"Well, sir," I told him, with what I hoped would pass as an earnest mien: "I rather thought I should settle down and do some work."

"What?" my academic Virgil responded, the bristly bushes of his eyebrows arching over his pipe in mock dismay. "And spoil three happy years?"

Well, I did get my undergraduate degree at the end of that last year. Just barely. And paraded with my Caius classmates through the Gate of Honor to the university Senate, right next door, where I accepted my parchment scroll at the hands of the Chancellor. And headed out into the real world without the first idea what to do with the rest of my life. Just like you, Harry. I do know that much. You had your degree in psychology. You would have made an excellent psychotherapist—a familiar path these days but not an obvious one in the 1920s when you graduated. Back then, the career paths in that field would have been either psychiatrist, with a medical degree, or psychoanalyst, with a couch. I can understand that neither one would have appealed to you. Alternatively . . . you had been involved in amateur theatrics at Cambridge, and you were tempted by the dream of a career in acting. I believe I mentioned earlier that Peggy told me this. But I suspect your father played a part in your rejecting this path, whether consciously or unconsciously: a practical man, a scientist, an inventor, a businessman, he would never have approved of so frivolous a career.

And then there was the ministry, the path you chose.

As for me, my degree was in Modern and Medieval Languages and French Philology—not an immediately promising career path. I was a poet. I had been writing poetry since the age of twelve and it was at that age, Peggy told me, that I announced my intention to become a writer. I had been writing poems in my student days at Cambridge—pretty maudlin stuff, I could well imagine. Still, it could hardly escape my attention, as I approached that time to leave the sheltered world of academia behind and set out into the real world where a "job" was needed, and the livable income that went along with it, that poets are not known to make a lot of money. That they are, in fact, lucky if they make anything at all.

There was, too, another factor that had to be considered: National Service. The military. I had managed to postpone that requirement by heading off early to university, but now that I was out in the world, the obligation loomed once more. I flirted with a vaguely romantic notion of joining the RAF to become a pilot, where I could leave the mundane ties of earth behind and drift ecstatically among the clouds. But the aptitude test put an ignominious end to that aspiration. I proved to be singularly lacking in spatial depth perception—a quality obviously desirable if not essential for a pilot. (My failure at this test might also explain the deficiency in sports I mentioned earlier—that I was never able to locate a ball in space).

What then? Did we consult together about this? Did we have a serious family discussion about my prospects? If we did, I don't remember it. But there proved to be another option into which I stumbled without serious forethought—one that would conveniently kill two of those proverbial birds with a single stone. I learned that teachers employed in the state school system were exempt from military service, and that by enrolling at a teacher's training college I could earn myself a further year's deferment.

A teacher's life? It would be ideal, I airily convinced myself. Not much work, really. Short days, long holidays . . . I would have plenty of time to devote to my poetry!

From what Olympian heights did I condescend to look down upon a world awaiting nothing better than the flowering of my genius!

How wrong I was, Harry.

As always, your delusional son,
Peter

5 October 2021

Dear Harry,

I realize, belatedly as usual, that it's time to acknowledge what has become obvious even to someone as obtuse as my stubborn self! The time has come to give up the original conceit that these letters are about *me* trying to get to know *you*. The truth is the opposite, they are about wanting *you* to get to know *me*. About needing your recognition and your love. The "tell me who you are" turns out to be reversed. But I suspect you probably understood that from the start.

From the time I left Cambridge and strode out onto the world's greater stage—with a quite few stumbles yet to come—I have had very little actual contact with you, other than what I have now discovered to be a remarkably extensive correspondence. In fact, the time we spent together, father and son, was sporadic and, over the years, relatively brief. Even from the earliest days, being away at boarding school for the better part of the year meant that I had less contact with you than most boys do with their fathers. Then, after Cambridge, I spent only two brief years more in England, in the big city, before leaving the country for good. For the rest of your life, I returned only for short visits. I moved first to Germany for two years, then to Canada for another two before arriving here in the United States, where I spent four years in Iowa

City at the Writers' Workshop, then moved out to California in 1968. I have lived here ever since. In short, the progression of the years kept putting an ever-greater geographical distance between the two of us.

It was not long after I left England that you retired—I think in part for reasons of poor health. I learned most of this from Flora, who stayed closer to home than I did: there were recurrent headaches, bronchial problems, a sometimes-severe depression. Retiring from your pastoral work if not—never!—from the priesthood, you spent the remainder of your days with Peggy at Glenview, that little cottage by the Cardigan Bay in Aberporth, where Peggy's parents also lived until their death. You set up your woodshop beside the cottage in what had been a small car garage and worked for many years at your lathe, a minister-turned-craftsman, while Peggy took care of the cottage and the cooking. You had your pub within walking distance, and when walking became difficult you took to a nicely decorated Alpine cane to help you up the hill. With that, your bent walk, your heavy, rain jacket and your French beret, you became a familiar sight in the village, something of a local institution on your daily trips up to The Ship in the middle of the day.

We'll talk more about our visits there, and the grandchildren's, in due course. In the meantime, it's good to have arrived at a greater clarity about my purpose in writing you these letters. You have become, curiously, perhaps perversely, your own son's confessor!

With love,
Peter

8 October 2021

Dear Harry,

Next stop London, then. Though not many geographical miles more distant from your Sharnbrook parish, the nation's capital city seemed somehow further removed from village life than did the university. Oh yes, I continued to come home quite often at the weekends, though I'm sure less frequently than from Cambridge. And when at home, I dutifully followed what I imagined to be your rules. I went to church on Sunday mornings. Took communion, at my mother's side. I did this, knowingly, to please you, keeping up the pretense that I was somehow still a good practicing Christian, as I thought you wanted, when in fact I had long since given up the practice. At Caius, despite the Dean's friendly interest in my welfare—the Dean's job, of course, at Cambridge, was not the purely administrative position that I filled over here in my last years in academia; he was more like the collage chaplain—I barely ever showed my face in chapel.

Even on my visits to you at the Vicarage, I had begun to feel more a stranger. In London, far from home, I felt untethered, relieved of obligation and responsibility, free to go my own misguided way. I signed up for a year of postgraduate study at a teacher's training college at the end of the King's Road in Chelsea, where I joined a small cadre of graduate students, half a dozen of us, rather snobby in our attitude toward the hoi-polloi of students working for a mere two-year teaching credential. I was assigned a tiny room on the top floor of the main college building, just big enough for a creaky bed and a desk and chair. The little window was placed too high on the wall to afford even a peekaboo view. It was here, in this dreary little accomodation, that I finally—finally!—found the courage to do what I had dismally failed to do years before, in my much more spacious and welcoming rooms at Caius: I made love to Susan, my unforgotten love from Cambridge days.

I've no doubt that it will tickle you, Harry—as it humbled me—to learn that many years later, when Susan and I reconnected (electronically: another story!) as old people, old friends on two sides of the Pacific Ocean—I discovered that Susan, the great obsession of my young life, the woman I had always thought of as my first true love, had not the slightest recollection of this monumental event! But with the frank admission that it might have never happened, this is how I "remember" that encounter. We had both chosen to come up to London after graduation. I no longer recall how I got back in touch with her but we arranged to meet. Perhaps we had dinner. Perhaps I invited her to come up to see my dark, little college room on the fourth floor of the college building. And perhaps she agreed to lie down on that little iron bed with me. Who knows if this is true? But as I recall, I had no further hesitation, no more reticence, no timidity. As I remember it. She does not.

And afterwards, she said, graciously (as I remember it; why would I remember her exact words so well if she never said them?): "You actually make love quite well, you know."

By this time, Harry, everything I learned growing up about the sanctity of sex had long since flown out the window. There was still in England in the 1950s, a lingering pretense of social and moral disapproval of sex before marriage. Surely, such reticence had been discarded many years before. What about those flappers, Harry, in your young day, the Roaring Twenties? When you yourself were in your twenties? Were those girls with their page boy haircuts and their short, shimmery skirts all innocence until they married? I don't believe it. If I know anything, it's that young people were bedding each other merrily before marriage even in your young day, Victorian moralism be damned. That post-Puritan period in the sexual history of humankind was the exception, surely, rather than the rule.

I bring this up to confess to something I suppose you might have known, or at least suspected; once initiated into the pleasures of the shared bed, I had absolutely no compunction about hopping into bed with whomsoever I could persuade to join me. I suspect that Flora was a little more circumspect about such things than I, but I'm sure that she, too, had what were referred to, in genteel circles, as "flings." Yet, none of this could be acknowledged in our family. Amongst the four of us, when we were together, it was as though we, the young members of the family, never swerved from the proprieties of our good Christian upbringing.

I have to tell you too that it did not end well with Susan. It was not long before she began to cool on (what I remember as) our relationship. It was perhaps in part the distance—we lived at opposite ends of town, a long tube or bus ride—but also because I soon became overbearingly possessive. I demanded, unsuccessfully I knew to my exasperation, her exclusive devotion. For the first time, but not the last, I discovered the intensity of my jealous rage—that "green-eyed monster that doth mock the meat it feeds on." And it was truly monstrous, hot, and wild, so uncontrollable that it could spiral in an instant from anger into a violence that I never suspected in me. I confess it now; I slapped two women in my life, Harry, and one of them was Susan. I'm relieved to know that this, too, is something she has blotted out from memory.

The other one was Ellie. Of all the misbegotten myths that have survived into the twenty-first century one of the worst is that of the male right to take ownership of women. Too often, even today, we men behave like those (apparently slandered!) Neanderthals, dragging our women into our cave and demanding total fealty. Anything less and we react in fury, provoked by what we perceive as an intolerable insult to our manhood.

Mea culpa, Harry. *Mea culpa*.

Your son,
Peter

9 October 2021

Dear Harry,

The slap that ignominiously ended my relationship with Susan had a surprising and, well, rather shameful sequel. On my way back to my room, still shaking with righteous rage, I ran into Marie. You might remember her, but if you don't you'll shortly get to know her better. The moment I saw her strolling in all innocence down the main corridor of the college, my hunger for Susan was instantly superseded by a new wave of lust. I did not even know this woman's name and had never exchanged a single word with her before virtually dragging her up the stairs (though, I protest, she offered no resistance) to that little room I recently described to you and there, Harry, yes, no other word for it, I fucked her.

I know. Crude. It's a word I never liked and I'm sure not one you ever used. But yes, there it is—I fucked her.

And to be honest, she fucked me right back.

But let me explain.

Marie was not one of us, not a graduate student, but you could tell at once that she was different from the other two-year teacher-training students. For one thing, she was clearly older than the students she habitually sat with in the dining hall where I first laid my concupiscent eyes on her. In fact, she was a couple of years older than me. She stood out not only for that reason, though, but especially for the joyful energy she projected, her constant merriment, and not least for the radiant shimmer of her golden hair.

As I mentioned earlier, we graduate students kept for the most part to ourselves. In the dining hall, we ate together, a small group of friends. But for months now, at mealtime, my eyes were drawn back time and again to the vision of that blond hair, that seductive, bubbling energy, that joyful smile.

So that day, still trembling with rage on my way back to my college room after handing out that slap, I swept her up. And afterwards, impulsively, still bathed in the afterglow of those hot, erotic moments, I asked Marie if she'd like to join me on a camping trip I had already planned in Germany that summer; and to my astonishment, she immediately agreed. That trip is a whole story unto itself, Harry. Enough to say here that for months and, as it turned out, years after that first encounter, we sinned away hungrily together, on and off, until our hunger for each other's body proved to have consequences we could never, at that moment, have foreseen.

Mea culpa, Harry. *Mea maxima culpa.*

Your wicked son,
Peter

10 October 2021

Dear Harry,

I'm sure you would have been troubled when you learned that Barry Evans and his family moved to London around the same time I did. You were convinced he was a "bad influence." You were right about the influence—and probably right, too, about the "bad." He was an important friend and ally with whom I could always talk about what was happening in my life in a way that I could never have dreamed of doing with you. You know the kind of thing I'm talking about.

Barry and Mary had found a place to live in Putney. It was exactly the kind of place you'd expect to find a Bohemian artist and his brood. They rented the floor above what once had been the stables of a grand old Victorian home on a street called Rayners Road, with a wide back gate leading into a cobblestone courtyard whose walls were overgrown with ivy. The flat itself was long and narrow, with a kitchen at one end, a big, comfortable living room in the middle and, off at an angle, bedrooms for the parents and the children. Below, the stables were converted to a spacious studio where Barry worked when he was not out on a job. He and his partner, William Kempster, had by now established a national reputation as muralists and illustrators, and work was readily available. They were working on travel posters for the railways, airline posters with eye-catching, tilted views of European capitals seen from the viewpoint of a landing airliner. Barry was still profligate, maybe, but no longer the impecunious artist we first knew.

Was it pure coincidence? I have forgotten now how it came about, but after finishing my year's teacher training I was offered a job teaching French and German at a boys' grammar school called Rutlish, in Wimbledon, not far from Putney, a little further to the south and west. I heard of a group of former Caius men who had reunited in London to rent one half of another large Victorian home on Mercier Road, quite literally around the corner from Barry and Mary's place. Conveniently, the nearby East Putney tube station was a mere two stops from Wimbledon on the District Line.

You knew some, but not all of the men who became my flat-mates; Hugh, for example—High deVere Welchman, to pay him full respect—was now a stockbroker in training and wore a tailored, pin-striped business suit and a bowler hat to work every day and sported a rolled black umbrella. Hugh loved old things, especially cars and furniture. Among his most treasured possessions was an elegant Sheraton sideboard which he kept assiduously polished. His room in our house was immaculately kept, an elegant exception to the hodge-podge of other quirky personal styles. Frank Brennan, the Irishman, painted the walls of his space in alternating colors of telephone black and telephone box red; Dick Booth—a big, taciturn, rugger player of a man whose frequent, furtive visits to the USSR had the rest of us convinced he was a spy with MI-6—maintained a space of studied anonymity; my friend Frank—later Graham— Rooth shared the top floor with me, his room a spare attic, his bed a mattress on the floor. He had a baffling infatuation with a mysterious and at that time virtually unknown sect called Scientology.

My attic room was the smallest in the house. I had the expert help of Mary in choosing colors for the multiple, mostly sloping walls; and Barry painted a Cubist-inspired mural on a rectangular space above the non-functioning fireplace. The cramped space allowed only for a desk and a single bed, the latter occupied most often by my lonely self, but on occasion— well, as frequently as possible—also host to any young woman I could persuade to join me there. My most frequent overnight company was my new friend Marie . . . but more about her shortly.

Barry continued to play the willing Pandar to my now insatiable appetites. It was at a party at his house that I met Violet, for instance, a small, pretty, vivacious woman who was in town for a weekend's visit. She was married. I didn't care. She seemed not to care. We were both more than a little tipsy, and Barry spurred us on. Violet's husband was in the RAF, and she made clear that she planned to use her weekend of liberty to gratify needs that went unmet at home. Only too happy to oblige, I took her home with me to my little attic room. As Barry commented the next day when he came over to visit after she left, the place looked as though a tornado had blown through. I'll spare you the details.

You would be disappointed in me in those early London days, Harry, and not only because of Violet. I spent my evenings and nights in this kind of debauchery as often as I could, but not nearly as often as I would have liked. I was looking for something, and to give me small credit I think a part of it was love. All I had was sex, and not enough of that. Absent that, of an evening, I found ready compensation in the pubs, and all too often nursed a hangover on the way to work. A walk to East Putney station through the London mist—sometimes, in those days, a heavy blanket of smog—was of help to clear the head, as was the walk from Wimbledon Station to the school. I would arrive in good enough shape, by a hair, to check in at the teacher's staff room for a cup of strong tea before heading off to class.

Who was I? The truth is, I had no idea. Was I the civilized, well-bred, well-spoken, socially acceptable young man, public school and Cambridge, straight-arrow, dutiful and honest to a fault? The young man you would have wanted me to be, perhaps even imagined that I was? Was I the hard-drinking, libertine, flamboyant Bohemian poet, careless of rules and social conventions, the one that Barry Evans flattered me to believe myself to be? Was I the carefree, polyamorous Romeo, seducer of women, ace lover that I'd like to have believed myself—but secretly feared that I was not, and could never be? Or was I the quiet, introverted, peace- and nature-loving, rather lazy, country boy who dreamed of pleasant, day-long idleness with a straw between his teeth and long, dreamless nights?

I was all of these, Harry, and none of them. Above all, I suppose I was like many young men in their very early twenties, unsure who I was, what it was I wanted, and whither I was going in my life.

Were you aware, I wonder, of this inner conflict? I tried to hide it when I was at home with a confident exterior, an easy social charm at village events, and outwardly—for the most part—gentlemanly behavior? Would it have helped if we'd been able to talk about these things? Had I not felt obliged to hide them from you, in order to protect both you and myself from guilt, embarrassment, accountability?

The only thing I know for sure is this: that I will never know.

But we can talk now, can't we?

Your son,
Peter

11 October 2021

Dear Harry,

Did I ever show the proper appreciation for the car you bought me, or at least helped me buy? I forget whether, or how, I participated in the purchase. Or how, not long afterwards, ungratefully perhaps, I sold it.

It was my first car, a little Ford Anglia. Its color would best be described as dun, not an attractive color by any means and not the color I would have chosen. But the price was right at the used car dealership in Bedford where we bought it after a thorough examination—you knew more about these things than I—and debate about the value for money. You determined that both body work and engine were sound; and I liked what was the rather sleek, quasi-American design for this little English car.

So, we bought it. It's possible that you got a better deal on account of your clerical collar—a courtesy you mentioned more than once in your letters. In those days, in the late fifties, the clergy could still count on being treated with consideration and respect. A tip of the cap, a nod of the head. Such things still counted.

I was immensely proud of my little Anglia. I brought it up to London and parked it proudly on the street outside our house. I had to admit that it was no match for Hugh's elegant black monster—was it a vintage Bentley? A Daimler?—but unlike his fine antique machine, mine actually worked. I did not have to tinker under the hood, which was how my friend Hugh spent a great deal of his weekend time. Now, instead of having to walk over to the tube station and take the train, I could drive up to the top of Putney Hill and cut across the common towards Wimbledon. I could drive into the teachers' parking lot and park my (nearly new!) Anglia with pride of possession alongside the odd assortment of my ill-paid colleagues' junkers. I could feel, well . . . almost like an adult. A man in control, and not only of his means of transportation but his life and destiny.

Which was obviously just one more delusion, Harry, as you'll understand by now. But thank you anyway, for this generosity and the trust it represented. And my apologies for proving, so soon afterwards, that the trust you'd shown in me was misplaced.

Regretfully,
Peter

12 October 2021

Dear Harry,

Is Marie still with us, in some corner of this poor, exploited planet? I don't see why she shouldn't be. She was just four or five years my senior, and these days many people live well into their nineties, more and more into their hundreds. If she is still alive—as I hope, so long as she is also well and hearty—this peripatetic infatuation of my youthful days will be a very old lady now! I hope she still remembers me with the same fondness and gratitude that I remember her, because I share equally in the blame for the havoc she eventually brought into my life.

Did I ever bring her home with me to Sharnbrook? I seem to remember that I did. Maybe more than once. I wonder what you could have thought of her? She was not outwardly the kind of girl who normally attracted me—not actually beautiful and not particularly pretty in any conventional way. Could you call her, in that long discarded and properly discredited male appraisal scale, a "blonde bombshell?" Maybe. Sort of. In a way. To me, and I know for sure to other men, she projected an irresistible sexual energy. But I should qualify that; her energy was not only sexual. I saw it more as a joyful lust for all the pleasures life could bring and damn the consequences. Remember my having invited her so impetuously to join me that first summer on a camping trip in Germany? Well, we survived that, miraculously. It proved to be a disastrous, rain-soaked trek down the Rhine and the Moselle Valley and back through muddy Belgium to the coast. And then we continued to see each other in London in the fall, each of us teaching at different schools in the south-western area of the city.

I am not proud of the young man I was at that time, Harry. Aside from everything else I had discovered in short order—no surprise—that teaching was not the poet's sinecure I had envisioned. The short hours I'd looked forward to were lengthened interminably by such chores as department meetings, teacher conferences, sports supervision and . . . my God, correcting homework! I found myself spending hours attempting to make sense of illegible schoolboy handwriting, in smudged exercise books in which I was obliged not only to correct the countless infuriating grammatical and punctuation errors, but also to add comments, commendations, questions, and in exceptional cases the exasperated "See me!" The long holidays I had looked forward to as opportunities to write turned out instead to be much-needed periods of restoration to a small measure of health and sanity. Weekends proved to be an all-too-brief and welcome respite. The worst of it was that my teenage charges were quick to spot my hopeless deficiency as a disciplinarian—and to take advantage of it. All too often, bleary, if not actually hung over when I arrived at class, I was ill-equipped to fend off their jubilant challenges to any attempt to assert authority. The chief weapon I had to wield against my tormentors was the threat of detention, a punishment they knew I was reluctant to deploy because it required me to stay late myself to supervise them.

And then there were sports. Each teacher was assigned the responsibility of supervising some team activity and it fell to me, thanks to an ill-advised admission that this had once been my own sport at school, to coach the cross-country running team. Can you imagine this, Harry? The example of the previous coach was daunting. He happily donned running gear in all weathers, rain or shine, and set out with the boys on a hearty five-mile circuit around Wimbledon Common. Which, you'll readily understand by now, was not for me. I contrived to set up various check points around the common, where I could drive my Anglia and show up, stopwatch in hand, to cheer my charges on. As Ellie would likely comment if I were ever to confess this sad history to her—What a putz!

Marie loved teaching. I'm afraid to say I grew to loathe it. And in the meantime, inexcusably, I began to treat her with cavalier entitlement. Happy to exercise the seigneurial right to disport myself with other women, I blithely assumed unquestioning fidelity on her part, as well as instant availability at my whim. If I had nothing more interesting going on, it was time to call Marie. And in truth, she always was available.

Until she wasn't.

It was one Saturday evening. I called her at the last moment, in full confidence that she would come running at my behest . . . and found that she had other plans. She had been invited to a party, she announced airily. She would probably be home late but perhaps we could find time to see each other the next day, Sunday.

It had been a while since my jealousy flared so furiously, as it had done with Susan. But it fired up with sudden and—this was Marie! My own true love! No?—with shocking intensity when I called her late that evening from the telephone we all shared at Mercier Road (mobile phones were science fiction in those days!) and she didn't answer. Where could she be? My mind immediately started conjuring visions of her cavorting with some treacherous young man in cavalry twill trousers and a striped college tie.

I suffered through a sleepless night, obsessed by endless scenarios of betrayal, each one more galling than the last, and called her home number as early as I thought decent on a Sunday morning. There was still no answer. Impossible! Could she, would she have spent the night in another man's bed? Not impossible. A man who might be, God forbid, richer, smarter, more stable in his life than my woeful self. Who might be blessed—this was the nightmare—with something bigger and sexier between his legs that I had. Something she'd be more impressed with. More eager for . . . The image of Marie enjoying the feel of another man's penis up inside her whipped me into a rage I struggled vainly to contain. I called again, and again the ring went unanswered. And again . . . I called Barry, to ask if he had heard from her. He was surprised. He sounded infuriatingly amused by my predicament. I hurried down to the Anglia and drove over to the small suburban house that Marie shared with her friend, a woman who had never bothered to disguise the fact that she distrusted me. She seemed delighted to see me so upset. No, she told me, smugly, Marie had not been home at all the night before.

My hours that Sunday morning were spent spiraling down into in an ever-increasing state of deeply offended rage. I was convinced Marie had betrayed me, that she had (joyfully!) welcomed another man into that intimate place that was mine by rights. Until finally, still sunk in this state of derangement and confusion, not to mention, yes, truthfully, self-pity, I heard the phone ring and made a dash for it. It was Barry.

"I have a surprise for you," he said. "Come on over."

Which I did. I ran.

Barry greeted me at the door with one of his wicked grins and waved me in, leading me up the stairs to the empty living room . . . Then, with a dramatic gesture, he flung wide the door to his bedroom, his and Mary's, and there, behind the door, giggling, was Marie.

The initial overwhelming sense of relief at seeing her was tempered immediately by a flood of questions that I did not dare to put to her aloud: where had she been? Where had she spent the night? With whom? I dreaded the answers to the questions that I feared to ask, and instead pretended to believe the innocent story she came up with. But I didn't. It was the first of many times I suspected her of lying. No, knew for a certainty that she was lying.

Worse, a new and worse suspicion began to seep like poison into that same distrustful corner of my mind: *What was she doing here at Barry's?* The two of them seemed to be having a lot of fun at my expense. How long had she been here? Where was Mary? The bed, I could see behind her, was a tangle of sheets and blankets. It looked appallingly like my own bed after a night of sex. Had she . . . ? Could she . . . have let Barry . . . ? I could not put it past him. Could not put it past her.

Still, the relief won out. I wanted her too much and the need proved too powerful for the suspicions. I forgave her, rapidly, without even knowing whether she might need forgiveness, and for what. It was so painful to admit to myself that she might have fooled around behind my back that I declined to even contemplate the possibility. My ego simply would not allow it. Had I known about such things back then, had I had the language I have now, I would have known what happened: I went into denial.

Enough for this one letter, Harry. I'm exhausted. I'll need to continue this story in my next.

Your son,
Peter

13 October 2021

Dear Harry,

Among the many hurtful, harmful things Marie and I inflicted on each other and, worse, much worse, on others over the years, I can claim to have done at least one decent thing by her. It started with a late-night telephone call I picked up at our Mercier Road flat.

It was Marie's roommate, to say she needed me.

I'm thankful to be able to say that I had not the slightest hesitation. Within minutes, I was in the Anglia, driving over to the small house she shared with that friend who—as I have said—did not like me much. Perhaps she was right about me. Absent romantic or other social interest, she saw through the surface of my charm to the less admirable character who lay beneath. But on this evening, she was friendlier than usual when she came to the front door and let me in. "She's in her room," she said.

I found Marie in tears. She'd had a call from her mother a short while ago; her father was dead, killed in an instant in a car crash caused by a drunk driving American from the local US air force base. Quite aside from obviously being distraught at the news; she felt helpless. She had no further details and there was nothing further she could do that night. It was too late now to catch the last train home. She would have to wait to take the first one in the morning—she lived in a small village near Oxford—and in the meantime she asked if I would stay with her. Just to hold her. Nothing more. Just hold her.

Of course. Of course, I would. I had never stayed overnight in her home before. Her room surprised me. It was neatly kept, unpretentious, quiet, and simply furnished, not a bit what I would have imagined from the exuberant Marie I knew. We lay down together on the single bed and stayed there all night long, my arms around her while she tried to sleep.

It was a long night. Marie cried through most of it, and I felt strangely privileged just to be there, holding her, lying together for the first time without a thought of sex.

I thought of you, Harry. I thought about fathers, and the pain of final, irremediable separation that is death. I was twenty-two years old. I had never been bothered, I'm sure, by the thought that you or Peggy might die. It was in a way beyond my comprehension. And here was Marie, in bed with me, a living body, and her father was gone. Even though I obviously did not know then that it would be nearly a half-century before you were to die, I could not imagine you dying. Could not imagine you gone. I remember trying to imagine it that night, your life being taken suddenly . . . but your death was simply unimaginable.

In the morning we woke early and dressed quickly. Once she was ready, I drove her to the train station and we waved goodbye.

Sadly, your son,
Peter

14 October 2021

Dear Harry,

Was it the death of her father than changed things with Marie? I suppose so, partly. But there were other factors that contributed to the many changes that ensued.

After that weekend of terrible suspicion and finding Marie with Barry at his flat on Rayners Road, for example, I was never able to think of him in the same way again. The long friendship in which I had shared the most intimate of secrets of my life with him, the darkest of my dreams, the most erotic of my desires was now tainted with an edge of distrust from which it never fully recovered. (After leaving London, not long after, I saw him only once more, on a visit home from America. When we met for a drink—I think with Ellie—at a pub in Soho, I was distressed to find his leering attempts at intimacy quite repulsive).

With Marie, when we resumed our newly tenuous relationship after her father's death, the tables were turned. I became ever more possessive. I could feel her slipping away from me, and the more I felt her slipping away, the more desperate was my need to cling to her. And then one day she broke the news that she was leaving. She had found a job at one of the British military schools in then still-occupied Germany. Devastated, I realized belatedly that I could not conceive of life without her. I fretted desperately for a month or two before deciding that I had to follow her. Do you remember, Harry, how I walked away from my first good job in Wimbledon in the middle of that school year? How I hurriedly sold that Ford Anglia you helped me buy and reneged on my share of the lease on Mercier Road? The pretext I was quick to share with anyone who asked was that I had to put my talents as a writer to the test. I may even have convinced myself that this was true. I was lucky to get a part-time evening job, teaching English to adult students at a language school in a town called Düren, not fifty miles from where Marie was living now. I would have time to write all day and every day, I told myself. Besides, I thought, rather than adolescent miscreants, what a difference to be teaching reasonable, grown-up men and women who signed up for classes because they actually wanted to learn.

Then, at the weekends, I could find some way to get together with Marie.

I suspect that you and Peggy never knew that she was the real reason for my sudden flight. Or did you guess? It had never occurred to me, in changing my whole life, that she would be other than as impatient as myself for us to be back (in bed!) together. But greatly to my chagrin and surprise, it seemed she wasn't. Once I was settled into my new environment, the weeks began to drag by with, from my end, increasingly desperate and difficult telephone calls that were met, at the other end, with unending excuses, prevarications, protestations, and delays. When I finally managed to prevail on her to drive down for a visit, I couldn't wait to get her into bed, and made urgent, frenzied love to her in the small room I had rented in a bleak apartment building—the best thing I could afford on my part-time teacher's pay. As I strove mightily, repeatedly, to satisfy my need, I refused to notice that Marie's part in our love-making rituals had turned from desire to tolerance. Denial was more acceptable in my anguished state of mind than recognition of the truth.

After that first weekend, the interval between her visits began to stretch out interminably. She was paid well enough to buy a metallic blue Renault Dauphine, an all too popular model at the time. Every time I caught a glimpse of one on the streets of Düren, my heart leapt with anticipation, followed at once by frustration, despair, and jealous rage. I tortured myself with vivid images of her infidelities, submitting willingly (joyfully!) to the amorous advances of all those charming British officers at her army base. On the increasingly rare occasions of her visits, I began to feel more like a supplicant than a lover. And then that one last weekend we spent together, in the cold, dark cavern of a room we had taken at a hotel far out in the country, in the bleak winter landscape of the Eifel Forest, she told me she could not make love because she was pregnant. And the baby wasn't mine.

Not mine. It was a terrible mistake she'd made, she said. It was just one time. There had been a trip out on one of the boats that take tourists up and down the Rhine. She was a bit drunk. She hardly knew the man. She didn't know what to do. I would have married her right then, but no, she did not want or need my help. She would take care of things herself.

I was too naïve to suspect that she was lying. It was only later that I came to suspect her of being a compulsive liar, and perhaps even then I was wrong. Perhaps, it was just my jealousy that told me so. In any event, it would be years before I saw Marie again, and then she would wreak havoc in my life. No. I was the one who did the havoc-wreaking. But she was there.

Oh, Harry, believe me, your son had never felt so miserable. There I was, stuck in that tiny, furnished room looking out on a bland and frigid street somewhere in Germany, in mid-winter, pounding away on my portable Royal typewriter (a parting gift from Peggy) and churning out dreadful poems that no one would ever read. I had an immersion heater and a mug to make tea or instant coffee, and an electric hotplate to heat up a bowl of soup or make a melted cheese sandwich with a slice of thick German rye bread and a slab of Emmentaler.

I had fallen so deep into despair that I could no longer conceive of a way up or out . . .

But then there was Winden. A friend helped me find a new place to live in this small village at the edge of the Eifel, in a house with a wonderful view out over a long, green valley to a hillside beyond and the edge of the trees. It was an easy bus ride from my job at Düren, and a great, inviting place to write. Reinvigorated by the springtime sun, I abandoned poetry and started work instead on the novel that I thought was guaranteed to bring me fame and fortune. Frau Hennes, a widow, was my landlady. Her husband was one of those tens of thousands of Wehrmacht soldiers deployed on Hitler's improvident Eastern front who never made it back from the Russian gulags after the war. She treated me like the son she never had. I loved the meals she cooked, *Sauerbraten, Rindsrouladen, Kartoffelpuffer* . . . the best of German comfort foods; and her breakfasts, *Speck mit*

Spielgeleier, ham and eggs. I never ate so well. I put back all the weight I'd lost to my long depression and added more!

At work, at the Berlitz School there was soon greater responsibility and a better salary as the school expanded to serve more students with more classes and added different languages. I was made Director.

And before too long there was the arrival of my first new colleague. Her name was Liz. I fell in love.

Your peripatetic son,
Peter

15 October 2021

Dear Harry,

You'll know by now how easily I lost my heart, and how much human destruction I left behind me as a result. It would take me many years yet to arrive at the understanding that love was something other than the satisfaction of my needs.

There followed many wonderful days and evenings in the new life I was creating for myself. Living in Winden, I was able to spend the better part of the day at my typewriter. I was gaining confidence, feeling more accomplished as a writer. Early evenings, I would take the bus into Düren, arriving at the Berlitz School in time to meet up with my new colleague for a cup of tea or coffee before classes started. I had not yet summoned the nerve to make my feelings known, nor was I sure of them myself. While I was aware of a familiar, powerfully physical attraction to this petite young woman with green eyes, dark hair, and a sharp and lively mind, I was content for once to take the time needed for us to get to know one another before trying to rush her off to bed. For her part, Liz was perhaps rightly wary of a man whose history she hardly knew and who was yet to earn her trust.

Still, we did build a friendship. After class, most often, we would go out to one of the nearby taverns for beer and a bite to eat—"Brat" or Knackwurst with Sauerkraut, or one of those breaded cutlets that German chefs do so well. I would sometimes order a big bowl of steamed mussels—a specialty at our favorite late-night haunt—until the memorable time when I must have swallowed down a bad one . . . I was so horribly sick, I scarcely made it home that night.

I was so sick that I have never dared to eat another mussel in more than sixty years.

We had friends in common. There were Willi and Helle, two aspiring young businessmen with a pretty girlfriend each and one with a brand-new VW Cabriolet for drives out to the country; there was Dieter, a slightly older man, forty-ish, old enough to have been a member of the Hitler Jugend. The ravages of war were still a vivid memory in Düren, at the eastern perimeter of what was the Battle of the Bulge. There were many people living there for whom the night of November 16, 1944, was a still recent nightmare, when waves of Allied bombers swarmed in the skies above the city and unleashed a murderous storm of high explosive and incendiary bombs. Of the 22,000 inhabitants of the small community, three thousand died that night, most of them trapped beneath the burning buildings in the cellars where they had taken shelter.

We became close friends, Liz and I, as well as colleagues. We stood out as the only two young English people, foreigners amongst the natives. There was a mutual respect as well as a tenderness. It took me a good long while, as I recall, to tell her awkwardly that I loved her and soon to ask her if she would consider marrying me. Until that moment we had still done little more than kiss goodnight, but she said, Yes. It was kind and brave of her to agree to take me on, because I was not much of a prospective husband, with only a part-time evening job and vague hopes of eventually earning recognition as a writer. I was impractical, penniless and—though I may have managed successfully to hide it—emotionally not much past my adolescence. As I look back on it, I wish that I could have been—your phrase, Harry!—more man for her woman. I was not.

She took me on anyway. Now, many years later, I continue to thank her for the immeasurable gift of love. It saddens me to acknowledge that I was unable to prove myself worthy of the trust that went along with it.

More of that later, Harry.

For now, your son,
Peter

16 October 2021

Dear Harry,

I know you believed in what the church called "the sanctity of marriage." I'm assuming that you observed the principle yourself. You belonged to a generation where divorce was still an unconscionable alternative, where it was spoken of amongst respectable people only in hushed whispers, not only a sign of a failure of character but also a family disgrace.

What a bitter, deeply distressing experience for you and Peggy, then, to know that the marriages of both your children ended in divorce.

There are matters too delicate and too hurtful still, after many years, to write about without due compassion and respect, so I want to keep this, insofar as possible, between you and me. I blame no one and take full responsibility for my own part in these events, no matter how long ago they occurred.

You'll remember that you came across to Germany, with Peggy of course, to officiate at the church ceremony where Liz and I were married. (This was after an obligatory civil event at the British consulate—and another of those ridiculous details that find a place in some odd corner of the mind and never want to leave, this one the giggle-inducing name of the officiating consul who raised his hand and intoned his name: "I, Robert John Claude Pease . . ." Hard to keep a straight face after that).

Flora and her new husband John were there too, as was my old Cambridge friend Hugh Welchman, who was my best man. It was a moment of mutual commitment, hope, and love. The families got along, in that tentative, first-time manner of getting to know each other. Then we spent what was, for me—I hope it was, too, for Liz—a wonderful week on honeymoon in Amsterdam. Returning to Düren, we settled into a downtown apartment for the first months of our life together.

Were we ready for the responsibilities of married life and, soon enough, of bringing children into the world? Perhaps Liz was, but I wasn't. For the time being, and for too many years to come, I allowed myself to drift along with little foresight and less planning. We were still in Düren when the possibility of pregnancy loomed and I first began to realize the need to get a real job and settle down to adult life (as though such a thing were possible for me, Harry!) Impractically hopeful as ever, I wrote off in response to a three-week old announcement in the "wanted" column of one of the leftist New Statesman weeklies that Peggy used to forward me from England. A private grammar school in Nova Scotia, Canada, of all places, was looking for someone to teach English. They were offering an annual salary of five thousand dollars, a prospect of wealth I had never dreamed of!

I applied at once, albeit belatedly. The response came in short order and it was no surprise, given the late date of my application, that the advertised post was already filled. But the school was now looking for a French and German teacher. Was I interested?

I telegraphed my eager assent.

And this was how I came to cross the Atlantic Ocean for the first time, Harry, never pausing to consider that it would put an even greater distance between you and me.

We settled in Halifax, Liz and I. Nova Scotia was good to us. As anyone who has traveled there will tell you, it is a truly lovely province with its wild, rocky coastline and scores of inland lakes where, in winter, I enjoyed the novel spectacle of car races on ice. It was cold, yes—colder by far than anything we'd ever known in Europe. There was real weather, blizzards in winter, hurricanes in the summer, a blaze of color as the seasons changed in the fall. We had a tiny basement apartment with a black and white TV set where we watched ice hockey every Saturday evening. There were only six teams back then, two Canadian, four American. We rooted for the Maple Leafs. We had a gray cat named Plato. We bought a brand-new car—the first I'd ever owned, a tiny, powder blue Mini Minor. Liz was seriously pregnant by now, but I insisted foolishly on taking us out for a spin on our new car's first day, despite weather forecasts predicting the imminent arrival of a hurricane. What did I care about hurricanes? They were only a word to me . . . (I learned only later that this was Ginny, a Category 2 storm, one of the most destructive to ever hit the Nova Scotia coast). We drove merrily out of town and before we knew it, we were in unfamiliar territory, lost in the rocky wilderness on a side road where the tarmac abruptly ended, giving way to a rough dirt surface, and the storm was hurtling all around us. I drove on. What else could I do? I was terrified, yes, by this time, but we were committed. Then suddenly, inexplicably, the road descended to sea level and we found ourselves driving alongside the ocean, dark and angry, with massive waves crashing down across the road.

We survived. My reckless insistence had exposed not only myself but my wife and our soon-to-be-born child to grievous danger. What saved us I will never know. Your God? More likely it was the little Mini's front wheel drive, gripping the mud and pulling us valiantly through the storm. When we finally reached the highway that led back to Halifax, I stopped to check on the car and opened the hood. The entire engine of my beautiful brand-new Mini was coated in a layer of thick, red, salty mud.

Hubris? I learned, at least, to pay attention to storm warnings in the future.

And then to our great joy, our first son, Matthew, was born.

All of which was fine, except that I had apparently forgotten the lesson learned at Rutlish: I was not cut out to be a teacher, particularly not at a secondary school for boys. It was a lesson I re-learned rather quickly at the Halifax Grammar School. It would be ungracious to complain too loudly. I was fortunate to have a good job. To be earning what seemed to us in those days a fine salary. And the school was a progressive one, with a well-qualified staff of committed colleagues and interesting, socially active parents—all good, compatible, caring people with whom Liz and I would socialize at evening events and on weekends at the shoreline where crabs and lobsters were thrown liberally into pots of boiling water on the beach and gobbled down with gusto on warm summer evenings.

We moved. We had no room for a baby in our tiny basement flat, so we found what I recall being a rather bleak modern apartment with an extra bedroom and a shared laundry room that came in handy with the diapers. We had a portable stereo and a collection of classical records that we loved, and French-Canadian folk songs. (*Ah, si mon moine voulait danser, A la claire fontaine* . . . I remember them). We discovered the lovely, haunting voice of Joan Baez . . . I think, no, I'm quite sure that we were happy, just the three of us.

And yet, and yet . . . There was still that poet in me, "yearning to be free"; the one who kept nudging me to write and making me feel empty and unaccomplished when I didn't. In fact, I had returned to writing poems. I had belatedly discovered the work of e.e.cummings and my poems were heavily influenced by his whimsical play with language. Meanwhile, more and more, the hours I spent in the classroom reminded me that teaching was not a passion but a requisite, money-earning chore.

It was at the end of the first school year in Nova Scotia that the son of one of my colleagues arrived with his wife to spend the summer with his parents. We hit it off well. He was a poet, a well-known poet, a successful poet even—a concept I had previously never entertained. In my ignorance, I had not heard of him before; I had been writing poems in my own little backwater, uninformed of the greater world of my contemporaries. What I saw in Mark Strand, a tall, powerful man, confident in himself both as a writer and a man, was everything I longed to be and clearly was not yet myself. He was kind enough to read my poems, assuring me that he found them to be intelligent and interesting; they showed promise. Nova Scotia was no place for me, he said; I should be at the

Poetry Workshop at the University of Iowa in Iowa City, where he had a teaching job.

A poetry workshop! Here was a new concept, Harry! Iowa! Who would have ever dreamed?

Sadly, Mark died before his time, a few short years ago. I still owe him a debt of gratitude. He recommended me to Paul Engle, the poet, founder and at that time still the man who ran the Writers' Workshop, and the rest followed with relative ease. I was offered a grant and a teaching assistant's job in the French Department which provided me with an adequate income for the family, and a place in the Ph.D. program in Comparative Literature. I was given an on-campus office of my own and low-cost graduate student housing in a Quonset hut just a short walk from the campus . . . It was everything I could have asked for.

I was thrilled with this unexpected change in my prospects that had fallen from the heavens into my lap. School-teaching was forever behind me, vistas of life as a genuine writer opened. There were, I soon discovered, more poets per square block in Iowa City than I could have imagined possible. And the Ph.D., I was assured by my new professors in comparative literature, would be a breeze for someone with my language skills and a degree in languages and literature from Cambridge University.

I hope you were proud of your new son, Harry, when all this began to happen. Or did you, in your wisdom, already intuit disaster looming in the years to come? I'd love to have known.

Your all too often deluded son,
Peter

17 October 2021

Dear Harry,

I need to share all this old stuff with you, in part because I feel I let you down. Not so much to excuse myself as to let you in on what was happening in my life, but to help you understand the not irrelevant context of events that you saw only from afar.

Our family was doing fine, I thought, through our first years in Iowa City. I was busy with my poetry, busy with my studies. We were overjoyed when our second son, Jason, was born at the nearby university hospital. We made friends—though now I see that in my self-involvement I never stopped to think they might be *my* friends, not *our* friends. In fact, it never occurred to me that this was *my* life, not *ours*. I had uprooted Liz (when did I start to call her Elizabeth?) from everything she had known, from family and friends, from the teaching career she eventually rediscovered and, I think, loved, and had isolated her with two young boys in a Quonset hut in the middle of the American Midwest, with nothing much else around except for poets and their boozing, narcissistic ways. Summers were oppressively hot and humid; winters unbelievably cold and isolating.

Then we/she (which of us was it?) decided she should take some time during our third summer there to fly back to visit friends and family in Europe. I was obliged to enroll in summer classes—so I insisted—to catch up with needed credits and promised to rejoin them all in England later. Which would have been a reasonable plan, except . . . while the family gone, there was a new and totally unanticipated arrival in Iowa City, one that led eventually to a crisis from which we would never fully recover.

It was 1967, the year that exploded in America into what became known as "the summer of love." You may never have heard the term, over there in your small village in Wales. The war in Vietnam continued to rage pitilessly abroad, but here at home it was the summer of hippies with long hair and bell-bottom trousers, marijuana, psychedelic rock, the summer of the Beatles' "Sergeant Pepper" and the Jefferson Airplane's "Surrealistic Pillow", with Grace Slick's seductive voice calling us irresistibly down the rabbit hole with Alice.

Alone, and at this vast distance from everything I'd learned from you and my superior English education about propriety, good behavior, dutiful respect for social convention and so on, I found myself torn loose from those salubrious moorings, seizing the opportunity to thumb my nose at everything I had ever known. My new "family" was a group of poets, hard drinkers all, who gathered every evening at someone's home for food and booze. There was George, scion of a patrician family back east, a brilliant experimentalist in the new fiction, and Sam, poet and translator, recently returned from a prolonged stay in Japan with Yumiko, his partner in both life and literary work, whom he would later marry. Together they translated the collected poems of Ryuichi Tamura, one of Japan's great modern poets, who also came to visit—though that was a bit later. There was the heavily bearded, mostly reclusive Norman Hoegberg, whose friendship led to a huge change in my life. More of him when I write next.

Our evenings started out, invariably, with generous lashings of Olde Bourbon, the cheapest brand we could find at the Iowa State liquor store—the only place you could buy alcohol in those days. Then we'd cook up a stew or barbeque a steak, or Yumiko—an expert in the preparation of delicious Japanese food—would conjure up our favorite *shabu-shabu*, a big communal broth into which we each dipped from our plate of chopped vegetables and thin slices of raw beef with—in my case—rather dubious chopstick skills. One memorable night, high on a mix of bourbon, rotgut wine and marijuana, we all climbed up on the roof of the house where George was staying—it happened to be at the home of your grandson Matthew's kindergarten teacher—and stretched out stark naked, flat on our backs, to gaze out into the vast night sky and watch the spectacular display of a meteor shower.

You see how magical it might have seemed, that summer?

Day times we went our different ways—but always to write, and write, and write. It was an intoxicating time, with more than alcohol, more even than marijuana, to feed with wonderful illusions the freedom-loving poet I'd always dreamed I'd be.

Always dreaming, Harry, always dreaming . . .

Your son,
Peter

18 October 2021
Matthew's birthday!

Dear Harry,

I was writing about the arrival of your oldest grandson, Matthew, just a couple of days ago while we were still in Nova Scotia. He still has his Canadian passport to this day. Would you believe that today's his birthday, his fifty-eighth!

I called him in England on my cell phone to wish him a Happy Birthday and we spoke for a good half hour. Do you remember, Harry, what a rigmarole they used to be, those transatlantic calls? Dialing the operator, looking for a connection—if there was one to be had—and waiting for the phone to be picked up at the other end? Shouting into the phone, in order to be heard? The distant scratchy voices, often clashing with each other as everyone tried to get a word in. Not to mention counting the minutes, for fear of the expense.

Today, with your cell phone, Harry, it's so easy. You just select the number on your speed dial list and punch it in, and usually the person you're calling picks up right away at the other end. No cost, except for the monthly agreement that you've signed on to. And it's just as easy to make a video call— there are several different ways to do it—and actually see the person that you're talking to. You'd be amazed.

So anyway, yes, it was good to talk to Matthew on his birthday. I put my mobile on speaker phone and we could all talk at will, hands free, all without shouting, without even raising our voices. He and his wife, Diane, just celebrated her 60th (!) with a trip up to the Lake District. She's a wonderful photographer and used her mobile phone to send us a stream of beautiful pictures, instantaneously, of the two of them hiking up the fells. I could almost smell that mossy scent of the water and the ferns that grew around a tranquil tarn at the mountain top and recalled the long walks that we took as boys when Windlesham was evacuated up to Ambleside, all those years ago.

Birthdays, Harry! Yours would be coming up in a month or so. One hundred and sixteen, by my calculation!

With love, your son,
Peter

20 October 2021

Dear Harry,

So, I promised you more about Norman, the fellow poet whose friendship contributed to a huge, irreversible change in my life and the way I see the world.

It was that same summer. He was invited down to visit friends on a farm some way to the south, not far from Hannibal, Missouri, and asked me if I'd like to join him for the drive. Of course, I agreed. I was free, after all, to do anything I cared to. The drive was a spectacular one, through lovely hilly, wooded countryside to a spot so remote, amidst the hills, there was no other human habitation anywhere in sight. To complete the dreamscape, Norman's friends—a man and a woman with a horde of untamed children—came out to greet us in the flowing white garments of true flower children. I could have imagined garlands in their hair. Our supper was a simple one: artichokes, with a butter dip for the leaves. I had never seen this kind of artichoke before, let alone eaten one, and I found the taste delicious.

Was there bread? Wine? Perhaps. I don't recall.

But I do remember the thunderstorm that followed, in the night. I promise, Harry, you have never experienced anything like a storm in the American Midwest. Our English storms are polite affairs beside these monsters, with lightning strikes that split the endless sky, thunder that roils the countryside, and often hail—sometimes the size of golf balls, sometimes even larger; on one occasion, in Iowa City, great chunks of ice came tumbling out of a black-green sky, so big that the bodywork of every car in the city unprotected by garage or carport was left badly dented). You would be awed, as I was, always, by these giant storms and by the threat of killer tornados they bring with them. I remember standing at the window of my room that night and gazing out in wonder, and perhaps some fear, inspired by the raw power unleashed by nature at its wildest.

The next morning arrived bright, still, serene, the grass and leaves still glistening from the rain the night before. Was there breakfast? I have no memory of sitting down with the family to eat—but I found Norman and his friend standing by the refrigerator engaged in serious debate, which was resolved only when they showed me a little tab and asked me if I'd like to join them on an "acid trip."

Acid! While I had been smoking marijuana quite a bit that summer, I still harbored a good deal of fear when it came to drugs. I had heard about LSD, of course, who hadn't? Psychedelics flourished, and not only in the music I had come to love. It had certainly never occurred to me that this might be the purpose of Norman's trip; but now, confronted with a new challenge to my fears . . . I could not say no. I laid the proffered tab on my tongue and washed it down with a glass of water.

We walked out away from the farm, the three of us, down towards what I'd learned was called the Femme Osage Creek. There was the legend of some Indian woman involved, many years before. Perhaps she still haunted this lovely landscape . . . At first I was unimpressed. I thought that nothing much had happened, aside from perhaps a sharpening of color, a brightening of perception. I began to wonder what the fuss was all about.

But then it hit. I realized I was no longer in the world I thought I knew. I found myself sitting naked in the creek, gazing down into the shallows where crawdads darted along a bed of smooth, brown stones below the surface of the water. I could see Norman sitting way upstream from me, naked also, gazing like myself into the wondrous aspect of a world that had started to reveal itself, everywhere, in its true nature. Everything—trees, rocks, birds, fields of grass, wildflowers— everything was suddenly, vibrantly alive, and everything, everything was in the process of communication, all things with each other, and everything with me. The normal barriers of perception vanished; I could *see*, I could *hear*, and better still I could absolutely *understand* everything around me. We were one. There was no mystery, only glorious, all-embracing clarity. *It all made sense.* The sudden, scarlet flash of a cardinal against the lush green of the trees was a message I could readily understand, reflecting the inner untrammeled elation that I felt.

How long did it last, that feeling? I don't know. It could have been hours. It was only later that day that I began to realize I had been separated from my friends. Where was I? Had they left me? The realization that I was all alone and still in this strangely altered state of mind began to translate into a gripping fear. I was cold. Darkness had begun to fall. I was disoriented, unsure which way would lead back to the farmhouse, back to other people in this vast emptiness. Had I lost my mind, along with my sense of direction? Something like panic started to set in as I looked around in vain for some recognizable landmark . . .

I walked and walked. I walked until I was so tired I was not sure I could walk further and only then, with inexpressible relief, caught sight of the farm we'd started from. Norman came out to greet me. "We were quite worried about you," he said. "We wondered where you'd got to." I fell into his arms.

Was this a kind of religious ecstasy, I ask myself in retrospect? Did you, Harry, ever experience anything of the kind? The reason I tell you about it is that the experience proved to be not limited to that one day. It left a profound and permanent mark on my understanding of the world and my place in it. I never again experimented with the drug. I never felt the need or the desire to do so, knowing that the change had already happened, that my perception would never again be quite as it had been before. I wrote a series of prose poems and gave it the title "Femme Osage."

If you challenge me, I will readily admit that there was something false, something artificial in this new sense of liberation I'd acquired. But there was also something profoundly true. Aldous Huxley wrote about it in *The Doors of Perception,* and while I have not read this book for many years, I know it was an effort to expand the realm of consciousness to areas yet unexplored. I'll have more to share with you about all this in due course, when I tell you something of my own ("religious"? "spiritual"?) conversion.

> In gratefully remembered ecstasy,
> your son,
> Peter

21 October 2021

Dear Harry,

As I've suggested, my sense of a newly acquired freedom was not restricted to the realm of consciousness. You raised me with a personal sense of loyalty and honor that I confess look somewhat tattered after all these years, in an age that today shows little respect for such quaint concepts. That summer—the summer of love—I was ready to cast it all aside without a second thought.

Oh, Harry, were you ever unfaithful? Do you know how hurtful, how destructive it can be? Of course, you do. Even if you yourself never cheated on your wife, on Peggy, you were a keen, compassionate observer of the effects of infidelity on marriage in your pastoral work. You know about the temptations of the flesh and how easily any one of us can be led astray, and how hard it is, impossible even, to heal the wounds that infidelity leaves in its wake. The anger, the pain, the resentment, the mistrust—these emotions roil within, and breed, and multiply.

I mentioned an unexpected new arrival in Iowa City that summer in an earlier letter. It was Marie. With her, she brought that old infatuation. Her presence reawakened that old, familiar hunger.

She had learned somehow that I was at the University of Iowa and stopped off during a cross-country drive to San Francisco from where she was now living, in New York City, on the off chance she might find me. Amazingly—unerringly perhaps—she did. Having surrendered our Quonset hut with plans to move into a rented house at the start of the fall semester, I was "without fixed address" all summer. At the time of Marie's arrival, I happened to be house-sitting for a respected Southern gentleman, one Dr. Gerber, chairman of the English Department, while he and his wife were away on vacation. I sincerely hope they never knew the story of what took place in their elegant, colonial residence on that shady back street in Iowa City while they were gone! Once she arrived, Marie stopped in the center of town and started asking around to see if anyone knew where she could find me. By sheer chance or stroke of fate, she happened upon a friend who knew where I was staying and gave her a phone number where she could reach me. Minutes later she showed up, the glowing presence I remembered, at the door to my provisional mansion.

I won't hide it, Harry. No excuses. I, we, wasted not one single moment before scurrying up the stairs to my bed in Dr. Gerber's spare room and ripped off each other's clothes.

I refuse to blame Marie. This was not her fault. Well, not hers alone. Before she arrived in Iowa City that summer my irrepressible—and, yes, Harry, alright, deplorable!—libido had already made its familiar appearance, tongue lolling out, the moment my family left for the Old World. It landed me first, without a moment's hesitation or remorse, in the bed of the English Department secretary, a divorcee and single mom who welcomed me there with a lust that easily equaled mine. Which is what I told myself, at least. So, what followed in the next few days was not primarily Marie's fault. And the sense of deprivation that consumed me later, after she left, was undoubtably all mine.

My group of poet friends welcomed this new presence into our midst without question or judgment, and soon she was having a merry, inebriated time along with the rest of us. There was, for example, the time when it was my turn to act the host and we all gathered at Dr. Gerber's home for an evening's revelry. Norman was our resident expert when it came to hamburger stew, and we all joined forces in chopping the onions, the peppers, the potatoes, and the other vegetables that he used. The task demanded refreshments, and Dr. Gerber's excellent bourbon was on hand to fill our glasses liberally as we worked. Come dinner time, his cellar provided us with the kind of wine we could never have otherwise afforded—and which I could not have afforded to replace. At the end of the evening, when the others left, Marie and I surveyed the damage with despair and, yes, for me, a remaining sense of shame. Together we set out to clean up as best we could. (I would not be telling you this story, Harry, were I not quite sure that the good Dr. Gerber and his wife had left us long ago.)

It chagrins me to say this but the truth is that those two weeks or so were sheer joy, before Marie had to move on. I gave no thought to the possible consequences, to the pain I'd cause to those I loved and the harm done to my marriage. I was too busy trying to gratify an insatiable hunger for the ecstasy of sensual pleasure than to bother myself with tiresome thoughts of what might lie ahead. I basked in the joy of being, as I thought, free, alive, "in love", the true libertine poet I foolishly imagined myself to be.

> I remain, in spite of all this,
> your son,
>> Peter

23 October 2021

Dear Harry,

It was also not just me, of course, who was to pay the price for my extravagant behavior. I no longer recall exactly how it happened, but I was unable to conceal the truth from Elizabeth when she returned from Europe with the boys. The hurt, the understandable sense of betrayal and the fury that she felt were immeasurable.

We did our best to patch things up. Well, to be honest, it was she who did her best. I was too moon-struck with my selfish desires and memories than to be present with the kind of love and support she so much needed in the predicament I'd created. We tried marriage counselling, but I think we both still harbored old world prejudices about the power of psychotherapy. I know I did. Back then—and indeed for many years yet to come—I was actively hostile to the notion that someone as mature and well-adjusted as myself could possibly need help. Shrinks were good for the mentally disturbed, perhaps, but definitely not for the strong and sound of mind, like me! I was still convinced, in those days, that it was a sign of moral weakness to be guided by the emotions, and still worse to waste one's time examining them—a habit I haughtily dismissed as "navel-gazing." Even the word "heart" was an embarrassment. I had still not even learned to say the words

"I love you." Naively, I equated love with sex and sex with love and saw no difference between them.

Where did I learn this nonsense, Harry? Not from you, I hope. But one thing I had learned from an early age, my first years away from home at boys' boarding school, was how dangerous it is to show your feelings and risk either public ridicule or bullying. Safer to keep it all bottled up inside, whether sadness, fear, or anger . . .

It was at Windlesham I learned the cost of anger. I've no idea what caused it, but I got into an angry head-to-head with a boy named Fitch. See, I still remember his name more than seventy-five years later? I remember the freckles on his face, his ginger hair. He was older than me, and bigger. The teacher on supervision duty, noticing our spat, intervened at once; he told us that we should settle our differences "like gentlemen," and produced two pairs of boxing gloves. The rest of the boys formed a rough boxing ring and the teacher had us go at it. I didn't stand a chance. When Fitch landed a punch to my face, I was just puzzled that anyone would want to hurt me. More punches, though, and I got angry. More blows succeeded in enraging me. Uncontrollable, now, I started flailing out impotently, left and right, while Fitch kept his cool and easily punched me senseless. All around, the boys were cheering when he was declared the victor and I was left, sobbing ignominiously, with a bloody nose. Lesson: if you're angry, never show it. If you're scared, still less.

Old stuff, Harry, yes, and buried deep. But during all those years I learned to hide my feelings well.

So, no discussion of the emotional problems, then. We settled for band aids in the hope that they might heal the deeper wounds inside. But we did manage, nonetheless, to put a reasonably good face on our marriage for another couple of years. In 1968, at the end of the following academic year, now qualified with a brand-new Ph.D. to teach at university level, I accepted the offer of a job at the University of Southern California. It was that move that finally broke us, along with my return, not too much later, to my familiar bad old ways.

More to come,
Peter

24 October 2021

Dear Harry,

I need to talk to you for a while about desire. I believe it to be the most powerful motivating force in the human mind, and the most destructive. Did you ever experience desire so intense, Harry, that you were willing to destroy even what you thought you loved the most?

I ask this because it happened to me two years after the summer of love that I described when I wrote to you a couple of days ago. We had moved from Iowa. I had taken that job as Assistant Professor of Comparative Literature at the University of Southern California—how proud you were of that! I was so pleased with this new opportunity that I hardly noticed at the time that it added another thousand miles to the distance between us.

So, this was the first summer of our new life in California, the summer of the historic landing of an American astronaut on the surface of the moon. Could you believe that, Harry? We humans were scarcely off the land here on Earth when you were born. And this was the summer when I met the woman with whom I have spent almost every day of my life since.

I need to refresh your memory of that summer, Harry, because you and Peggy were among those I caused such great unhappiness. The other victims were my wife and sons.

It started when I encouraged Elizabeth to return to Europe with the boys to spend time with you and her family and to take care, as I recall, of some recurring dental issues. But yes, I won't lie, I encouraged her. I was already, half-consciously perhaps creating space in my life to reignite that fire in the loins that I had never fully managed to contain. I had invited a friend, Jim, one of my graduate students who was in trouble with his own marriage to take over a room in our Hermosa Beach apartment for the month, and it was he who brought home with him one evening a young woman he himself was hoping to date. A bad idea. This was the young woman you came to know as Ellie.

You will have noticed, Harry, throughout these letters I've been writing, that I have a ridiculous propensity to fall in love. Perhaps it's the poet in me—or is that merely the excuse of the incurably romantic? With Ellie it was instant. She had short, dark hair and the kind of green eyes that—I don't know why—I fall for. There was, too, a mischief in her eyes that beckoned irresistibly.

From the moment she showed up in my life for the first time I was, as we used to say in England, a goner.

It was late. There we were, the three of us, tired after the introductions and the small talk, and we needed sleep. Well, neither Jim nor—by this time—I was willing to surrender masculine courting rights to the other and Ellie, besides, was certainly not ready to favor either one of us, so we all three bedded down innocently enough—no, really!—on the sitting room floor, two guys with Ellie tucked in between us. With the desire in me now fully awakened, I remember that even at that early moment I did not try to hide it. My hands strayed toward Ellie in the darkness and I was exhilarated to discover that my tentative explorations were not immediately rejected. But that was all. It could go no further in that strange circumstance. I'm sure that I slept little that night, and in the morning I had to leave. I had previously arranged to spend a few days with a friend, like me a recent Ph. D. in Comparative Literature from Iowa, and his artist wife. He had taken a job at the University of California in Irvine, and the couple were lucky to have found a wonderful old Victorian house to rent in Laguna Beach, a place called the Captain's House. It has since been lifted from its foundations and moved inland to allow, sadly, for commercial development, but in those days it was located high above the ocean at the south end of the bluff overlooking Main Beach. Such a romantic spot! And I had nothing but romance on my mind as I pined away for what was not yet even a new love.

I wrote and wrote. Poem after poem. And when the time came to return home to Los Angeles, I had a bunch of them, a whole suite of poems, all neatly typed out and bound together as a skinny book.

Did I drive straight to Ellie's apartment when I got back to the city? Did I wait for a respectable few hours? A day? I don't recall. But I do remember standing there at her doorstep, poems in hand, and her surprise when she came to answer the door. The poems were the clincher. It took little else to persuade her to escape for an illicit weekend together, and we drove north up the coast toward Santa Barbara, without any destination in mind. After much dithering we happened upon a motel memorably called The Pilot House, in Goleta, at the perimeter of what was then the tiny Santa Barbara airport. We booked a room.

It took us only a few delirious moments to get rid of the irksome clothes and find ourselves in bed. If it weren't such a horrible cliché, Harry, I'd be tempted to say: the rest is history.

With love,
Peter

25 October 2021

Dear Harry,

I wrote in an earlier letter that I wanted to keep this between you and me, and I'll try to stick to that. I have already alluded to the relevant details of that second summer, two years after Marie's appearance in Iowa, when I disingenuously arranged for myself to stay alone in California while the family returned once more to Europe for a reunion with the grandparents. No need to revisit events that can still invoke the same feelings of betrayal, guilt, and pain that they did more than fifty years ago. I alone bear the responsibility for all of it. Back then, I managed to persuade myself that it was self-preservation, a liberation I could not live without. In Ellie, I found, and continued for many years to find, a fuller, more expansive version of myself. Let it be enough, then, to remind you of your well-intentioned efforts to intervene; your desperate letters, your transatlantic telephone calls, your pleas to save the marriage "for the children."

None of which succeeded, Harry. After a bitter and eventually futile struggle to restore what we once had together, Elizabeth packed up and left with the children, returning to Iowa where she had grown comfortable with a job, and friends, and an environment that suited her better than brash Southern California—and created a needed geographical separation from myself. I lived for many years with guilt, and many more with the pain of watching from afar as my sons grew from little boys to big ones and from big boys to young men, all without the benefit of daily contact with their father. No matter how lovingly they were brought up by their mother, I saw myself as a glaring absence in their lives. The one month, once a year, when they flew to California to visit me was barely adequate time for me to be the father my judgment tells me I should have been; and this unhappy truth has weighed painfully on my mind every day since the dark day of our separation.

As for our part in this—yours, Harry, and mine—it was perhaps the story of a clash of cultures, a conflict between the values of old Europe where you still lived, both literally and metaphorically speaking, and which I had long since left behind; and those of the new world, where I had been living already for ten years. For me, also and specifically, it was a conflict between the heart which I had long distrusted, even scorned, and the head, with all its conflicting arguments, judgments, prejudices, and beliefs. Adding to this problematic mix was that other troublesome organ, the imperious one that sought to rule me—too often successfully—from its throne between my legs.

I can only imagine your distress, and Peggy's, when your efforts proved eventually unsuccessful. I know there were times when you called yourself a failure—a word that comes up often in your letters—and Flora later reminded me that you suffered through bouts of severe depression in your life after retirement. Perhaps this was a part of it. I know you tried just as earnestly to patch the rift in Flora's marriage, and equally without success. I know little about the problems that led to the split between her and her husband, John—a truly decent, honorable man himself—but I recall the anger with which Flora told me, much later, of the advice you pressed on her: that a woman's duty was to submit to her husband's natural desires. Which of course is the kind of old-world thinking I was referring to.

This I know: that despite all the broad-mindedness you sought to embrace, and often with success, you were inescapably of your time. For all your understanding of human nature— it was nothing if not compassionate—there were judgments you were unable to shake when crises hit. Your jokes would have been considered tasteless, if not reprehensible in the culture of the American twenty-first century; your attitudes toward women, like the one above, almost criminal. What you considered innocent flirtations would have been damned as bordering on abuse. In this regard as in others, surprisingly, perhaps, you shared a lot in common with Ellie's father, Mike, though he, an American, was perhaps less bound by the strictures of outdated social norms than you. It was a pleasure that you got along well together and enjoyed a kind of mutual understanding and respect. That you both, without intending to, left sometimes painful scars on your daughters' psyches is a measure of the cultural distance we have traveled in the days since you were born, more than a hundred years ago.

Your son,
Peter

27 October 2021

Dear Harry,

The year is 2021. It is now fifty years since the events I am recalling for you, Harry, as well as for myself. My two sons are middle-aged men, themselves much older already than I was when we were separated, father and sons. A quirk of time. It's a joy to be able to speak to both fairly frequently on the telephone these days. Jason, the younger of the two, comes out to California almost yearly—usually in January—to spend some time with us. It's a nice respite from the cold, Iowa winters. Because Matthew and his family live in England, we see them only every other year or so. Now especially, our planned reunions are continually postponed thanks to the pandemic that continues to plague our modern world. They live only a few miles distant from Aspley Guise, where I grew up as a youngster.

Both my sons are fine young men. Well, I call them young even though they are now undeniably middle-aged. Matthew will be sixty in just two short years!

I love those boys. I have always loved them. I love that Matthew has been such a devoted father to his three grown children and that Jason has built himself a life that suits him well. A confirmed bachelor, he has long held a job where he'll grudgingly admit he is clearly valued and respected. He has a house he loves and cares for meticulously. A dog, the same . . . I love that he has managed to pursue his one true passion in life—the guitar—with single-minded devotion to perfecting his mastery of the instrument. It distresses me deeply that he has had to contend with life-threatening disease, major surgery, and long and painful recovery—but he has done it all with phenomenal dignity and courage. Both men are blessed with sound values, a respect for others, a creative intelligence, sharp perception, and a wry sense of humor. I am immensely proud of them. You would be proud, too, of these boys you once played with on the beach at Aberporth.

There is a big part of me that argues I have not earned that right, to be proud of who they are. There are the genes, of course—yours and mine. But who can claim credit for their genes? I deserve none of the credit for the daily, weekly, monthly, yearly work involved in guiding them as they grew from boys to men. That all belongs rightly to their mother, and I honor her for that. Still, I am, I hope, more of a father to them now than when they were growing up. They see me for all my faults and seem to accept me generously for who I am. These letters that I'm writing to you, Harry, are in part an inquiry into what it means to be a father. We were both absent fathers, each in our own way—though I can't deny the obvious truth that I was more absent, and in a different way, than you. You chose to pack me off to school and I saw you three times a year when I was growing up: two weeks at Christmas, two at Easter, four in the summer. I saw Matthew and Jason only during their summer vacation when they were boys. There's more to it, I know, than the actual time we spent together, but the wounds are undeniable.

There is no way to make comparisons, to see whose wounds are worse. I have a judge sitting on my shoulder who keeps insisting that the ones I inflicted are worse, by far, than those that I received. But how to measure them? How is pain weighed, attributed, apportioned? We all carry our wounds around with us, don't we? Some buried, some worn on the sleeve. We each learn in our different way to live with them. When I say I'm proud of my sons, it's not to exculpate my younger self for the wounds that I inflicted, but rather to allow myself the solace of the present.

What can I claim, then, of fatherhood? What can I claim to have learned, from you, my own father? Perhaps no more, nor less, than to be the man I am.

> With love from your son,
> Peter

28 October 2021

Dear Harry,

I'm thinking about desire again. I'm grateful to have learned a good deal about it in the intervening years. Like others of my flaws—the ones I know about and readily admit to!—I have learned not to fight with it and repress it so much as to make of it my friend. I try to see it as a boisterous, troublesome, interfering old friend who can be allowed to come out to play from time to time but not always get his way—especially never when the consequences are predictably inappropriate or hurtful.

Back then, desire burned hot and uncontrollable enough in me to destroy everything in its path. Its companion in destruction was jealousy, which burned equally hot.

I told you a while ago, in an earlier letter, that I had slapped two women in my life, and that the second one was Ellie. It happened after the delirium of that summer we first met, when we agreed to part to see if we could both make our marriages work; and after I had made the decision to leave mine and had moved into a small bachelor apartment on a quiet street near the eastern end of Hollywood Boulevard, so small that instead of a bedroom it had a Murphy bed that pulled down from the wall in the living room.

It was here that Ellie returned to visit me one evening after spending the previous night with the husband she had not yet been able to bring herself to leave. I asked her if she had slept with him and she said yes, and I was so enraged by what I saw as a betrayal that I hauled back and slapped her hard across the face.

Do we all have violence in us, Harry? We men, who go to war? Who kill each other over meaningless disputes? Were you ever aware of some ancient, instinctive urge to violence in yourself? I'm reminded, as I ask these questions, about that one time when you lost your temper and raised your belt to threaten me. But you stopped yourself. I never saw violence erupt in you. You would growl impatiently in suppressed anger or frustration sometimes, driving, or when something went wrong in the workshop. But actual violence? Slapping a person that you loved? I never saw that. Not at all. I was horrified to find it in myself.

It's a wonder that Ellie stuck it out with me, Harry, after that.

Shamefully remembered,
Peter

29 October 2021

Dear Harry,

And yet she did stick it out with me, for another fifty years and more. After some time together we were married. I woke up on the morning of 11/11, Armistice Day and decided it was time. We called our next-door neighbors, now good friends, and had them meet us at the office of a downtown Los Angeles judge. Ellie was eight months pregnant, belly out to there. How she made it up the steep hill to the courtyard we'll never know. But she did. The judge did the job. (Ellie's father, Mike, had been boasting to friends that he was soon to be an illegitimate grandfather so I sent him a telegram: "Illegitimate grandfatherhood forestalled by downtown judge." I think he was a little miffed!)

Sarah was born one month and two days later.

We have lived for our entire half-century together on the same hill in the Los Feliz-Silver Lake area of Los Angeles. For most of those years, we lived at the crest of the hill, looking west over the Los Angeles basin and east as far as the San Gabriel and the San Bernardino mountains. It was there you visited us once, shortly after Sarah was born. The first home that we shared was a small cottage perched on the south side of the hill, a fairly easy drive for Ellie to the County Museum, where she worked, and close enough to USC for me to be able to host seminars with my graduate students.

Still, Ellie was reluctant to introduce me to her parents. Was it in part because I came from a Christian family? The truth is—we have talked about this before—I had known few Jews before coming to Los Angeles. I'd lived in your pretty, sheltered English country parishes, went off to schools rooted in the Anglo-Catholic heritage. It seems strange to me now, but even at Cambridge and in my London days, the only Jewish family I knew, that I recall, was that of one Dr. Green, a physician for whom Flora worked for a spell as a receptionist. Strange—well, perhaps not so strange—that he too, like Mike, was an avid art collector. I was invited on one occasion to his house and was mesmerized by the extraordinary, baffling paintings on the walls, thick with impasto, at first sight abstract, impenetrable, powerful, yet on further adjustment of the eyes unmistakably evocative of figures or landscapes while insistent that their surfaces were nothing but pure paint. I think you were there, too, Harry, and were as awed as I was. I did not know it at the time, but this was my first exposure to the "contemporary art" that was later to become my professional interest as a writer.

Other than this Dr. Green, then, I was not aware of knowing any other Jews in my early life. And then there was Ellie, who was Jewish. So, there was that. That I was not a Jew was not the only reason for her hesitation in introducing me to her family, I suspect. She may have been unsure about bringing home this rather unkempt, rather unpromising British poet when her parents were still so proud of the aspiring French film director to whom she remained nominally married. But

I decided in due course that it was time for them to meet me and took the responsibility into my own hands. I drove across town one day when she was visiting her folks in Westwood and knocked on the door at what I knew to be their address.

The maid who answered the door gave me first a doubtful once-over but conceded finally that it was alright to let me know that Ellie was out with her dad for his habitual post-prandial walk. I drove around the block and, when I spotted them, pulled up alongside them in my battered old VW Beetle.

Which is how I first met Mike, the famous screen writer and novelist, one time President of the Screen Writers' Guild and Board member at the Los Angeles County Museum. And more importantly, remember, the man who taught me how to hug. I was welcomed into the family, Harry, almost immediately as a son. Unsurprisingly, that first visit was a little awkward. I sat on the sofa in the living room while Ellie's stepmother, Dossy, fussed around nervously with drinks and bites to eat. For many years thereafter, I would sit on that same sofa, always awestruck by the paintings on the walls—paintings by artists whose names were unfamiliar to me on that first visit, but who I'd soon come to recognize as masters of their time: Guston, Franz Kline, de Kooning, Claes Oldenburg, Ed Kienholz, Jasper Johns, R. B. Kitaj . . . I was even to come to know some of these giants at the dining table where Mike and Dossy loved to entertain.

They changed my life, those paintings. Not just the paintings, but Ellie and her family, the passion for art that she inherited. Aside from that one astonishing brush with contemporary art at Dr. Green's home in London, I had known nothing previously about the work of the artists of our time. Picasso, yes, of course, and the modernists. Matisse. Paul Klee, the Surrealists. I had a passing knowledge of their place in history. But Abstract Expressionism, Minimalism, Pop Art . . . ? Conceptual art? I'd never heard of any of them. Among my contemporaries, I knew only writers. But from that time on, my own work as a writer and an academic was to take a radical turn away from literature . . . and into the world of art.

My horizons began to expand in other ways at Mike and Dossy's. I'm not sure that I'd call Mike a religious Jew—there was too much of the secularist in him for that—but he had an unmistakably rabbinical streak. Over the years, we celebrated more festivals than I can count in their dining room—Yom Kippur, Rosh Hashanah, Passover—and I learned much about Jewish history, Jewish lore, Jewish religion. Dossy had converted from her Episcopalian origins to Judaism after meeting Mike many years before and supervised the preparation of the traditional foods with a watchful eye on the kitchen help. You and Peggy, as I've reminded you a couple of times before, were the honored guests at one their Passover seders. Your letters—Peggy's, too—are filled with affectionate memories of that occasion and a multitude of other references to Mike and Dossy. Dossy, I know, made the trek to visit you one time in Aberporth. But for the distance, you would all have been great friends.

I have never chosen to embrace Judaism, as Dossy did, but I have always been respectful and supportive of Ellie's need to keep the traditions alive. I never chose to return to your faith either, Harry. I choose not to believe in the existence of any God, Hebrew, Muslim, Christian . . . You'll be happy to know, though, that I have discovered my own spiritual path in my late years, and I think we could agree on many aspects of what I have chosen to believe and how I choose to practice.

More of that in due course. In the meantime, I'm finding a lot of pleasure in being able to assure you that not everything I learned from you is lost.

With love,
Peter

30 October 2021

Dear Harry,

Light relief!

While I think of it, I recall another of your favorite Bishop stories, this one not so bawdy.

The Bishop is visiting the parish and this young lad, an altar boy, has been instructed how to bring him his morning tea: you knock politely on his bedroom door and you say, "It's the boy with your tea, my Lord!"—because bishops, of course, are by their annointment also lords of the realm.

The lad is nervous. He fetches the tea from the kitchen and to be sure he won't forget them he keeps repeating the words as he climbs the stairs: "It's the boy with your tea, my Lord, it's the boy with your tea, my Lord, it's the boy with the tea . . ." Then he reaches the door to the Bishop's bedroom, knocks politely, as instructed, and announces in a loud and confident voice, "It's the Lord with your tea, my boy!"

You got such a laugh out of that one, Harry. I did too. We laughed together. Thanks.

Your son,
Peter

2 November 2021

Dear Harry,

To pick up where I left off in my recent letter, I have some thoughts about another aspect of your core understanding of our nature as human beings that I have come to share with you, after many years of skepticism in my younger days.

I'm thinking about the interdependence of the intellectual, the emotional, and the spiritual aspects of our lives. For most of my young adult life—in fact, until I was well into my middle years—I lived almost entirely "in my head." As you know by now, the heart was an alien, suspicious place, and I was frankly scornful if not actively hostile to those who saw fit to pay any serious attention to that secret inner side to our existence. I derided their work as "self-indulgence," failing notably to see how my own thoughts and actions were effectively controlled by the dark, hidden side of consciousness. In the 1970s, already in my forties, I remained adamantly blind to any number of insistent signals that, had I paid attention, I could have seen coming in from different directions, beckoning. I balked at every opportunity to wake up.

There was, for example, a brush with the Esalen Institute, home in the 1960s to the human potential movement. Ellie and I ran into a couple who were well-placed there and who urged us to liberate our minds and bodies by sharing in the

Esalen experience. But I was not to be persuaded. I had heard of naked people, men and women, sitting in the hot tubs on the cliffs. I knew or thought to know about those infamous "encounter groups" where otherwise reasonable people were encouraged to expose the worst of their human weaknesses, examining their wounded childhoods—as though everyone didn't have one—their sexual deviance, the emotional turmoil of their lives. Not for me, Harry. I was well-adjusted, strong, dignified. I could keep my feelings to myself. Not for me to let them spill out messily and "share" them with others. No thanks.

As to the spiritual aspect of my life, I remember a well-intentioned student who was dying to have me read Ram Dass, insisting that *Be Here Now* would change my life. I dismissed it without reading it, of course, secure in my superior conviction that it was all gobbledy-gook, fake spirituality—a word I studiously avoided—pop culture, a tawdry stand-in for the religion I had long since abandoned.

It took me another twenty years and a good deal of intense heartache to recognize the damage I had done to myself and those I loved by keeping so much pain and anger bottled up inside. I could have spared myself by listening to you more closely in the first place—you, who already intuitively knew so much about all this before the Esalen Institute was ever thought of. Remember that simple action with the skipping rope? I know, I keep coming back to that. But it reminds me that you understood the nexus between the emotional and the physical, between mind and body, long before it became a part of commonly accepted lore.

We'll return to all this, Harry, at the proper moment. Meantime, I send belated thoughts of deep respect as well as love.

Your son,
Peter

4 November 2021

Dear Harry,

My earlier mention of Flora and the break-up of her marriage gave me pause to reflect further on our sibling relationship and the role you played as father in both our lives, both as children and later as grown-ups with families of our own.

I miss Flora. It is now already six years since she left us, so suddenly it came as a shock to everyone who knew her. She was—as you well know—my only sibling, leaving me the sole survivor of the four of us, our nuclear family. I am lonely for you. For Flora, especially. As adult siblings, it took us many years of estrangement before we rediscovered the strong bond between us, but we were both happy when we finally found it.

We squabbled endlessly in our early years, as little children do. Sharing a room in the Rectory at Aspley Guise—"the nursery"—we each had a corner bed with a window over it, the light sealed in with black-out curtains during the war. Mine looked out to the east, over an expanse of flat land and past the tall chimney stacks of the Bedfordshire brickworks; Flora's looked south toward London, where we could see the orange glow on the horizon as the city burned during the Blitz. Closer to home, in the daytime, she looked out over the dark green rhododendron bushes, past our neighbors' garden, and down towards the center of the village. The big walk-in doll's house you built for her one Christmas stood at the foot of my bed, the dark, gaping apertures of its glassless windows scaring me horribly at night as a little child, obsessed with the notion that burglars and murderers would come crawling through them out into our room. Flora had pigtails that I liked to pull when I was cross with her; she would retaliate by pinching, scratching, biting—the weapons wicked little girls would unleash on little boys. Our fights would inevitably end in tears and rage, and you or Peggy would come rushing up the stairs to sort things out. You always took Flora's side. The war between us lasted until I got my own room, the tiny one between your bedroom and the nursery, and there was no more territory to fight over.

Were we also good friends? I suppose so. I remember us all together in the kitchen where our mother would make the fruit from the orchard into jam, blowing on her wooden spoon before giving us tastes of the sweet white "scum" that rose to the surface. I remember hating having to hold hands with her—well, with any girl—when we went out for walks with Mrs. Smith, up the hill past the blackberry bushes to the sandpit. And I remember us sitting, trying to be good, one on each side of our mother in the Rector's pew in church.

Then we both went away to school. As I remember it, I went first. I think Flora was sent away a little later because she was a girl, but I could be wrong. My uniform was light gray with black and white stripes as trim; Flora's was cornflower blue. (How easily the name of that color comes back to my mind, and its unique, deep shade of blue!) From then on, we saw each other only during the holidays, two weeks at

Christmas, two at Easter and four weeks—maybe six—in the summertime. Christmas was best. The toys you made, the tall, fir tree in the drawing room, with lights and tinsel, glittering balls, a shining star on top, Father Christmas climbing noisily up the stairs to our room on Christmas Eve, and the crowded dinner table with assorted aunts and cousins (uncles were away at war) mixing in with the billetees. Those were great times. Summers, it was always the caravan. Flora and I each slept in our own little tent. We loved the beach. If you could save up enough petrol coupons during the war, there were the long drives west—before motorways!—to Aberporth, and Penparc Cottage where Grimp and Grane lived, the beaches and the tide pools where we'd poke the prawning nets you made for us under long strands of seaweed to catch those strange, transparent sea creatures for dinner. The walks over the rocks or along the cliffs to Tresaith.

I had a hard time understanding Flora's gloomy moods in her teenage years, the sense that she was always pushing me away. Even then she became something of a stranger.

Then she was gone. I stayed home a year or two longer than she and went off to Cambridge. She went to secretarial school in London. That's how things were in those days. Boys went to university; girls learned to type and take dictation from the men who went to university. Sad, Harry, when you think of it, no? Flora lived for a few years in London where, after her job with Dr. Green, she worked in an advertising agency. Her boss was the brother of Donald Maclean, one of those Communist spies known as the Cambridge Five. She had a photo taken with Cary Grant, who needed a pretty girl on his arm for a PR picture during his London visit. She fell in love with the wrong man—he was married, perhaps? I never knew—and fled the city, unhappily, for a spell as a "purserette" on the Cunard line between Southampton and New York. She worked for a while on the Queen Mary. By this time, in her early twenties, she had become little more than an exotic stranger who dropped in at the Vicarage from time to time to visit. I have the impression, Harry, that even then you and she had a touchy relationship. She kept her distance. She feared you even as she loved you, resisting the heavy weight of what she felt to be your judgment.

We both married at around the same time, and you officiated at both weddings. Flora's was in your own church at Sharnbrook. You approved of John, her husband, one of those many young men who were deeply influenced by you, especially in the matter of the Christian faith. He had grown up without it and became, I tend to think, a kind of acolyte. It may have been in part the closeness between the two of you that eventually drove a wedge between Flora and her husband. As I recalled for you in an earlier letter, Flora confided in me once that your advice to her, when they were experiencing difficulties in their marriage, was to give in meekly to the male needs of her husband. She found it hard to forgive you for that advice, because it was John you sided with. You saw him to be a normal, healthy man; she, on the other hand, was and always had been, "difficult."

For many years after our divorces, we remained strangers to each other, Flora and me. There were too many old judgments and unexamined assumptions that came between us. So, it was a welcome moment, much later in life, when we began to find common ground in our need to heal old wounds. Flora had been working at this for years, committed to a journey of inner discovery that, in my willful and persistent ignorance, I dismissed along with everything else I condemned as self-indulgent twaddle. It took an unwelcome confrontation with the hidden pain and turmoil in my own life for us to begin to bridge the gap between us, brother and sister, and acknowledge some ancient wounds. I had always been the blue-eyed boy, as she saw it, the one who could do no wrong; she was the dark one, the troublemaker, with her hidden secrets. The great trauma of her earliest years, I learned—you would remember this—was having been isolated in hospital with scarlet fever at the age of two or three. Her deep consciousness was scarred with the searing memory of having been cut off from her parents for a long period of quarantine by a thick panel of glass—and by the knowledge that her little brother was living happily at home with them. The envy burned in her, unrecognized, for years, along with another agonizing, ineradicable memory from the same time. When she was finally ready to be released from the hospital, the nurses seized her treasured stuffed monkey from her arms and would not let her take it home with her—the only friend she had been able to hold and love.

I expect that Flora shared all this with you, Harry, at some point later in her life. I hope you managed to come to an easy, loving relationship in the years before you died, and that Flora found the release she needed in mutual understanding and forgiveness. I know how hard she had worked to heal those suppressed wounds from the past, and to find some measure of inner peace.

I'm sure you'd be pleased to know that we, your "children"—why do we have no proper word for adult children in the English language? Is there something about us that wants to stay forever children, beholden to our mummies and daddies?—rediscovered the sibling bond between us in our later years. It was a surprise to both of us, I think, to finally recognize that we had much in common once I had given up my pride and had joined her on the path toward a greater clarity about myself and my relationships. It was only then that we were able to begin to work together to heal the long-buried wounds that had festered in the space between us.

More in my next.

Your son, Flora's brother,
Peter

5 November 2021

Dear Harry,

Now, years after her death, Flora's absence continues to haunt me. She was only eighty when she died, but the inner work to which she had devoted her full attention in her later years allowed her to meet death with reassuring equanimity.

It was a shock to all of us. She had been experiencing stomach pain for about six months, perhaps a bit longer, but doctors had not been able to attribute it to any particular source—until one day, when she went in for another diagnostic test and this time was told she had cancer, with maybe another year to live.

We happened to be in England at the time, Ellie and me. We were enjoying a quiet stay at a hotel in the New Forest when Flora's daughter, Charlotte, called with the news, and we drove over the next day to Cheltenham where she was in hospital. It was a bleak place, we discovered when we got there; a hospital with long, echoing corridors, creaking elevators, and crowded wards. None of the niceties. We found Flora lying in a stereotypical "hospital bed"—iron bedstead, separated from her neighbors on either side by flimsy screens. But crisp, clean sheets and cheerful, helpful nurses. Despite the pain of the cancer, diagnosed too late for successful medical intervention, she was quick to let us know that she was quite ready to set off on what she called "the next great adventure." She was happy to have seen her grandson, Hugo, grow to manhood and was secure in the knowledge that she had given him everything from his grandmother. She was at peace with her two daughters, both of whom now lived nearby. And now that her brother was here she felt complete.

We left the ward, the two of us, for a stroll out onto a little sun porch, Flora pushing her IV stand in front of her. We found a place to sit quietly in a pale patch of sunlight that found its way in between stone pillars. I don't remember either of us having very much to say, but it was pleasant enough just sitting quietly and letting the minutes slip by as we watched other patients take their slow, halting exercise, old ladies all, smiling and nodding as they passed us by.

Then it was time to leave. Flora watched us with her own smile as we said our goodbyes. For the time being, we said. We promised to come back again for a visit before it came time for her to leave us. Thinking back on that moment, I feel sure she knew that would not happen, that she had already decided it was time for her to go. It was more to reassure us that she accepted our promise and said a perfectly calm if sad goodbye. And waved to us as we left the ward. No tears. I wonder if they came later once we were gone.

This was the last time that I saw her. When I got home to Los Angeles I wrote a poem, "Bluebells", recalling the two of us as children in the woods together, filling baskets with those beautiful wildflowers to bring home for Peggy. I hope she was able to read it before she died, just a few days later, at the convalescent center where they sent off for a period of "recovery" from her hospital stay. She left us peacefully, I heard. And yes, I am convinced her death was a decision on her part, a choice to leave rather than suffer the further indignities of prolonged pain and the humiliation of dependency. She just set off on her journey, confident that no matter where it led it would be preferable to further mortal suffering.

It does feel strange, Harry, when I compare her death to yours. (I'll have reason to talk more about this later. It's not about chronology. You were already long gone when she died . . .) No longer a believing Christian, like myself, she did not deny, delay, or struggle as you did. It was as though she knew where she was going and was perfectly content to be going there. Still, I had a hard time reading "Bluebells" at her funeral. Could not get through it without tears. She insisted on being buried as she had lived, with respect for the well-being of our fragile planet. Her degradable wicker coffin would soon rot away, returning what remained of her physical body to the hungry biological embrace of Mother Earth.

Which is something that I thought you'd like to know. Your daughter, Harry, was a truly lovely person whose view of the world became increasingly compassionate, conscious, spiritual as she aged. You would be as proud of her as I am.

Your son,
Peter

BLUEBELLS
For my sister

It's bluebells time. I find myself once more
In England at this season, knee-deep in them,
Strolling through woods near Harpenden
With my son, Matthew, who's now fifty plus,
And his young daughter, Alice, sixteen,
Already a young woman; and Joe and Georgia,
Twins, rowdy kids still at thirteen, romping
Up ahead.

               And I'm remembering those days
When we two, as children, would ride our bikes
Down that steep, narrow hill toward the airfield
Where we watched Spitfires sputter in to land
On their return from battle. Here, the woods
Were a magic carpet, blue and green; we'd pick
Great baskets full of flowers to bring back home
To our mother at the Rectory. Primroses, too,
And cowslips . . .

               And now, not five days later,
I'm at your bedside in the Cheltenham hospital
Where they rushed you, to the disbelief of all
Who know you, to operate on what proved to be
Inoperable. And yet I find you in good spirits.

We are both—let's say the word—both old now,
You at eighty, I at seventy-eight. The memory
Of those bluebell woods is distant as a dream.
I hear you say, with what sounds a kind of joy,
"I'm ready," and it grieves me. It grieves me
Because I know that I'm not ready. Not ready
To let go the world I left some fifty years ago!

Here's the strange thing: I did not feel this
When our parents died, but I do feel it now,
The long-neglected, buried pain of separation,
Of disconnection from my early life, those days
When we picked bluebells in woods.

                                    Back, now,
In arid Southern California, where I chose to live
My adult life, these fifty years, the gulf of time
And space between us overwhelms me, I,
At four-thirty in the morning in my bed, you,
mid-afternoon, in yours, in the England that I left.

And yet, despite the sadness, I do not nurse
Regrets. I've lived a good life here, am grateful
For it all. I'm grateful, too, for this: that, having
So diverged, and for so many years, our paths
Came strangely back together, not geographically,
Perhaps, but in more important, deeper ways,
That probably surprised us both. You in your way,
And I in mine, we found the need to reconnect

With something of our father's we had lost,
Rejected, even, in our anger over things long past;
Call it his search, his struggle, the ever-present,
Ever painfully examined, and yet ever unexplained
Gut pain that he lived with all his life—the pain,
Perhaps, of separation from the God from whom
He sought salvation. He struggled, too, with death,
When his time came.

                              That you are "ready" now
Speaks well of the work that you have done
To come to terms with life, and with yourself,
To learn the ways of loving freely, both yourself
And others. That I am "not yet ready" speaks
To my unwillingness to accept the disconnect
That you, with grace, have found; have found
Within your heart: the strong will to let go.

7 November 2021

Dear Harry,

That last letter about Flora was one of the longest I have written. It must be obvious how deeply I still feel her loss. Sometimes it's hard to realize that she's gone. I have a picture of her over the desk in my study, smiling, and, close by, a small collection of the lovely, ceramic bowls she made toward the end of her life. A reflection of herself, they are intensely colorful, strong in their fragility and, rejecting formal perfection, left purposefully unfinished at the rims. It is in good part through her that I have come to understand that love, once recognized, acknowledged, and properly embraced, survives all ravages— including time and death—and will never vanish from the heart that nurtures it.

There was some tension initially between Flora and Ellie when they met. Flora admitted freely enough that her old feeling of envy was reawakened by the happiness of our relationship. Seeing us together, she felt alone, and lonely. I was the lucky one. And I'll confess that there is some truth to Peggy's firm belief that no matter what happens, "Peter always ends up on his feet." While I've had my share of troubles in my life—there's more of this to come, Harry, that's a promise—I believe I've also had more than my share of blessings. In bleak moments, when they come to me, I often wonder whether it has all been more than I deserve.

It was one Christmas time in the early 1970s when I first brought Ellie back to England to meet you. When I told you of my plans to visit, I mentioned that I would be bringing "a friend" but offered no further detail. Nor did you request it. Poor Ellie had caught a bug of some kind—psychosomatic, you would likely say!—and was deathly sick when we arrived at Heathrow after the long flight. Fortunately, I had pre-booked a room for us at a railway hotel in London, near the station, to be ready for the train journey to Wales the next day.

There you were, you and Peggy, to greet us when our train pulled in. I don't think I had ever given much thought to the fact that Ellie was Jewish (no, that's not true; I had) and I had not even mentioned that it was a girl I was bringing with me to visit; but somehow you had intuited both facts about her prior to our arrival and there was some initial awkwardness as you packed our suitcases into the trunk and arranged for Ellie to sit with Peggy in the back seat. Ellie recalls a kind of recoil on Peggy's part, sitting next to her, squeezed as far as possible into her own corner of the back seat of your Triumph. I like to think this was caused by Ellie's cold and not her Jewishness!

You, too, were nervous. On the pretext of showing your guest something of the Welsh countryside you loved, you drove hither and yon without apparent purpose until there was nothing left for it but to bring us back to the cottage in Aberporth. Once there, while we were retrieving our luggage from the trunk and with Ellie and Peggy safely out of earshot, you put the question that must have been on your mind: "Your mother and I have no idea about your life together in Los Angeles, but we have made up every bed in the house and you can tell us which arrangement you prefer."

It was remarkable, Ellie and I agreed later, that you would be so open to our situation. We, too, had been unsure how to handle this problem; we had been "living in sin"—remember that quaint old phrase?—for quite some time now, and had never even bothered to consider marriage. I made bold to tell you as much, and you insisted on letting us have the only double bed in the cottage, the one that you and Peggy shared, while the two of you would occupy the attic room upstairs.

Such was Ellie's introduction to her *goyische* in-laws-to-be. After a few days in Aberporth, you drove us over the Harpenden, just north of London, where Flora and John lived with their two little girls. To spare us the expense of a hotel they had found a room in a vacationing friend's house—the coldest room we ever had the misfortune to sleep in!—and Jewish Ellie was introduced to Father Christmas, stuffed stockings for the girls, and that whole family tradition. It was her first-time meeting Flora, too, and John, at a time when were none of us were able to foresee how the story of their marriage would end up.

Thank you anyway, Harry, for the kindness that you and Peggy showed to Ellie on that first visit. It was long remembered, honored, and appreciated.

> With fond remembrance,
> your son,
> Peter

8 November 2021

Dear Harry,

I was wrong! I misremembered. I let that last letter stand because it tells you something about my state of mind.

You did know in advance that it was Ellie I was bringing over to England with me that Christmas. The year was 1971. It's true that we were not married yet. But I have been re-reading some of those letters from you and Peggy and you both made it clear that you would welcome her—that you would go out of your way to greet her and make her feel at home. You even made the long drive to Swansea (it was not Carmarthen!) to meet us at the station, and Peggy wrote in advance that she was looking forward to introducing Ellie "to our lovely Welsh countryside."

You see? I have been wrong about so much. You'd think by now I would have learned about projection. All the hesitation, all the prejudice, all the judgment . . . It was me, Harry! It wasn't you or Peggy. It was me! Forgive me. We remember things as we imagine them to have been, not as they were, and in doing so we show ourselves for who we are.

Affectionately.
Peter

10 November 2021

Dear Harry,

Back to what it was I was about to say . . .

I woke in the middle of the night last night and found myself thinking about your letters with such a sense of shame and sadness that it was hard to get back to sleep. I read more of them yesterday and have many more yet to read.

It's about projection, I think. I finally get it. I have been too glib, too ready to apply the term to others without bothering to think about how it might just as well apply to myself. A bit like you and your psychosomatics! So, you were not the remote, impossible-to-reach father my memory made you out to be— that was me! Your letters are filled with warmth, affection, interest, concern. Your sometimes barely legible scrawl fills out those blue air mail forms edge to edge, and still finds room for more words added in the margins. You often say how much you miss me, how much you love your grandchildren, how you regret the distance that separates us. You read my books of poems from those early days—*Aspley Guise*, *The Lost Garden*, *Parapoems*—with serious curiosity and understanding and responded to them with thoughtful, carefully chosen words. You shared them with your friends and glowed with pride when they responded to my work with praise. You even loved the sometimes-outrageous clothes—pink shirts, gaudy ties, striped pants!—we sent from California as gifts at Christmas time and birthdays, wearing them with ridiculous pride to show off at the pub. Aside from the actor, there was something of the clown in you, too!

Your self-awareness in those letters is honest to a degree I must have missed when I first received and read them. The humility and self-doubt are often poignant, leaving doors open for me that I never chose, or dared, to enter. It would have been up to me to ask about the frequent allusions you made to doubts about your faith. Foolishly, I let them slide, and now that I pay attention and seriously want to ask about them, it's too late. You talk about your "failings" as a father, as a husband, as a grandfather, and I regret so much that we can no longer sit down together, face-to-face, for me to ask you to go further, to tell me more—and give you my feedback. You write about your passions, the creative drive that led you to spend so many hours in the workshop and create so many lovely objects on your lathe. You talk about your physical ailments earlier in life, and later, as you watched your body age. Now that my own body is deteriorating with the unavoidable effects of the passing years, how much I'd appreciate the opportunity to talk about these things.

It's obvious from your letters, too, how much you loved your Peggy.

An impertinent and nosy son, I have presumed to ask about your sex life. Given how open you are about most other things in your letters, it would not surprise me to find you willing to talk about even this. On more than one occasion you spoke—a bit boastfully! Surprisingly, a bit macho—about your continuing activity well into old age. I long for details!

It is your self-deprecating humor, above all, that stands out. It tempers even the most serious of our "conversations" and brings a smile to my face as I read.

So, no, Harry. If anyone was remote, if anyone was hard to reach, it was me, your son. It was I who was the distant, impossible-to-reach father, I who was aloof, averse to the risk that goes along with intimacy and physical touch. It was I who needed to protect my all-too-fragile self from letting others in to places where I might get hurt. It was I who needed to work so hard, once I was finally exposed to all this, in the effort to change my life. I'll have more to say about this soon. Enough, here, to cop to it, in that old, expressive phrase, and to open my heart just a little further to the man you were.

Yours, as you would often say,
affectionately,
Peter

9 November 2021

Dear Harry,

I woke in the middle of the night with the urge to pee and that old English euphemism rattling around in what's left of my brain: Spend a penny. As in "I need to spend a penny."

I wonder if the phrase is still current now that its context has been long forgotten? We used to have those pay toilets—I hope they don't have them anymore!—where you had to put a penny in the slot to gain admittance. Pennies, of course, were not today's chintzy little things, they were impressively huge pieces of hardware, weighing in at a hundred times their monetary value. A "pocketful of change" would weigh your trousers down and jangle loudly when you walked. That's when there were, quite sensibly, twelve pennies to the shilling (a much smaller coin) and twenty shillings to the pound. There was no pound coin. Just pound notes. And fivers. That was something, in those days, to see one of those impressive fivers, plain white with big, ornate black lettering, as big and flimsy as a handkerchief . . .

Now they've gone and spoiled everything, of course.

With love, your son,
Peter

11 November 2021

Dear Harry,

I'm continually finding more ways in which we are alike and now I have come upon yet another. We are easily upset and irritated when disturbed in the performance of our rituals.

It happened the other night. Oh, it's a silly ritual, hardly worthy of the name. I like to settle down and watch something on the television after dinner and before going to bed. Ellie and I are not always in sync on this ritual. If it happens to be something in which she is not interested and she happens to be tired, she goes to sleep. (She even snores a bit!) Meantime I, who am easily hooked by a story line and want to follow it, get irritated by her lack of interest and, particularly, by her—to me, at least, seemingly—ostentatious display of boredom.

Silly, yes, but last night it blew up into one of those serious arguments we still get into after all these years together, and it put me in mind of a much more serious and hurtful occasion, when you were similarly interrupted in that evening ritual of your pre-dinner glass of Guinness, and which may have seemed equally trivial to you. It was not.

It was on one of our visits with you, over on your side of the Atlantic. You and Peggy had been kind enough to offer to take care of Sarah for a few days while Ellie and I took a side trip by ourselves, the kind of little honeymoon we still like to take from time to time. I seem to recall that you even lent us your aging Triumph for the trip, and we headed south from Wales for what was to be a jaunt around the southwestern counties, Exeter, Somerset, Devon, Cornwall. Arriving in Plymouth in the evening, our first night out, we decided to check in with you to see how Sarah was doing and found a pay phone down by the docks—one of those tall, red telephone booths, as familiar as "bobbies" in England in pre-cellphone days. Getting through to you at Glenview, though, we were alarmed to hear there had been an urgent call for Ellie from California; she was to call back as soon as possible.

In those days, a transatlantic call was still a major undertaking, let alone a call from a telephone booth with piles of coins and operators to contend with. Harder still was the news from the other end. Ellie's father, Mike, had taken a serious fall and was in a coma in the hospital. He might not survive.

We had to get back home to California—and as soon as possible. We drove through the night to Aberporth to pick up Sarah and started early the next morning on the journey back to London with you and Peggy, arriving there late afternoon and reserving seats on the first available flight to Los Angeles the following day. Meantime, distressed by the delay and desperately anxious, of course, for Mike, we all stayed the night at John's flat. (John, by this time long divorced from Flora, was still, and always, a member of the family). Once settled in for the night, you were anxious to get started on your ritual of the pre-dinner Guinness while we placed another call to California to check on Mike's progress. Ellie could only get through to Vicky, the Black woman—more of a family friend, really—who took care of Mike and Dossy's house and helped in the kitchen; it was from Vicky, she learned that Ellie's uncle, a physician, had decided there was little to be gained in prolonging life in Mike's condition and had ordered his removal from the medical devices keeping him alive. Ellie's dad, Sarah's granddad, and my good friend was dead. (I thought then and have often thought since that this was an act of cruelty on her uncle's part, one that made it impossible for Ellie to say her last goodbyes).

Ellie was understandably distraught. She'd had a close, complex, and deeply loving relationship with her father. To lose him in this way, when she was half a world away, was devastating. She wept. Of course, she wept.

Which is when you stepped in, Harry, assuming the role of paterfamilias. Reliving in memory how it happened, I still find it hard to believe this . . . well, it amounted to an act of startling callousness on your part. You told her to stop crying. Forbade her. "You must think of the child," you said, not thinking of Sarah, I suspect, but of your Guinness—a ritual that brooked no interruption. You, who understood so much about the emotional needs of human beings. You, and your skipping rope! How uncharacteristic, yet . . . how typical! No one could ever accuse you of being a simple man, devoid of contradictions.

Ellie should have been allowed to weep until the tears no longer came. Should have been encouraged to cry for as long as she wanted. For as long as she needed. But incredibly you stepped in and shut her down. Of course, this was also a moment when I should have stepped in myself. I should have told you to back off. But I didn't. I submitted to the wishes of my father.

I did once have the opportunity to talk to you about this, along with many other matters that had long been left unspoken between father and son. But this conversation took place, alas, only in absentia. The context was a weekend of intense and challenging confrontation between myself and the dark side of my nature. I'm anxious to tell you about that weekend and will do so soon. In the meantime, I must ask myself what prevented me from taking a stand that evening? Would it have been otherwise had I been confronted with the reticence that held me back before that occasion instead of after? Would I have been better able to listen to the heart's needs at that moment, to have had the confidence to stand up to you and say that you were wrong?

Would I have been able to find my voice as a man, I wonder, rather than capitulate before my father's will?

I like to think better of myself now, Harry. I like to think that I would have spoken up and given voice to the anger at my father that I would not allow myself to feel.

Your son,
Peter

13 November 2021

Dear Harry,

I could not have anticipated when I left England for the first time in 1960, to live and work as an exile in a foreign country, that I would never return except as an occasional visitor to the country of my birth. The distance between you and me, between father and son, first created when I left for school many years before, was now established as a geographical fact. While Germany was close enough, those first two years, the distance grew with each move, from Germany to Canada, from Canada to Iowa and from Iowa, finally, to Southern California, where I have now lived for more than fifty years. And now that geographical distance has expanded even further, since your death, into the unknowable divide between the living and the dead.

Finally finding a home here in California, I have long since settled into my life as a husband and a father. As I already noted in a previous letter, while Ellie and I have not yet quite matched the Diamond Jubilee that you and Peggy celebrated a few years before you died—the family joined forces and bought you a new toilet for Glenview!—we will soon have five decades to celebrate. There are few marriages these days that last as long as ours.

The years have been good ones for the most part. Through my association with Ellie and her art maven family, I began to write about the work of contemporary artists working in the Southern California area. I morphed from (primarily) poet into novelist, essayist, and art critic. Reading through your letters from that period of change, I am much moved by the interest you took in the early books of poems that I published. *Aspley Guise* was of course of particular interest, with its evocation of your Rectory and St. Botolph's church. You shared it with many of your old friends and took obvious delight in their responses. *Parapoems*, too, you read with a measure of care and thoughtfulness that I had forgotten, and I was quite surprised, on re-reading your letters, to discover such detailed comments and questions about its literary intentions. You even gave a meticulous reading to the text I wrote for that tiny hand-made book, *The Lost Garden*, and your (Freudian!) analysis of the battle with the cactus it describes was both amusing and amazingly astute! I did not realize—yes, I must have known, but for some reason overlooked—the pride you took in my professional life both as a writer and an academic.

I've mentioned that I was not qualified to teach art or art history, the field that had become the center of my professional life as a writer. I made a career switch from teaching to administration and started a promising career in art schools and colleges. After ten years, by the mid-1980s, I was in serious contention for vice-presidencies, even presidencies at the small art colleges I had come to love. I traveled throughout the country for interviews. I was offered good jobs . . . but found myself eventually unable to tear myself away from the metropolis where I was now known and respected as a critic. Your letters show that you followed this odyssey with love and support through all its vicissitudes. You supported me even when I finally managed to remind myself, in 1986, that I was supposed to have been a writer, not an academic, and quit the academic world almost overnight. You'll be relieved to know that I have managed to live happily without a job since then. Work, yes. I do work. I have persisted in my work as a writer every day, long past other people's "retirement age." But there has been no daily grind, no dreaded commute to work, no office hours . . . and, of course, no salary!

The first years were hard. The fact that we survived financially was largely due, at first, to Ellie's work as an art consultant, advising private and corporate clients on the acquisition of contemporary artwork for their collections. The last years of the 1980s were a good time for that profession, with seemingly enough disposable cash and corporate profits to underwrite art purchases, so her income made it possible for me to write. With a small but steady income writing reviews, articles, and exhibition catalogues, I even re-imagined myself from those early days in Germany as the next great novelist; and actually succeeded in publishing a couple of books in the mystery-thriller genre that you loved to read. Your passion was my inspiration. That career, however, never quite took off. It did not prove the source of income I had naively hoped. Most of my work since then has taken the form of essays, art catalogue contributions, memoirs, and off-beat reflections on the vicissitudes of life. For the past twenty years, I have maintained a presence on the Internet (don't ask; enough to say that it's a new worldwide communication system) with a series of blogs that have attracted a world-wide audience of readers I would not otherwise have had.

And yet . . . despite the long-delayed achievement of my freedom as a writer, all was not well in our lives. I plan to tell you how I was brought face-to-face, in my fiftieth year, with the need to finally leave the wounded boy behind, grow up and take full ownership of my life; and to make a better account of myself as man, a husband, and a father than I had been able to do till then. And how I sought to do it.

Your son,
Peter

14 November 2021

Dear Harry,

Another aside. Forgive me. Can we indulge a little in what we jokingly call, over here, the "organ recital"? Which is when we old folks get together to exchange the tedious details of our declining strength and health.

The reason? I must go down to see the doctor this morning. Again! I seem to spend half my time these days in doctors' offices! Did I mention that I had a hip replaced on my right side earlier this year? Amazing, the things they manage to do these days. This time it's a bad knee. Actually, I'm in quite a lot of pain. The hip replacement surgery was more than three months ago and I really thought I was recovering nicely. I have been following a strict physical therapy program to regain strength and flexibility in my leg, and up until a month or so ago I was back to walking a mile or more without undue stress or pain. Then the knee gave out on me, also on the right side. It has been getting increasingly painful in the past few days and my walking has gone, well, backwards.

It's distressing, of course, to watch the body age. It's distressing to be in constant pain because pain, especially when severe—you should know, you had enough of it!—is not restricted to the affected area. It becomes debilitating to the mind as well as to the body. So, as I watch my own body suffer the effects of age, I wonder how old age was for you? With more than 5,000 geographical miles between us, I was not able to observe that process at first hand, except at the intervals of two or three years between our visits.

I did see how your body bent with age—as mine has begun to do. Ellie keeps trying to straighten me up! You relied more and more on your walking stick, while you were still able to make your daily uphill progress to the pub on the cliff above the bay. I know there came a time when you were no longer able to spend those precious hours in the converted garage that had become your woodshop even long into retirement, where you had been able to turn out bowls, and salt and pepper mills, and candlesticks, and other truly lovely wooden objects on your lathe. That must have been a huge, heart-breaking sacrifice. (Is it not interesting, though, that Flora also turned to making bowls, later her in life? Hers were ceramic, of course, yours wood. But there you were both of you, making bowls, containers, beautiful receptacles of silent, empty space . . . father and daughter, reunited in a singular preoccupation).

I wonder whether those skilled hands of yours were affected by arthritis? I suppose they must have been, though they never showed the tremor that bothers many people as they age. Mine too—my hands—have aged, though less chronically than the legs. I have what's called Dupuytren's Contractures, with subcutaneous growths pulling the fingers out of alignment, and I wonder if you had these too? They're supposedly hereditary. But I don't know. I must have watched a thousand times as you used your fingers, deftly, to make your hand-rolled cigarettes . . . Were you still able to manipulate those little rolling devices in old age? At least until the time you had to give up smoking altogether when Peggy's doctor told her that your second-hand smoke was polluting the air in that little cottage and contributing to the bronchial problems that would kill her if you didn't stop. After which you never smoked again. Bravo for you!

Was it that life-long habit that killed you, eventually? Even from an early age, I remember that familiar rasping cough, especially when you got up in the morning. Am I right in thinking it got worse with age? I think I never knew the official cause of your death but given the difficulty you had breathing in your last days; I suspect that emphysema was some significant part of it. I do remember your adamant refusal, when the time came, to take the last steps through that final exit door into eternity. But that's for another letter.

Meantime, I need to get myself off to the doctor's office. More tomorrow.

This comes, as ever, with loving memories.

Your son,
Peter

17 November 2021

Dear Harry,

We do not know what suffering means until we watch our children suffer. Don't you agree? How much it must have affected you and Peggy, watching your children's marriages fail and families break apart. Your letters speak so often of tears and breaking hearts—but always also of the love and support you had to offer through it all.

I only came to understand the depth of my own suffering when I saw Sarah suffer. I need not remind you of the specific circumstances here—I have written about them elsewhere. Enough to say that her suffering taught me that I had to change my life. (Did I ever mention how much I have always loved those closing words to one of Rilke's Sonnets to Orpheus: "*Du musst dein Leben ändern*"? You must change your life! Even when I first read them as a young man, those words struck a resonant, challenging chord somewhere deep in the heart and mind. I should have heeded them earlier but I chose not to listen to the call. I have had reason to recall those words often since).

So, here's how it started. It was the first day of January in the year 1992. I went to my desk to consult my to-do list—yes, I keep those running lists of reminders!—and saw there were five telephone calls to be returned. Which would have been quite normal, except that this time every name on the list was a Peter: Peter Shelton and Peter Erskine, both Los Angeles artists; Peter Goulds, a friend and art dealer; Peter Norton, one of the early self-made millionaires in the burgeoning field of computer technology and the creator of the Norton Utilities—also, back then, a fledgling but enthusiastic art collector, and a new friend; and then there was one other Peter whose identity is now lost to a shaky memory. But I do remember there were five.

I joked to myself; this has to be the year of Peter.

Our family was in turmoil. I had always thought of myself as Mr. Fixit, the kind of practical man who could solve any problem that confronted him or those he loved. But here was a serious, even life-threatening situation that I could not set to rights with a wave of my trusty paternal wand. After years of scorn and prejudice—I have told you about this!—I'd finally had to concede that this was an instance where psychotherapy might be called for, and I was frankly shocked when the therapist we consulted put it to me bluntly: "If you want to help your family, you need to work on yourself."

Work on myself! I was appalled. I had no idea what that could mean, still less how to go about it.

That was the year that Ellie and I went to Rome. Not to consult with the Pope, as you might have guessed, but thanks to a writing assignment I'd accepted. I wrote in an earlier letter, if you recall, about that moment of epiphany when confronted with my namesake's chains in the church of San Pietro ad Vincola and the sudden, stunning realization that it was time to cast off my own. (I'm not the only one: "Man is born free," Jean-Jacques Rousseau wrote famously, "and everywhere is in chains." Along with him—a Romantic, then!—I have come to believe that we all carry our own chains around with us, and our life's work is to liberate ourselves and rediscover the freedom of our birthright.) On my return to Los Angeles, clear in my mind as to *what* I needed to do but not *how* to do it, a chance encounter at an art world cocktail party left me understanding exactly where I needed to go. A friend listened to the story of my revelation and told me about the men's "training weekend" he had just completed. It had changed his life, he said. It was called the New Warrior Training Adventure.

Warriors? Training? Adventure? Absurd! It sounded ridiculously childish, the last thing in the world I would ever want to do. And yet some inner angel—demon?—prompted me to inquire further, and I called to get more information. The weekend would demand of me everything I had, I was warned—physically, intellectually, emotionally. Take no prisoners! I recoiled at the idea. Besides, it cost $500—a very large sum of money to a man without a job or reliable source of income.

I resisted mightily. But one piece of wisdom I have since acquired is that resistance is often the reminder of exactly where I need to go. Perhaps I already knew this, at some level below consciousness, because I signed up right away.

I arrived at the weekend two hours late. I had a ready excuse—the traffic—but if I expected sympathy for what had been a nightmare journey of unprecedented tie-ups on the freeways, I got none. Would I have been so late, I was asked, had it been a matter of life or death? Of course not. In the next hours and days, I was put through the wringer, allowed no excuses, no prevarications, no delusions. My "trainers" were unsparing in holding the mirror up for me to see my deluded self, all the anger and all the fears, the ironclad suit of armor with which I had learned since boyhood to protect my vulnerable self (and yes! with great success!) from the world out there—without realizing how it also prevented me from simply showing up to my own life. I found myself reconnecting both with the vulnerable little boy, so playful and imaginative but so thoroughly constricted by the armor I'd created; and at the same time with that old, fierce, primitive male barbarian who survives unacknowledged in the hearts of men, caged, in shackles, roaring to be free.

Warrior to the rescue!

In the climactic act of those two grueling, almost sleepless days, I was challenged to revisit the deepest and most painful of old wounds that continued to shape my life. My first thought was for Mr. Ellis, the man who had abused my boyhood innocence. But no, my mentors saw beyond this incident and would not allow me to stop there. They insisted I go deeper, deeper . . . And when I finally arrived at the deepest, darkest source of everything that still held me back from the fullest realization of my power as a man, I found myself face to face with . . . none other than yourself, Harry! You, the man I loved the most but in whose love I never managed to believe. You, the man at the altar, as far from me as God Himself, the man I would never be able to reach no matter how hard I tried. You, too, the one who exiled me from my rightful place in my father's house and sent me off to school. There I was, face to face with you!

In the psychodrama that ensued, this "you"—in the guise of a tall stranger who played that role—stood distant, disdainful, and aloof. My challenge was to lay claim to your attention, to demand your recognition and your love by breaking through a gauntlet of strong, unyielding men—more with the power of intention than brute force—who placed themselves between us. You, my father, stood beyond them, back turned, scornful of my efforts, impossibly remote. Success meant finally wrestling with those chains that had imprisoned me and breaking free.

You should have been there, Harry, to hear the sound that came bellowing from my throat—not so much the "primal scream" of pain that John Lennon told the world about in song; though yes, that too. But this was more the untamed roar of rage I had kept locked up inside for decades, the outrage of a little boy exiled not only from the familiar warmth of family and home but, so it felt to him, from his father's heart. It was the lion's roar (yes, remember I'm a Leo!) I had never dared to show you, the roar that marked the ritual passage into the manhood that had so long eluded me.

You would recognize the process. The actor in you understood the power of ritual, dramatic recreation; the healer knew the power of the skipping rope you once tightened around my neck, the physical reenactment of long buried trauma.

What I learned that weekend—and what changed my life—was the realization that I had never understood what manhood was about. It was not merely about gender, about sex, about my ability to perform, to dominate, to deal with life's problems when they arose, to show the way. I had never so clearly understood that manhood resides neither

309

in the musculature nor the genitals, but in the heart. I had discounted the essential value of emotional strength, emotional commitment. I had failed to include love in the equation of my life.

Well, Harry, believe me, I was not healed of all my wounds that weekend. I did not leave a perfect specimen of enlightened manhood. But, as Ellie later told me, I left two inches taller, more confident in my power, more able to recognize and even reveal my vulnerabilities—and in that, paradoxically, to gain immeasurably in strength. I had learned to look into my heart for the truth it had to tell me. I had learned something about the meaning of accountability.

Wisdom, though, would have to wait for another day.

With love,
Peter

18 November 2021

Dear Harry,

A footnote to that last letter.

More projection. I realized only much later that it was not you I was so desperately trying to reach in that dramatic moment I described. It was not you who had abandoned me. Not you who had earned my anger. It was me. I was the aloof, the distant one. I was the one whose heart was closed, who was afraid to show and share either my anger or my love.

This was something that I failed to understand in that moment that felt so much like triumph. I felt so relieved to have been able to reach you, I was unable to see the deeper truth that had revealed itself.

You had always been there. I was just looking in the wrong place. Had I looked into my heart, I would have found you. It was my own authentic self that I was looking for.

With love, your son,
Peter

20 November 2021

Dear Harry,

There's something else that I brought away with me from that men's weekend: the realization that there was an important piece that had been missing in my life. I had spent the better part of my life drifting—from one job to another, from one situation to another, blown about by ambient winds, as though I had no choice. I had given little thought to a sense of purpose. Why was I put here on this planet? What was it I was "given to do"—to use another of those phrases that I like? In those old myths that left their mark on me as a youngster, the knight is defined by his quest, the warrior by his mission. They thrive as men of service. But what was mine? Yes, I had known since the age of twelve that I was meant to be a writer. I always felt right about myself, "on mission" as it were, when I had a writing project going; and, conversely, uncomfortably "off mission" without one.

Okay, so I'm a writer. But to what end?

I have never entirely lost that deep, sometimes hidden, sometimes forgotten, sometimes neglected sense of obligation that I learned from you, Harry, from what you modeled in your life rather than what you taught in words—an obligation to use the time I have to serve the needs of others as much as, if not more than my own. The experience of that weekend left me with a new clarity: that service is an essential part of what it means to be a man. We men, myself emphatically included, have learned—mistakenly, as I see it now—to define ourselves too readily by our dominance, our sexual performance, our competitive edge. You held yourself to a different standard. In all your parishes when I was growing up, you had a flock of parishioners to tend. They relied on you to help them in their time of need. You were pastor, spiritual guide, psychotherapist, nurse, marriage counsellor, gerontologist. You laid hands on the sick and held hands with the dying. You sprinkled holy water on your people at their baptism, brought in the bishop for their confirmation, oversaw the exchange of rings in marriage. You were there for the birth of their children, their grandparenthood, their death, and the burial of their remains.

You served. From my earliest days I was aware of this, and it was something every moment of my childhood and education led me to expect also of myself. In moments when I am hard on myself as I look back on what has already been a long life, when I call myself to account for how I've lived it, this is where I do not measure up to you or my expectations of myself. I have more to give to my fellow beings on this earth than I have found ways to make that possible

I have struggled with that.

You gifted me with a social conscience and, looking back, I think I genuinely started out with good intentions when I first went into teaching. It was a worthy avocation, a chance to prove my worth. And there were times in my later professional life as a teacher when I did well, when I was able to make a difference in other peoples' lives. But those moments were almost never in the classroom. It was not "teaching" in the sense that I was passing out information or knowledge to eagerly receptive minds from my own superior store of them; instead, those moments were in the setting of small groups, seminars, or personal, one-on-one encounters, exchanges having more to do with lived human experience than with knowledge, with body than brain, with listening than speaking. I had the satisfaction of knowing I was able to touch others in important, life-changing ways without having "taught" them anything at all.

When I left teaching, I no longer had a ready forum for these acts of service. But I soon discovered another, similar forum for the kind of teaching that I liked—mentoring, really, more than teaching—in the organization of men where I now found a place. For twenty years in this great and still thankfully expanding circle of men—the ManKind Project—I had the pleasure and privilege of sitting in intimate circles of my peers, other men, each one of them with their own particular plight to work through, pain or fear, anger or grief, and find the path to live authentic lives. As the years passed, Harry, I became a respected elder in this organization, a wise old man who had learned at least enough to know that I knew nothing!

I am still connected to this work of conscious living with a small group of older men who meet each month on our computer screens thanks to the miracle of Zoom (don't ask, Harry: too complicated!), to keep "in touch" as we observe the process of our aging. There came a time, though, when I needed to move on from my activity in the larger organization and create a greater space of freedom for myself.

How, then, to continue to be of service at this more solitary moment in my life? Could writing alone be considered an act of service?

There have been times when I have judged this great, enduring passion of mine to be a selfish, self-indulgent way of life. I was able to reach others through publication, yes, and for years I published frequently in national magazines. I also published, as you know, two books of poetry, two novels, a substantial monograph about a world-famous artist. Even so, it could never seem quite enough; I longed for ways to find a wider audience, more ears to reach, more minds to change.

I had left that training weekend with my own life-changing commitment, a new sense of mission: to "write honestly," was how I phrased it. Not that my writing had been dishonest, but it was always objective, outward-looking. I realized now that I needed to show not just what was in my head, but in my heart and over time, my understanding of that new sense of mission became deeper, broader. I found a new formulation to describe what I was after; not simply "writing honestly," my aim was "getting to the heart of the matter." It was about going deep. About being able to reveal what was in my own heart and learning what was in the hearts of others. More and more, I wanted to know what lies below, behind the surfaces we present to others. I became less of a "critic", more of an essayist—and felt comfortable with the change. I thought often of the *Essais* of the great French writer, Montaigne, and sought to emulate the way he shared his deepest thoughts and feelings.

I'd like to think of these letters that I'm writing, Harry, in that light. I want to go deep. When I have occasion to speak to others about these "letters to my father"—mostly, but not exclusively to men—I never fail to see the light of recognition in their eyes. Should I find some way, as is my aspiration, to put them out into the world, it might be that they too prove in some way a fulfillment of that profound and never quite fully satisfied desire.

As I say, I have struggled. You were always present, somewhere in my mind, reminding me that dedication to the needs of others was more noble than attention to one's own. You chose to create a platform for that, in your pastoral work, and you had a ready, needful patronage: your flock. My own flock, my readership, is sparse, and scattered wide, for the most part anonymous. From the responses to my work that come back to my attention, I know that I'm able to touch the hearts and minds of many of my fellow beings with my words; that even thus, remotely, I change lives. I am privileged in that.

And still I keep a place of sadness in my own heart, that judgment in my mind—that I have had more to give than means give it, to realize in full my need to be of service to the world.

With love, your son,
Peter

21 November 2021

Dear Harry,

I had some further thoughts this morning as I re-read that last letter to myself. There's another phrase from the literary heritage I have acquired in years of writing, another one that frequently reverberates in my mind. It's a short one, two words only, from E. M. Forster's novel, *Howards End*: "Only connect." (The passage continues, "Only connect the prose and the passion, and both will be exalted, and human love will be seen at its height." Lofty words, but the two simple ones are enough for me).

Only connect!

"I do it for myself." I have heard this many times from creative people of all kinds. I don't do it for myself. I want to connect. And it's not easy. For most working artists, the vast majority of them, I'd guess, it's hard if not impossible to find a gallery to show their work. By the same token, most of us who write find it almost impossible to find anyone to publish what we write. The competition in this contemporary world is immense and daunting. You were gone already when *Persist*, my little book of essays on this subject came out. (I did find a small, independent publisher for that!) Its subtitle was "In Praise of the Creative Spirit in a World Gone Mad with Commerce." Still, I fundamentally disagree with that defensive posture. I do not "do it for myself." I never have. I do it, precisely, to connect. I recall, Harry, how you connected through your sermons. They may have been a torment for you to write, but they were certainly loved by your parishioners. I recall that somewhere in my own boxed archives I have ancient recordings of a few them on those old cassette tapes. I would love to hear your voice again, but in all probability, even if I could find those tapes and they have not eroded, the machine no longer exists to play them on.

You had your pulpit. I have been fortunate to find publishers—small presses for poetry, national magazines for my writing about art and artists, commercial book publishers for my novels (I recently re-read my mystery novel, *Dirty-Down*, published back in the 1980s, and was pleased to find an accurate representation of the Los Angeles art world there!) But I'm also fortunate to have lived at the dawn of the digital age, with the vast universe of the Internet at my fingertips. For twenty years and more I have been a blogger—something you would not have heard of, Harry, a kind of diarist in this new medium, a sometime essayist, commentator, able to share my thoughts and observations with readers literally throughout the world. And responses come, too, from literally throughout the world, long-distant echoes reverberating back to me and reassuring me that my words have been listened to, and heard, and that they have touched hearts and minds, as your words did in the confines of your church. Which was enough, back then. Which is enough for me now when I allow myself the credit.

Your son,
Peter

23 November 2021

Dear Harry,

There was a further step I needed to take in my work with The Mankind Project. If the New Warrior Training Adventure was boot camp for the heart, ahead of me still was boot camp for the soul. I found it in the form of a week-long retreat that was called, appropriately, Warrior Monk.

Remember how you once gave thought to becoming a monk? I believe you even spent a while as a novice in a monastery—how long before Peggy rescued you? For myself, it was no monastery but a retreat center at Glen Ivy Hot Springs, an oasis nestled in an otherwise arid valley that lies between the hills to the east of Los Angeles. Devised and led by Bill Kauth, one of the founders of the initiation training that led to the MKP organization, Warrior Monk was a week-long exercise in what might best be described as spiritual discipline— nothing so rigorous, of course, as the years of training required of the Zen monk or the Benedictine, nor the exercises that traditionally undergird the Jesuit priesthood, but something along those lines. Monk lite, we might say, here in America. The call I felt to sign up for the retreat was prompted, I think, by the need to probe even deeper into the structure of my own psyche—and perhaps, I realized only much later, to set out on a path that you had modeled for me. I was not interested in finding Christ, nor the salvation that He offered but I was beginning to feel the absence of spiritual commitment of some kind and wondering how that might look. Through reading, thought and practice I had come to embrace the notion that there are four essential components in the fully integrated human being—four quadrants, if you will: the physical, the emotional, the intellectual, and the spiritual. Some call them Lover, Warrior, Magician, King. Some find their attributes in the four corners, east, south, west, and north. The ideal, I learned, was to achieve as perfect as possible a balance between the four to achieve a mature "integrity".

So, I went in search of spirit, and the Monk week put me through my paces. Each day our small group marched in solemn procession to the nearby hilltop to greet the rising sun and celebrate the four directions; we alternated periods of silent meditation with rigorous exercise; we walked in solitary silence, attentive to the movement of each muscle with each steep; we ate simple meals from a single bowl and cleaned our bowl carefully after each meal; we chanted, men's voices raised in unison; in the sufi tradition, we danced every evening like whirling dervishes. The climax of the week was a night-long vigil, each in our own "cell", a dark night of the soul in which we were each exhorted to do battle with our inner demons. I stripped naked, fasted, fought off fatigue and engaged the enemies: my pride, my guilt, my sexual desire, my ever-demanding libido. My self-pity, my pathetic feelings of inadequacy, my need for recognition. They all came visiting in turn. In the pitch darkness of my cell, I made a point of welcoming each of them as though a physical presence, a body to be wrestled with and sent packing. When the daylight finally broke through and the bell rang, summoning us to morning devotions, I felt cleansed.

I am no monk, Harry. I have no urge to be one. I am not tempted by the material sacrifices that the spiritual life demands. I understand that week as drama, akin to the drama of the warrior weekend. It was play. But we know, Harry—is this not true?—that play is serious. Along with our tragic heroes, we purge our weaknesses and flaws every time we watch them played out on the stage. It is that much more powerful when we play them out ourselves. What I brought away from that week at Glen Ivy was a reconnection with a part of myself that I had not lost, but neglected, the part that sat as a small boy and watched you at the altar, the part that, as an older boy, served you at Communion, the part that sang in the choir and knelt beside my bed each night to pray.

As you served, Harry, so did I. Gladly. I served as a staff member in the drama of the many warrior weekends, most often in the role of the Elder, entitled to bless. I served as a staffer on at least one Warrior Monk week—maybe two. That feeble memory, again!

With love,
Peter

24 November 2021

Dear Harry,

How you would have loved to spend time with your grandchildren, now that they are no longer the little children you remember playing with on the beach at Aberporth. That rubber dinghy! How they loved it! What a great time you had! Can you believe that Matthew and Jason are now middle-aged men? Matthew is approaching his sixtieth birthday in a couple of years, Jason passing his mid-fifties! Even Sarah—that pretty little girl!—will soon be fifty! You would be so interested, so proud of each of them. Let me tell you a bit about the good people that they are today.

Matthew, your oldest grandson, lives in England, not much more than a stone's throw from your parishes in Bedfordshire and Hertfordshire, Aspley Guise, Braughing, Sharnbrook. He has been married for almost twenty-five years to a beautiful woman—her mother Finnish, her father from an English Jewish family, both still alive and in their nineties. Together, Matthew (he goes by Matt to everyone but me) and Diane have three grown children, two still at university, one out into the world. They have worked for many years in the financial world, writing, editing, and translating from Japanese into English for international banking companies. Matthew has been much wrapped up in being the wonderful, dedicated father that he has been to their three children; for most of their lives, he has been the family's chief cook and bottle-washer. From you, Harry, he inherited the thespian gene. He has loved the stage since high school days and even recently, until our current pandemic struck, was playing supporting and lead roles in local amateur theatrics, particularly musicals. How you'd have loved to see him ham it up in *The Pirates of Penzance* or *The Producers*!

Jason, too, has the creative gene. He is a dedicated, skilled, and passionate guitarist—has been all his life since he was a teenage boy. He still lives in Iowa, near where he and Matthew lived with their mom while they were growing up. He makes a good living working for an educational testing company where he is clearly much valued and respected after years of rising through the ranks. I'm sad—more for myself, I suppose—that he has chosen not to marry and have children like his brother, but he seems happy with his choice. He has created a great life for himself, with an impressive, professionally organized music studio in his small, tidy house, along with a much-loved dog, Louis, a sporty car and two motorcycles. He plays gigs, mostly jazz and classical, and mostly solo these days, after years of performing with bands. He has emerged just recently from a successful, but to all of us a truly anguishing battle with bladder cancer. While a bit of a cynic, frankly, but a cheerful one, he has a good heart, and observes his fellow humans with a bemused and skeptical eye.

As for Sarah . . . she was with us just yesterday. In fact, to be close to her son's elementary school, she has taken to working here in our house every day. Like so many people today because of the pandemic, she works remotely, away from the office, thanks to the ubiquitous computer. (Don't even ask!) She has been working now for a good number of years for the widely known and universally respected American Film Institute, where she manages the catalog that documents a hundred years of American film. A couple of years ago, she was awarded a major grant from the National Endowment for a project to study the neglected contribution of women in early Hollywood. She now has another grant application under review, to expand the catalog's reach to include overlooked communities of color. You would appreciate her social conscience, her dedication to equality and justice, and to the well being of our shared global environment. Most importantly, though, she is the single mom of a nine-year-old boy—a tough, full-time occupation in itself—and is making a wonderful job of it. We wish for her the stable and satisfying partnership she longs for, like yours, Harry, with Pegs, or like ours. As it is, she has a good, solid, caring man in her life— who sadly lives in Amsterdam. Which is not an easy commute, especially in the time of Covid-19.

So, there you go, Harry. Your grandchildren. Even spending time with them—always too short!—as little kids, you must have known they would grow up to be substantial people, committed to the values we have always shared as a family. They have good roots, creative genes (apart from her other talents, Sarah is a truly gifted writer), and a sense of responsibility to their fellow beings on this planet. In short, they have much of you in them, and much of Peggy too. And I hope a little of their parents. I wish you could have known them as they are today.

But that was not to be. Matthew must have been in his early twenties when you died but living at that time in Japan; Jason in his late teens, and Sarah not much more than ten years old. How quickly the time passes, Harry, and I've noticed as I'm sure you must have too, how its passage continues to accelerate as the years accumulate.

With love,
Peter

26 November 2021

Dear Harry,

So strange! As I wrote down the date above it struck me that it's on your birthday that I'm writing to you about your death! These non-coincidences—I refuse to accept them as coincidences—persist in haunting me as I write . . .

It was my former brother-in-law and still our good friend, John, who called to let me know that you were dying. It was not unexpected. You were old, as I am now, and had lived through a great deal of sickness and suffering. You had witnessed the historic barbarity of two world wars and the horrors of the Holocaust, of Hiroshima and Nagasaki. You had watched the progress from the first primitive flying machines to jumbo jets and supersonic fighter planes, from the crackling static of early cat's whisker radio to high-definition television, from the clumsy upright typewriter to the personal computer (I had my first, a Kaypro, several years before you died. It weighed a ton and had exponentially less capacity than today's slim laptops). You saw atom bombs and nuclear bombs and you watched men walk on the surface of the moon. You died before the advent of today's ubiquitous smart phones with their capacity for video chats and immense data storage, but I tend to think you didn't miss much on this account. I hate the things—but like everyone else on the planet, I use mine all the time. Since when you were born, the world has changed immeasurably, and not always for the better.

The doctors told John and Flora, both in attendance, that you had little time left to live. If we wanted the opportunity to spend a few moments with you one last time before you left this plane of existence we would need to grab seats on the next flight from Los Angeles and make our way to the hospital in Cardigan.

Of course, I wanted to say goodbye. This was not long after the men's weekend I recently described and I was still full of the elation that resulted, proud of having faced you down and eager to share with you my need for liberation from our past. And now here was perhaps my last and only chance to close the gap I had always sensed between us before it was too late, to show you that my heart was open to forgiveness and love—and to ask for yours.

Ellie and I flew to Heathrow and took the train to Wales. Your narrow bed was in a rather grim hospital ward, just one in a row of identical others, reminding me of those scenes in old black and white war movies, with wounded soldiers lined up in anonymous rows. The doctor greeted us, confirming in a whispered conversation what John had told us; you had not long to live.

Oh, Harry, you looked so lost and vulnerable! You lay there like a child, seeming to try so hard, without success, to understand what was happening to you and around you. Your eyes were milky, distant, searching for some assurance, some anchor in the world you were about to leave. We each of us spent some time in turn alone with you, each seeking in our own way to say what needed to be said.

I took your hand in mine when my turn came. Fresh from my recent experience and full of self-assurance, I wanted more than anything to be honest with you in a way I had never been in the past. I cannot know how much you understood of what I said, but I tried so hard to say it all. It seemed important, for example, to share my loss of faith. For years, I had kept up that pretense. I would go to church to please you and avoid having to admit the uncomfortable truth for fear of hurting you; it was many years since I abandoned the last shred of belief in the God you spent your whole life serving. Equally important, it seemed to me, was to let you know that I had never felt your love, and how much I needed it. Honesty required me to tell you the whole truth, I thought, in my newly acquired commitment to total authenticity.

I hope now that you didn't hear any of this nonsense. As I look back on it, it seems a needless, rather selfish act of cruelty. Such things should have been shared courageously, while you could still hear what I had to say and be able to respond. We could have talked things out between us, man to man. My now more careful reading of your long-neglected letters assures me that you would have listened, that what I chose to keep hidden for fear of causing you pain was more cowardice on my part than consideration for your feelings. You were always perfectly capable of listening, anxious even. Your letters made this clear; the door was always open. It was I who lacked the courage to step through. We could have had a good old talk and come together afterwards with a hug and a mutual assurance of our love.

One thing was unquestionably real, though, at your deathbed. I did need your blessing. At the end of our one-sided "conversation" at least I knew enough to ask for this. Whether or not you heard or understood me, I reminded you of the blessing you used to give me as a child at the altar rail every Sunday, before I was old enough to take communion. Your now feeble hand no longer had the strength to do what I asked of you, so I took it in mine and laid it on my head. It mattered little that your mind could no longer summon up the words, nor that I no longer remembered them. I received your blessing anyway, wordlessly, and it has been with me in the years that have passed since then.

So now I can thank you for that blessing, Harry. It was the best of all ways to say goodbye.

In loving memory, your son,
Peter

27 November 2021

Dear Harry,

But then you did not die. You refused to die as you were supposed to do.

It was shortly after that "final" blessing that you rallied! Ellie recalls you sitting up cheerfully suddenly in your deathbed and demanding ice cream!

You were still obstinately alive when the time came for our planned return to Los Angeles.

I have thought about this often, Harry, puzzled by the fact that you were so reluctant to meet the merciful , all-loving God in whom you struggled to believe. Perhaps the doubts you hinted at so many times—we never got to discuss them, did we? More's the pity—came back with sudden intensity to delay your passage at that moment. Perhaps your intellectual skepticism kicked back in when you were confronted with the imminence of either heaven or hell—though you surely could not have believed that you deserved the latter? No matter the reason, you declined the opportunity to leave us when the time came. It was with a certain naughty pride and self-satisfaction, I believe, that you chose to prove the doctors wrong.

We left eventually Ellie and I. We were thousands of miles away in California when you could no longer resist and deigned to surrender up your spirit to the inevitable call of death. I wonder, was my trusty namesake waiting for you at the gate when you arrived there, rattling his keys? I always liked that image, even if I never believed in it as a reality. If Peter was waiting, though, I can be sure that he unlocked the gate and waved you on through. You had earned your place in Paradise. Heaven could wait!

I had wanted to be at your bedside when you died, but I was not. Flora called us in Los Angeles to let us know you were gone, and we chose not to return to Wales so soon for your funeral. We could not afford another trip, we told ourselves. (No, that's an evasion: *I* told *myself* . . .) I came to understand later that this was a mistake. I used money as the pretext. I persuaded myself that you would neither have wanted nor expected us to have gone to such expense. But I should have known better. There are more important things than money and the proper fulfillment of such once-in-a-lifetime ritual responsibilities is one of them.

I chose instead, wrongly, as I see it now, to leave those responsibilities to Flora. She had your mortal remains cremated and I have wondered ever since if I should have tried to persuade her otherwise. I think your choice would have been to return your body to the earth, like those many men and women that you buried in your time. You stood over so many open graves, your black cassock and white surplice shifting in the breeze as you recited the haunting words of committal from the Book of Common Prayer: "We therefore commit this body to the ground, earth to earth, ashes to ashes, dust to dust; in sure and certain hope of the Resurrection to eternal life."

The words resonate, Harry: "We commit this body to the ground." I believe this is what you would have wanted and am saddened by the thought that I failed to insist on the same ritual you performed for those countless souls who went before you. As for that "sure and certain hope of the Resurrection to eternal life . . ." Well, as you know Harry, I'm not sure and certain about that eternal life, and I suspect you were not either. But that's for another letter.

> With love, as always, your son,
> Peter

29 November 2021

Dear Harry,

You'll know about it now, of course, if there is anything to know. The afterlife, I mean. That "Resurrection to eternal life." The alternative is what I believed for most of my adult life: that death is not only the end of the physical body but the end of consciousness as well. That we live, then die into oblivion.

Now, I'm not so sure. As you may have noticed, we tend to grow less sure of things as we grow older! The only thing I am sure of is the not-knowing. Which I suppose is a good place to be.

I say it again: I do not believe in God. I do not believe there's either a heaven where we can enjoy eternal life in fields of bliss, or a hell to keep us burning horribly in that same forever. That's for Bosch. Hieronymus, I mean. I do not believe, as some do, fervently, that we shall all be reunited with our loved ones when the last trumpet sounds. I do not believe in my seven virgins, in the unlikely event that I happen to die a martyr. It would be nice to think, like those ancient Egyptians (among others: I think of similar Norse myths and burial practices) that I could sail away to the next world in a bark laden with all my earthly possessions.

Not a chance. I would not want them anyway. I'm beginning to feel burdened enough by them while I'm still alive.

I have the same difficulty when it comes to the Buddhist concept of rebirth. (You'll be reading more shortly, Harry, about my near-embrace of Buddhism). The Buddha himself is supposed to have looked back over 554 previous lives before entering the realm of the deathless. I had the rather more modest experience myself of visiting two "past lives" in a session with a kind friend who believed in such things; I was not the only one he led back in trance states to what he sincerely believed to be prior existences. He encouraged me to take that trip with him at a time when I needed healing from a period of great emotional and spiritual upheaval. It was an interesting and in truth a deeply compelling experience.

It started as I lay back on a bed and closed my eyes, listening to my friend's reassuring voice at first as he led me back, purportedly through centuries of time, and invited me to encounter the being I once was. All at once I found myself (really, Harry!) in the early Middle Ages. Everything around me, everything that happened had that hyper-reality of dream. It felt, well . . . true—and quite terrifying. I was in the act of committing murder. With a dagger. My victim was clearly known to me, although in some corner of my mind I struggled to know who he was—an enemy. I found myself, felt myself, physically stabbing him, not once, but multiple times until he was dead. My punishment followed immediately. I was to be hanged for my crime. Again, I literally felt the noose around my neck, tightening as they hoisted me on the limb of a tree and left me hanging. There, on the bed, in the present moment, I was squirming violently, grasping at my throat. (Yes, Harry, how perfect! Shades of your skipping rope! Figure that one out!

Was my punishment being recapitulated at the moment of my rebirth, centuries later? Was this, um . . . "karma"? These are mysteries, we can agree, that we are not given to understand).

My friend must have been alarmed. He calmed me down and was intent on guiding me back through the centuries when I made an instinctive, unanticipated stop in Victorian times. Again, the context seemed very real, very immediate—a formal dining room not unlike the one in the Rectory at Aspley Guise. I was a child, a pre-teenage boy, so fat my belly was bursting out of the waistline of my pantaloons like Tweedledee. No matter, I was unable to stop gorging myself. I kept shoveling ever more food into my mouth until, like a balloon, I literally burst.

Past lives? Nightmares, induced by that trance state? Life experience, my deepest fears made manifest in the form of the grotesque? I do not know and cannot explain to you, Harry, what was happening to me on that bed. I can only assure you that it felt overwhelmingly real, overwhelmingly convincing.

I hope that my other past lives, if other past lives I had, were less horrifying than these. From what I understand of karma, the moment of our death is important in determining our next incarnation and a part of the purpose of the meditation practice is to prepare us for that moment, to assure our passage in a calm and fearless state of mind. I see the point . . . and I do spend a good amount of time, in meditation, with thoughts of death. My death. I know some older people hope for nothing better than to pass on peacefully in their sleep. I understand this. But my own hope—and I acknowledge that I will have little choice in the manner of my death—is to die consciously, fully aware of what is happening as I make that final journey. I have read of monks who died sitting quietly, motionless in meditation. They had put in far more training, obviously, than I will ever do, and were better prepared for death than I will ever be, but it would be wonderful to have the strength of mind to emulate that amazing equanimity.

There is a pleasing logic to Buddhist thought and ethics, Harry, which is what appeals to me about it. No external agency governing our lives, punishing, or rewarding us according to a set of rules we do not fully understand. No, it all comes back, always, to ourselves, our actions, how we choose to live: "We are", the text of the Sublime Attitudes reads, "the owners of our actions, heir to our actions, related through our actions, and live dependent on our actions. Whatever we do, for good or evil, to that will we fall heir."

I'm pretty sure this thinking would appeal to you, too.

With love,
Peter

30 November 2021

Dear Harry,

So yes, coming back to your death, I was sad not to have been present. I would wish to have been at your side, supporting you with love as you started out on your final journey. It seems to me the kind of job a son should do, so it bothers me to feel that I failed you in some respect. I have watched other people die and I found the experience, strangely perhaps, to be a joy and a privilege. I watched one person die in pain and anger, another in serenity and peace. Both deaths were liberations from the burdens of the flesh, but I know which one I'd choose.

Let me tell you about Ellie's mother, Laurie. You did not know her well—not as well as you knew Mike and Dossy, but you met her. I believe that she, too, visited you once in Aberporth. She died sometime after you and she had the good fortune—the fulfilled intention?—to die at home. I must admit quite honestly that I was not able, during her life, to return her love in quite the measure of generosity that she gave it. *Mea culpa.* I nursed judgments that were too often unkind, projections that reflected poorly on myself. She was an artist. We have one of her quite beautiful and skillfully executed early paintings, not untypical of the 1930s when they were painted. It hangs over the bed in our Laguna Beach cottage, a reminder of her spirit. When she moved from New York to California, she transitioned in her art from painting to ceramic sculpture, and we also have an elegant clay pelican standing by the Buddha fountain in our back patio. She converted the garage behind her house into a studio with, alongside it, a large kiln, and she not only made her own work there for many years, but she also used the studio as a place to welcome her devoted students. A sprightly woman even as she aged, she continued teaching until well into her nineties.

She died an exemplary death; I think at the age of 93. Perhaps sensing the imminence of her life's end and without the energy or will to resist it further, she took to her bed one day and never again left it. She lay there quietly for about two weeks, taking no sustenance but the sips of water we applied to her lips, wrapped up calmly within herself and no longer speaking or paying attention to anything around her. Hoping to repair some remaining tension between mother and daughter before her death, I encouraged her at one point to assure Ellie that she loved her, and without a murmur, she found the strength to move her now enfeebled, scrawny hand to touch Ellie's face, stroking it with only the gentlest of pressure and returning just a moment later, quietly, to that place of internal serenity where she was resting. More days passed peacefully in this way before the hospice nurse informed us that the end was very near. We sat and held her hands and watched as Laurie's breaths began to come further apart, and further, lighter, and shallower until, sensing the approach of death we began to count the intervals between those breaths and monitor the interval as it slowly increased. And finally, quietly, the moment came when the next breath simply didn't come at all, and she was gone.

It was at that moment that Ellie happened to glance through her mother's bedroom window, across the lawn to the studio, and saw a dove fly off from the studio roof and disappear into the sky . . .

Laurie's death was a final gift to her daughter and myself—a death so beautiful it leaves me regretful for not having been more responsive to her kindness and her childlike vulnerability while she was still alive.

I would wish such a death for myself and those I love.

Your son,
Peter

1 December 2021

Dear Harry,

It was no surprise that your darling Peggy did not survive you for too long (you always called her darling and she, you). After you left us, she no longer had the physical strength or will to take care of herself in your beloved Glenview cottage, but it must have been a wrench for her to leave the place where you had spent so many years together. Having now reached that same age myself, I am thankful to be mostly fit in mind and body, but I dread the prospect of dependency, of needing help to do the smallest and most intimate things, and especially of having to move from a treasured home of many years into some kind of impersonal assisted living facility. All of which is possible . . .

I flew across to visit Peggy once she was installed in her new home in Newcastle-Emlyn, a few miles over the hill and inland from Aberporth. She was reasonably comfortable and well taken care of so far as I could tell, a "lady" much liked and respected by staff and fellow residents alike. She was content, quietly accepting of her situation, but she was not happy. How could she be? You had rarely been apart. As well as everything else, you were solid companions on the journey of your life together. Now she spent almost all her time alone in her own little room, and much of it in bed. Her window looked out over the lush green valley of the lovely river Teifi, and in this sense, in the countryside of her native Wales, she felt at home. She had always been a great nature lover. On our walks, when I was growing up, she could name every different tree and wildflower that we passed, and every bird just by its song, its plumage, or its flight pattern. Like her mother before her, she would bring flowers home with her to press between the pages of her books, just as Victorian ladies used to do.

I held her hand a lot. It was so soft, so emptied of energy and resistance. We talked, exchanging memories—though there was much she had forgotten. I think it's fair to say that she looked forward to the moment when she could take her leave of a life that had become a burden she no longer wished to carry. Did she hope to join you in the afterlife? Perhaps she did, and I would like to think she got her wish.

Again, having spent time with her shortly before her death, I chose not to make the long journey back for her funeral. She, too, was cremated. Her ashes are interred alongside yours, Harry, in a tiny, shared plot in the cemetery of St. Cymwyl's church in Aberporth, high up the hill overlooking the Cardigan Bay.

Ellie and I visited there once, some years after your death, and Peggy's, and stood together for a while in silence, the wind off the Irish Sea blowing through our hair. As I think back to that occasion, what comes to mind is Goethe's lovely poem, "*Über allen Gipfeln*". In Longfellow's translation it's titled "O'er all the hilltops." Here it is, in its original mellifluent German (I know you can't read it, but let me enjoy the music of the language for you):

Über allen Gipfeln
Ist Ruh.
In allen Wipfeln
Spürest du
Kaum einen Hauch;
Die Vögelein schweigen im Walde.
Warte nur, balde
Ruhest du auch.

In Longfellow's translation, the poem reads thus: "O'er all the hill-tops/Is quiet now,/In all the tree-tops/Hearest thou/Hardly a breath;/The birds are asleep in the trees:/Wait; soon like these/Thou too shalt rest." The translation is literally quite close to the original, but what it fails to capture is the music, the lyrical perfection of this tiny poem. Its magic reaches a climax in the barely pronounced, lilting "e" sound at the end of those three words, *Walde, warte, balde,* sounds that trail off quietly, imperceptibly into silence, as though leading the reader's mind into the infinite . . . "*Warte nur, balde, Ruhest du auch*"—you too will rest. Those words in the final line come beckoning, the gentlest and most seductive of all invitations to leave this mortal life behind.

And I confess, I take it personally.

Your son,
Peter

2 December 2021

Dear Harry,

Nothing ever really "belongs" to us, does it? Not really. Everything we think we own, everything we think gives meaning to our lives, everything we gather around us as we go—it all disperses. Scatters. Some of it will belong to someone else. Some of it, Harry . . . well, most of it, perhaps, is junk.

Was it before or after Peggy's death that Flora and I stood together, with Ellie, for one last time in your Aberporth cottage? It was to be sold. No point in hanging on to it. The decision between me and Flora was that old adage: everything must go. Emptied of your presence, both of you, the little house felt almost alien, as though we were strangers arriving on a strange, now long forgotten planet. There was the tall, wingback easy chair where you would sit every morning without fail to read your "office", the *Book of Common Prayer* spread open on your knees; where you would sit later the same morning, tamping down the shredded tobacco in your intricate little machine to make yourself a smoke. Above it, on the wall, the colorful Frank Brangwyn print of Venice I so well remembered from its place in the drawing room at Aspley Guise. There was the old-fashioned television set, its screen empty, a big, dead eye, where you used to watch the news each evening and maybe a mystery. More rituals. There was the three-legged stool, its chevron seat hand-carved with the coat of arms of our old Cambridge college, Caius ("2 serpents in pale," the heraldry handbook quaintly reminds me, "their tails knit together, all proper.")

In the little dining room, we contemplated for the last time the table we gathered around to enjoy the food that Peggy so deliciously prepared in the kitchen, where you stood to say grace before the meal, where you honed the carving knife (the sound of steel on steel still rings in my ears), touching the blade with a finger to test its edge before carving, meticulously, the roast. Against the wall, the lovely antique Welsh dresser from Penparc cottage, Peggy's parents' Aberporth home, its shelves lined with the Blue Willow plates and bowls, platters, and vegetable dishes that you used for every meal. The napkins and tablecloths folded neatly in the drawers. The silver service chest with its gleaming knives and forks and spoons.

On the sun porch at the back of the house, past the dining room, a pile of half-read magazines and a bag of unfinished knitting beside Peggy's favorite chair. Beyond, beneath the now neglected fruit trees, the lawn you used to mow was overgrown, unkept . . .

We had to choose. Obviously, Ellie and I could not hope to take that beautiful Welsh dresser back to Los Angeles with us, nor the dining table and chairs. We had to content ourselves with small stuff. I chose the oak clock with the delicate deco inlay, the one with the familiar, reassuring tick and chime that had stood for years on the mantlepiece in the nursery at Aspley Guise. The broken Delft platter, a family heirloom that had once, so the story went, belonged to William of Orange. The Burleigh tea set with a delicate iris pattern which is now displayed, lovingly, in your granddaughter Sarah's house not far from where we live. And of course—how could I resist—the stool with the Caius College crest. It is now in my own study, here in Los Angeles. One day, I hope it will be in the hands of your great-granddaughter, Georgia, now a Caius girl—there were only Caius men, in our day! My cupidity aroused by all these wonderful relics, I was aware of the desire to take them all, to bring them all home with me—as though I needed them. And then there was the delicate matter of Peggy's jewelry . . . Who would get what? Who would get the better, the prettier, the more valuable pieces of those sometimes-handsome baubles that you, Harry, had bought for her over the years? Ellie gladly ceded the field to Flora, of course.

It was all so sad, Harry, these objects that were a familiar part of your daily lives, objects by which you and Peggy defined yourselves: this is who we are—everything touched more often by your hands than all the years could count. Things to be passed on now—re-cycled, is the word that's popular today— repurposed, resettled in a new environment where they are no longer quite the same things that they were before. We plundered what we could, your heirs. Took what we thought might be useful, what might be valuable, what might remind us of you, of our childhood and of times long past.

The rest? We had it picked up wholesale by the local auctioneer with instructions to sell what he could. Who knows what he did with what he couldn't sell? It could have been donated for charity; I suppose. Or just thrown out. Like junk.

All of which has me thinking of that great Buddhist mantra: This is not me; this is not mine; this is not who I am.

Sadly,
Peter

4 December 2021

Good Sunday morning, Harry,

Because it's Sunday here in Southern California as I write these words. The month is December, and the year is 2021. I am now 85 years old. I was writing just a couple of days ago about Peggy. Had she lived, she would have been one hundred and fifteen! Imagine! As usual, Harry, I will not go to church today. But I'm remembering all those Sundays that we did, as a family, in Aspley Guise, Braughing, Sharnbrook . . . your parishes. We never missed, as children; nor did I ever dare to miss even after leaving home when I came back to stay with you. It still saddens me to remember that, even though I no longer believed, I felt compelled to keep up the pretense.

Before the current terrible pandemic that rages here in America and throughout the world, I had adopted a different Sunday ritual, joining a little meditation group that gathered in a home near our cottage in Laguna Beach. It was closed when the pandemic hit when we could no longer sit together safely. Though we called ourselves a "sangha", this was actually not a correct use of the word which originally applied to the groups of monks who followed in the Buddha's footsteps. None of us, certainly, was a monk. Or a nun! I joined the group in its early days, in the mid-1990s, soon after I first became interested in meditation. It started when a friend invited me to learn about the practice of a group that he was involved with, Nichiren Buddhism, which involved the constant, repetitious chanting of a single phrase from the Lotus Sutra, *nam myoho renge kyo*. You could chant, he told me, with specific intention, to achieve whatever it was you needed in your life—all the way from finding peace of mind to healing a sick child . . . to getting that new car you always wanted! I found that chanting helped me to develop considerable inner strength and serenity, not to mention quite startling success in achieving my intentions: at one point I was chanting obsessively for a seaside cottage in Laguna Beach and . . . well, you know how that ended up!

Still, the time came when I began to feel uncomfortable with the practice. There was, as I saw it, an incongruence between its supposedly spiritual orientation and its material, goal-oriented intentions. At around the same time, it happened that I was introduced by another teacher—this time at the same Esalen Institute I had long maligned—to the alternative of silent meditation and I was soon finding it rewarding to sit silently for ten or fifteen minutes a day than chanting for a half hour or more. Then I heard about the Laguna Beach sitting group. I called to inquire about it and the nice lady (now my long-time, wonderful friend, Eva) explained that they would meet every Sunday and sit for an hour before opening up for a second hour of discussion.

An hour! The prospect was intimidating. An hour was as long as one of your Parish Masses on a Sunday morning, Harry, but without the distraction of a single word of prayer, let alone standing up occasionally to belt out a hymn! An hour of sitting in total silence on a cushion, with nothing but my always busy mind to keep me company! I had only just begun to learn how to minimize the intrusion of those fleeting thoughts for a few minutes by watching them pass by without latching onto them; I had only just begun to learn how to deal with the recurring distractions of physical discomfort—the endless aches and pains—and those ever-shifting emotions.

Ten minutes was a challenge. But an hour!

So yes, the first time I joined my sitting friends, the mind wandered off, looking desperately for something, anything, to keep it entertained. The knees, bent into that unnatural and unaccustomed cross-legged position, began to ache until they screamed. Seconds stretched out into minutes, minutes into an eternity. But then . . . the bell sounded. The hour was done. I had not just survived, I had triumphed!

That was the start. I soon became accustomed to that Sunday morning hour, even to enjoy the opportunity to let go of life's other contingencies and simply sit. And the years went by. Our group had been gathering every Sunday for twenty-five years and more before the pandemic struck.

I alluded to the Buddhist theory of karma in an earlier letter. Next time I write, I'll introduce you to the Thai Forest Buddhist monk who came once a month to lead us in our meditations. It was he who taught me about karma, along with other aspects of the Buddhist teachings in his dharma talks. I first came to know him as Than Geoff ("Than" translates as "monk") but his proper name is Thanissaro Bhikkhu and his birth name was Geoffrey de Graff. Since becoming abbot of the Metta Forest Monastery, his proper mode of address is Ajaan. He is a man of profound knowledge and compassion, of deep conviction, and you and he would have had much to talk about.

Enough, now, for this Sunday morning. More later!

With love,
Peter

5 December 2021

Dear Harry,

Since those beginnings, now more than twenty-five years ago, meditation has been my daily practice. I am more than grateful to have brought it into my life. When I first started, I was able to sit with relative ease in the conventional pose, cross-legged, with a straight back and hands folded comfortably in my lap. Now that my bones and joints lack the flexibility of youth—or, truthfully, the discipline of rigorous practice—I choose to use a chair, but the process is the same: unwavering attention on the breath and coming back to the breath every time the mind wanders off, as it still tends to do! It's a discipline that has helped me immeasurably with mental focus, clarity, and control, and one that helps me return to equanimity when emotions gain the upper hand. It gives me the opportunity to look at my life with some remove, to reflect upon my actions—what causes them and what their outcome is—and to change course when it seems necessary. The end goal, as the Buddha taught, is release from suffering, the happiness a person can achieve when no longer driven by ego, delusions, or desires. Am I "happy", then? Let's say that I catch glimpses of that happiness.

We have talked about service, Harry, and my practice has opened new opportunities to share its benefits with others.

About five years ago, I put out word on a local communications network (another concept you would have no reason to be familiar with!) inviting neighbors to join me for a weekly meditation session. A few accepted, forming the nucleus of a still-expanding group that meets regularly—virtually since the pandemic, with the aid of our computers—on Wednesday evenings. Drawing on what I have learned from Than Geoff over the years, I guide the group in meditation for the first twenty minutes or so, then leave participants to move on into their own silent sit for a similar amount of time. Then we talk. Sometimes serious talk about serious things, sometimes chit-chat. The whole thing takes just an hour, and everyone leaves feeling a little happier, I hope, and a little more in tune with their inner life. It's a bit like going to church. I'm a bit like you, dare I say, in leading the ceremony . . .

It's a "service."

The other way I have found to be of service through my meditation practice is something I call "One Hour/One Painting." Combining the ancient skills of meditation and contemplation, I invite small groups of participants to sit with me for a full hour in front of a single painting. I start out with a little basic instruction in closed-eye meditation, then walk my participants through an hour of alternating intense moments of open-eyed contemplation of the chosen painting and closed-eye meditation. Most people walk past paintings in museums and galleries with barely a second glance and imagine they have "seen" them. At most, they pause for long enough to look at the wall tag and read the name of the artist and the title of the painting. "One Hour/One Painting" offers a whole new way of looking at art—one that gives the painting the chance to work its magic. I have offered this experience at various museums and galleries for the past twenty years and more, and the response is reliably grateful and enthusiastic. In this high-speed world we have created, people have little opportunity to slow down, take a breath, and focus their attention, and when they're offered it, they respond with genuine delight. In some small way, then, I have been able to change lives. I have even been able, in my way, to do what you were able to do in your churches: connect people with an important part of their lives that too often goes neglected.

For this privilege, too, as well as for the desire to serve others in this way, I am grateful for the example that you gave me.

Your son,
Peter

6 December 2021

Dear Harry,

I promised to follow up with more about Than Geoff and Buddhism, and this morning I woke thinking about prayer, and the difference between Christian prayer and the metta practice that I learned from Than Geoff—the practice of sending out thoughts of goodwill and compassion.

First, though, Than Geoff. As I said, you would have liked him enormously, had you known him—and he, you. He is a soft-spoken man, but the softness of his voice belies a rigorous and gently challenging attitude toward the teaching of the dharma and the meditation practice. The Thai Forest tradition is what I hope to rightly describe as back-to-basics, no frills Theravada Buddhism. Than Geoff, though, is no straight-laced moralist. He is also blessed with a delightful, sometimes irreverent sense of humor. Like you, he is a great storyteller, enchanted with the vagaries of human behavior, and like you he loves the response of an audience. Tolerant of the beliefs of others, he is quite firm in his own. He takes seriously the questions of skeptics like me and answers them persuasively from the vast depth of his knowledge and experience. Like myself, he is a writer and translator, and has published more books than I could count. How he finds time to do everything is beyond my comprehension, let alone how he manages to do all of it so well.

Because I had it in mind to talk to you about this, I asked him just the other day about prayer. It was you and Peggy, of course, who taught me to pray. Me and Flora, both. Every night it was down on our knees at bedtime in our pajamas, hands clasped together in front of our faces, asking God to take care of us, our family, our friends, our country and our soldiers, sailors, and airmen in the time of war. If we had been bad, we could pray to Him for forgiveness, too. If we prayed hard enough, we'd be forgiven.

We never missed a night, not once. It was the evening ritual. First there was story time, then it was prayers before bed, and then lights out. I remember even having to say our prayers at Christmas time, with all the excitement and those empty stockings stretched out at the foot of our beds.

With the war going on there was good reason to pray.

We prayed in church too, of course. You would lead the prayers, up in front, and the whole congregation prayed with you. The words of many of those prayers, so often repeated, were forever imprinted on my mind.

I stopped praying when I was a teenager. I think I stopped even earlier at home when Flora and I each had our own room and no one came in any more to tuck us in at bedtime. By that time, I think it was just assumed that the children said their prayers. We still prayed at school, of course. We all had to go to chapel every day. There were morning prayers in the assembly hall and evening prayers in chapel. Sundays, we prayed three times a day, once in the morning, once in the evening, and a third time if you decided to attend the optional early communion service in the small chapel down below in the crypt. There was no way I could avoid being present in all this, at least in body. The mind was a different matter. My mind was always wandering off elsewhere. At some point, I stopped joining in with the general recitation of the words. I did not believe them; I could not bring myself to say them. I listened with a growing skepticism, with the scorn of an adolescent disbeliever while others said them. At bedtime, I no longer ever got down on my knees.

I have never prayed since. As I came to understand it, praying meant having someone or something to pray *to*, some superior being or powerful entity that could "answer" your prayer and grant you what you wished. Or not. For someone like myself, I thought, whose endlessly superior intelligence discounted the existence of that someone or something, prayer could have no meaning and no serious purpose.

As I learned more about Buddhism through Than Geoff, however, I came to appreciate what seemed a bit like what I remembered about prayer. As he taught it, the first essential step in meditation was the practice of *metta*, sending out thoughts of loving-kindness and compassion first to ourselves, then to those closest to us, those we love, then out in ever-expanding circles to every other living being: May we all find true happiness in our lives . . .

Sensing that similarity, I asked Than Geoff about what he saw to be the difference between Christian prayer and the metta practice that he taught. He pointed to intention. Metta, he explained, is not a request for intervention from some external power; instead, it sets the intention to achieve the desired result through one's own efforts: "May I be happy, may I be free from stress and pain . . ." The words of the Sublime Attitudes are not addressed to some all-powerful being, some "higher power"—as atheists like to say. Rather, they establish the mind's intention to realize change through thoughtful inner work, reflection, dedication, study, effort . . .

I don't think you'd find anything to quarrel with here, Harry. As I take the time get to know you better than I did while you were still alive, it's my impression that you had as much trouble as myself believing in that almighty God you had been taught to worship by the religious conventions of your time. Had you come to it in some meaningful way before accepting the Christian faith that was all you could have known, I believe you would have found a gratifying refuge in Buddhism as I have done, and a lot in common between yourself and my friend and spiritual informant Thanissaro Bhikkhu.

Your son,
Peter

7 December 2021
Jason's birthday!

Dear Harry,

Can we talk about pain and suffering? It seems like a good moment, now that we've broached the subject of Buddhism, because the cessation of suffering is central to the Buddha's teachings. Pain is unavoidable, he taught. Every one of us is subject to that fearsome triad, aging, illness, and death. No one escapes. But suffering . . . well, he gave us a path to end it, should we have the commitment and persistence to follow it.

You experienced more than your share of pain, physical, emotional, and spiritual. How to deal with it? Grin and bear it. This was your philosophy, your mantra, repeated more times than I could ever count. We have talked a good deal about the history of that pain, going back as far as I remember, and still further: I am haunted by the memory of an image that appeared in the pages of the local newspaper in Newcastle-on-Tyne. I believe the photo was taken before I was even born, in 1936. You are dressed in your cassock and dog collar and seated, a bit incongruously, at the fretsaw in your workshop. The lighting—a flash bulb, I suspect—leaves you looking tense, gaunt, emaciated. The story's headline reads "Desperate, Hungry, for Want of Two Shillings and Sixpence a Week", referring to the plight of miners and their families in the wake of the Great Depression. Peggy clipped that image with the accompanying story and pasted it with pride in the family album. At times, she would have me sit with her to leaf through the pages of that grand old album, and she always used to joke when we came to that page that it was you, not the miners, who looked desperate and hungry. What I saw was pain. I'm sure you were suffering from physical ailments even then. Perhaps it was your ulcer, and I'm thinking that ulcer was most likely the result of internalizing the suffering of others, your parishioners, whose lives at that time were bleak. Your natural empathy had you suffering along with them, dignifying their deprivation with an element of pathos—pathos in the noble sense, from the Greek word for "suffering."

It seems to me that Christianity sees something noble, essential, and enlightening in suffering, with Christ himself as the exemplar. No one, surely, could fail to notice the striking contrast between traditional representations of Christ and of the Buddha. Aside from those chubby babies—no disrespect!—perched on the lap of his (virgin!) mom, the most familiar image of Christ is the crucifixion. There he is, in every church in Christendom, in paintings, sculptures and stained glass, his face contorted in agony, adorned with a crown of thorns, hands and feet nailed to the cross and blood dripping from the spear wound in his side. Christ died for our sins; we are told—along with the constant reminder that we must continually repent for them ourselves. But then look at the Buddha. He sits there on his lotus leaf, eyes closed in meditation, hands resting gently in his lap. His lips are shaped into a serene, immutable smile that invites us irresistibly to join him. Or else, he's up on his toes, dancing, hands raised in celebration, with a big belly and a contagious laugh!

I ask you, Harry, which is the more appealing of these images?

Or compare the Christian Ten Commandments (okay, Old Testament, but adopted by Christianity) with the Buddha's Eightfold Path. A "commandment" is imperious, authoritarian; a "path" a simple invitation. There's overlap, of course, between the two. "Thou shalt not kill", and so on. But, as I understand it, the Buddha didn't command anyone to do anything, he simply proposed the option of a right way of going about one's life. If observed, he taught, that path would lead the practitioner to happiness *in this life*, through the cessation of suffering. Christ's best offer was happiness in the next life. The Buddha did not require his followers to worship him, nor did he condemn misdeeds as "sin" that required punishment. Instead, he rightly pointed out that ill-considered, selfish, thoughtless actions lead to undesirable consequences, resulting in harm to either the person committing them or to others, or to both. Karma is neither more nor less than the logical and necessary outcome of the things we do.

I wonder what Than Geoff would have to say to you about your pain? If karma was involved, he would surely have attributed it to some unknown cause in a past life, because your actions in your current life were, if not blameless, at least not worthy of so grievous a reward. You devoted your whole life to the service of your fellow human beings. I wonder if you'd agree with the thought I have expressed before, that the pain you experienced in so many various ways throughout your life was the physical manifestation of a persistent inner struggle with faith, the conflict between intellectual skepticism and spiritual yearning that lasted right up to the moment of your death? The Buddhist advice, if I may presume, would be to let go of the attachment to both skepticism and desire, and to settle instead for the not-knowing, or knowing that you cannot and will not know, and for the inner peace that acceptance will allow. As with everything about Buddhism, it's incredibly simple . . . and incredibly hard.

With love, your son,
Peter

8 December 2021

Dear Harry,

There is, too, the not-small matter of the ego—another thing we cling to, another illusory creation of the busy mind. And therefore, another source of suffering.

You had one. Quite a big one. The ego of the performer, the man at the altar with a flock to worship him almost as much as the God he worked to serve. I suggested a while ago that this was something you shared with Ellie's father, Mike. Big egos, both, and a lot invested in them. I say this without disrespect. I'm a Leo. I have my ego too! And, let's face it, you were both inveterate charmers with your egos. People loved you.

The ego is buttressed by a sense of self. It was from an observation of Than Geoff's that I came to understand that I have not one, but a number of these selves: the writer, teacher, husband, lover, father, the little wounded Peter (I'm still carrying him around!) I have not only the selves that I myself invent, but all those selves invented for me by others, the roles they see me play, the ones I somehow feel I need to live up to.

So many Peters, then! And all of them illusions, mental constructs arising from the need to "be somebody." It was a huge relief, Harry, with the help of everything I learned about the dharma, to arrive at the conclusion that I was nobody. Well, it was never a "conclusion" because those selves keep popping up again. No sooner do I think I've seen through one of them, another one appears. Or the same one, reasserting himself just to prove he's still in charge. But nobody is a good place to be when I can find him. I think of that lovely little children's poem by the American poet William Hughes Mearns (I always thought it was A. A. Milne. Wrong!)

> Yesterday, upon the stair
> I met a man who wasn't there!
> He wasn't there again today.
> Oh how I wish he'd go away!

A very Buddhist poem, Harry! I'm at my best when I can think of myself as "nobody," not in the bad, negative sense, but simply in the awareness that none of my selves can survive the test of radical questioning. Who am I? Who am I really? And finally, Who is this Peter?

I am only who I think I am. And my thoughts, as we know, are insubstantial, fleeting, no more than passing clouds in the sky of consciousness.

Oh, I'm not free from all those selves yet, Harry. But I like to think that at least I'm on the road to freedom.

See you when I get there!

> With love,
> "Peter"

9 December 2021

Dear Harry,

I cannot claim to be a Buddhist. I do, though, share your need to believe in something greater and more meaningful than the short-lived entity that, despite what I wrote just yesterday, I persist in thinking of as "myself." I never stop searching for something that allows me to feel that my being here in this life, on this planet, has a more than passing significance. That my life has some meaning, some reason, some purpose. Otherwise, it's all, well . . . kind of pointless, isn't it?

I already told you about my problems with your faith, Christianity. With Buddhism, I'm nearly all the way there but the sticking point is rebirth. I wrote about this, too, in an earlier letter. I have played with the concept of past lives, but the fact remains that I can't quite get my mind around the idea of being reborn countless times until I reach enlightenment and can be spared the necessity of another round. Than Geoff tells me not to worry about such things, to keep my mind focused on what it can know now rather than what it can't. It's enough to deal with real life karma, as it happens in the present moment, by monitoring my actions in this life. Still, I keep thinking that if I am to embrace Buddhism as a religion, there remains that "leap of faith" into what strikes me as purely fanciful, just one more illusion constructed by the mind seeking solace when confronted with the inevitable reality of death. I could just as well choose to believe in the literal existence of fairies, or of angels. Why not? Than Geoff seems perfectly fine with those mischievous devas, up to the impish tricks they like to play at the expense of human beings. They keep showing up in the stories he tells with such obvious delight. But I can't quite manage it.

This is precisely why I find the Buddhist path so much more appealing. I don't have to believe in that kind of magic. It's mostly very practical. Still, to use the terms that occur in the Buddhist texts I read and seems to fit, I'm happy to remain more of a "householder"—a lay follower—than a "monk"! I accept the wisdom of the precepts (note: *not* commandments!) against killing, stealing, lying, harmful sex, the use of intoxicants and follow them as best I can. (I still drink wine, Harry, like yourself. And I enjoy the occasional drop of Scotch or vodka. Aside from that one "trip" I described to you a while ago, I have never been much interested in drugs. It has been many years since I even smoked a joint). But I have not found my way from that respect to the leap of faith that religion would require. I'm hesitant to even call myself a student in the accepted Buddhist sense. Than Geoff is a teacher I respect enormously, and I have learned more from him than I can possibly say. But the true Buddhist teacher-student relationship—pretty much a requirement, as I understand it, for any serious aspirant to the Buddhist faith—is much different. It's a powerful, years-long bond of obedience and trust.

I catch occasional glimpses of the numinous core of Buddhism at moments when I can watch, as though from some remote part of the universe, as my mind slips irrevocably deeper into the fully rapt, unwavering attention that is meditation at its highest. At such times, I shift effortlessly over into a place where consciousness itself seems to expand infinitely in time and space and I find a few minutes, moments, really, of almost blissful certitude that this strange human attribute, consciousness, may be the one part of our human experience that transcends death. Only then does the concept of the deathless seem real to me.

Am I otherwise a skeptic? Yes. An atheist, a heathen? Yes. Do I mistrust religion? Yes. The history of religions, current as well as past, is hardly one to inspire confidence. They seem to promote hatred and violence in the human heart as much as the love they preach.

If I look at myself in the mirror with total honesty, I must confess that I'm also a bit lazy (see my postscript, Harry). I am disciplined in my meditation, rarely missing my half hour's morning sit, but you might well ask where my practice belongs in my life. I lack the total commitment of those of my friends who devote more time than I to dharma study, discussion, and meditation practice. Many of them make regular pilgrimages to Than Geoff's beautiful Metta monastery in Valley Center, set in an avocado orchard south from here. Some attend festivals and celebrations, other stay on for retreats lasting days or weeks at a time. I admire them enormously for their dedication—and, truthfully, feel a bit guilty that I'm unwilling to make the same commitment. To be the Buddhist I imagine a "real Buddhist" to be, I am too greatly attached to life's ordinary rhythms of marriage, work, rest, and entertainment.

A moderately contented householder, then, I am unwilling to take the time and make the sacrifices needed to embrace the Buddha's teachings as the center of my life. You, too, Harry, were something of a hedonist. Your working life was one of sacrifice and service, but I believe you would not find fault with my choice to keep religious practice within the perspective of life's other contingencies and joys.

Your son,
Peter

PS: You might be tickled to know that my remark about laziness put me in mind of a caustic note I once received, as a teenager, from the great English satirist Evelyn Waugh. Knowing that he was an "old boy" of my public school, Lancing College, I had the cheek to write to him in my capacity as one of the editors of the school literary magazine to ask if he had anything we could publish. On the back of an otherwise blank postcard, the great man declined, informing me that the only thing he'd ever learned at Lancing was a commitment to lifelong laziness. I wrote back, asking, first, if I could assure future editors that he would never collaborate; and, second, if he would give me permission to print the text of the postcard he had sent. He came back at me with an even more caustic note: "Yes to both questions, E.W.")

10 December 2021

Dear Harry,

It started the other morning as I sat in meditation. I could hear our grandson, Luka, stirring in the room behind me and the question popped up: what is the greatest gift I could ever give him? Not money, of course, nor any material thing. Not even a great education. It occurred to me that the greatest gift I could ever give him would be the skill I have learned myself over many years: the skill of meditation. Once you've mastered that—or, well, have begun to master it, since you're always at the start—it applies to everything you undertake in life and improves your chances of success. He's a restless 10-year-old at the moment, though, so that gift will likely have to wait a few years yet . . .

Thinking about this, though, I started wondering what might be the greatest gift I received from you, Harry, father to son. It was not your religion, which I soon abandoned. It was not my more than privileged education—though that was a true gift, one that has stood me in good stead throughout my working and post-working life. It was not even the skill you had with words—a gift that I myself have worked long years to hone. No, I believe the greatest gift you gave me was my conscience.

Not consciousness. That's something I had to learn I needed, something I have learned slowly through the years, the need to be present and to pay attention. No, I do mean conscience, an infallible, sometimes annoying moral compass, that indefinable place in the heart, brain, and mind where I quite simply know without question what is right and what is wrong. It can be a burden, when it turns back on me in the form of a "guilty conscience." Guilt rarely serves me well. More valuable than guilt is recognition, realization, and based on that the intention to do better when I fall short.

Not indistinct from that personal moral compass is the social conscience I also learned from you. Usually without much debate, I know what social justice looks like, and what injustice looks like, too. You took the side of underpaid, underserved workers in the coal mines in the north of England, where I was born. You militated for the improvement of working conditions that compromised their health long before the National Health Service came along. You were the champion of the poor, the sick, the underprivileged. You never questioned what you knew to be right, and never shirked the responsibility to speak out against the wrong.

It is a quality much needed in America today, and much lacking. I look to the politics of this country and find them dominated by the lust for power and the fear of acting forcefully for the public good. I look to business and see the predominant compulsion of the bottom line. I look to religion, for God's sake, where moral issues are subordinated to political advantage. We could use men of your conscience to model what it means to be in service to humanity, not self.

So, I do thank you for that gift, Harry. It's a hard one to honor in the observance in a world that so dishonors it, but I value it, nonetheless. Who knows, I might even find ways to share it with that restless great-grandson, who will need if he is to be worthy of the life you passed on to him through me and through his mom, your granddaughter. I trust that it may be so, or humanity will soon find itself in a sorry state indeed.

Respectfully, your son,
Peter

11 December 2021

Dear Harry,

I know it's something of a cliché—one popularized by no less an authority than The Beatles—but I have concluded that "love is all there is."

Religions preach it; their adherents too often fail to practice it. Christ preached it. Those who most loudly, ardently proclaim themselves to be Christians, particularly in my adopted country, choose intolerance over kindness and understanding for those with different views. "Turn the other cheek" becomes "smash them before they can smash you." It's the same with self-righteously pious people throughout the world—and across religions. The fanaticism of the most zealous followers of the prophet Muhammad allows them to commit atrocities upon those who also worship their Prophet no less than on those of us who seem to represent the Great Satan. The fervid conservative Jews in Israel are committed to the expansion of their plot of land at the cost of the hated Palestinians and are willing to inflame conflict to achieve their goals. Even Buddhists, Harry, are known to resort to deadly violence and warfare, mostly recently in the country that was known as Burma in your day, now Myanmar, where they openly persecute their Muslim compatriots.

Overall, I believe we would all be better off without religions and without God, or gods of any kind. An atheist myself, I don't particularly care whether others believe in their chosen deity, but I do object when they use their beliefs as a reason to cause harm to their fellow human beings, or even murder them. It was you who taught me that God is Love, which seems to be a shared fundamental tenet of every religion on the face of the earth. How tragic, then, that humans so readily convert that purported love into hatred for each other. And how loathsome that religious men use it—along with their superior physical strength—to force women into submission.

Oh, Harry, would that others shared your tolerance, your genuine interest in the beliefs of others, the "ecumenicism" that you reached later in your life. I would be more tempted to believe in the God you worshipped were he not the inspiration for so much intolerance, so much anger, so much violence. I was old enough to understand when you stirred controversy in your Aspley Guise congregation by refusing to depict Germans as the Antichrist from your pulpit. No zealots, surely, these good people concealed their own nationalist hatred under the guise of patriotism—a custom that persists in America today. Our current incarnation of the Christian patriot believes that "God is on his side" in the slaughter of opponents to his faith. With "love" of country goes hatred of the other.

The Buddha, not unlike your Jesus, taught compassion. At the core of Buddhism is the injunction: Do no harm. The metta practice—I mentioned this in an earlier letter, Harry—asks us to start each meditation by sending out thoughts of goodwill into the world, first to ourselves. If we are unable to love ourselves, how then could we love others?—and then in ever-widening circles to all living beings. It's the practice of love, the practice of compassion that opens the door to greater clarity, greater awareness of our predicament as mortal beings, and greater empathy for those who share the condition of our lives with us. The joy of this is that it's not a theory, it's a practice. It's the doing of compassion that makes it real.

I believe you were a man of great compassion, Harry. I believe the only person for whom you found it hard to feel compassion was yourself. I believe that this was the deep inner conflict of your life, the source of all your suffering. And I believe the Buddha could have helped you love yourself more than Jesus ever did. Judgment, particularly self-judgment, succeeds only in creating suffering. You did not need to agonize over doubt, lack of faith, weakness, inadequacy, sin. The exercise of compassion is less about repentance and forgiveness, as I understand it, than about acknowledgment and acceptance.

It's not easy. Luckily, the Buddha also taught us that we have a handy tool that helps us to put compassion into practice. It's called the breath. In twenty-five years of daily sitting quietly and watching myself breathing, Harry, I have come to understand that the breath is the greatest of all human resources. It is possible to dismiss all the familiar judgments of the busy mind, all the aches and pains of the aging body, and all the spontaneously arising emotions—fear and anger, grief and, yes, even joy—and simply breathe in love, and breathe out love, in the belief that this energy alone will make the world a better place.

With love, yes! Your son,

Peter

12 December 2021

Dear Harry,

It's time to stop intruding on your eternal rest with all these letters. Let's agree to end on a positive note, one that looks toward the future. Not for the two of us, of course; your life ended long ago. I do not have far to go myself. No, I wanted to talk to you about your progeny . . . my grandchildren, your great grandchildren. This will be a good note to end on.

You would be proud of them, yes. But more important, you would love them, and your love would radiate back from them to brighten your own inner being, your own consciousness, as it does for me. Some people have the good fortune to live long enough to know their great grandchildren. Not you. So let me introduce you.

There's Hugo, the oldest, who must now be 22 or 23 years old. That's my guess. He's Charlotte's son. You'll remember Charlotte, Flora's daughter, your first grandchild, born just a month or so before my son, Matthew. She was the one who started to call you "Fodder"—a little girl's attempt to get her tongue around "Grandfather." You were recently installed as a Canon of St. Alban's diocese and loved it that you could now be called "Canon Fodder." Ellie and I had a bright orange t-shirt made with the moniker emblazoned on the chest and sent it as a gift. In his teenage years, Hugo nursed ambitions to

be the actor you once wanted to be—a family trait, for sure—
and earned a scholarship to a well-known performing arts
academy. He used the fine diction he acquired to earn a nice
little bit of money on the side doing voice-overs for children's
stories and commercials. I called him the other day and we
had a long video chat on Zoom, thanks to the magic of video
communications. He's just now starting out on post-graduate
studies in the art of animation.

You have four other great-grandchildren, all on my side of
the family. Three of them are already grown adults. Home for
them is in Harpenden, in England, with their dad, my older
son Matthew and his lovely wife Diane. It's hardly more than
a stone's throw from your old parishes in Bedfordshire and
Hertfordsire. So that's nice. I have mentioned a couple of times
before—are you bored with this already?—that your younger
granddaughter, Georgia, is at Caius! It must be obvious by now
that I'm more than chuffed. What a great time you'd have had,
boasting about her to your friends at The Ship!

Joe, Georgia's twin brother, started out at Nottingham
University last year. It's a great campus—Ellie and I visited
there a few years back, when Alice, Joe and Georgia's older
sister, was a student there. Joe is a strapping young man, a
lot taller than his father now and slimming down from some
teenage chubbiness. (I may be doing him and injustice here;
we only caught a glimpse of him every couple of years or so.)
It has been one of our great sorrows that these three now
young people have grown up so far away from us—which
helps me sympathize with how it was for you, with your two
grandsons growing up in distant Iowa. Lucky for you, though,

that you had your granddaughters reasonably close. Anyway, Joe has chosen—surprisingly in this connected, digital, high speed internet world—to study ancient Greek! We are sad that their first year at university for both these young people was dominated by the strictures imposed by the COVID pandemic. No lectures, no social gatherings, none of the activities that broaden your horizons and prepare you, past your school days, for the world at large. The current year, their second, looks a little better, but not by much.

Alice, your oldest granddaughter, finished her degree—in philosophy!—at Nottingham and is now out in the working world. Despite all the problems with Covid, she managed to find a job at a school in Luton, not far from her parents' home in Harpenden. (You used to take us to the dentist there as children! A terrifying experience!) Having started out as an intern—an apprentice, as it were—she has since been hired on for actual job at the same school, teaching children with behavior problems! I don't envy her, but she loves the work, and is lucky to be starting on a career at a time when so many of her peers have a hard time simply finding jobs. She has a boyfriend, William, and we understand that they may have plans to move in together—another fine idea that would have been unthinkable in our day.

So yes, we love our older grandchildren, Ellie and I, even though it has been hard to watch them grow up from so far away. Alice was born in Tokyo when her parents were working there and we went across to Japan to visit when she was just a baby. The twins were born a couple of years later in London, where Matthew and Diane moved when Alice was a toddler.

The whole family has been out to the US a couple of times to visit us here in California, and Matthew's mum in Iowa. But it's a long journey, and expensive, as you might remember. You hated flying. We do love to go back to England to visit them, but the prospect of air travel grows less appealing by the year, and now the pandemic has prevented travel in either direction for the past two years. I'm dying to get back soon to visit all of them—and especially, of course, to see Georgia at Caius!

We're lucky to have at least one of our grandchildren children nearby. Luka, your youngest great-grandson, Sarah's son, is now nearly ten years old, and they live just twenty minutes away. It has been a joy to watch his life unfold from day to day and week to week and year to year. We have been very attentive, very present grandparents for this young imp. A single mother since his earliest days, Sarah has been grateful for our proximity and our ability to help, and we are more than delighted to provide it. Luka is an incredibly smart youngster, as you would expect. His elementary school is five minutes from our house in the Hollywood Hills, and we love to pick him up once, sometimes twice a week and bring him home for a sleepover. Among the many things we love about him is the joyful energy he brings to everything he does—including beating his grandfather at board games! What a blessing to have him in our lives!

How proud you would be of your progeny, Harry, these bright young people who show such promise for creative and productive lives. We leave them, shamefully, with a world in peril and huge problems to be solved. For generations—well, since the Industrial Revolution—we humans have created an ungodly mess of our planet Earth and have still not found ways to live with each other in peace and with mutual respect. It's hardly fair to rely on our children and grandchildren to make a better job of it than we have, but they'll have no other option. The promise of the socialism you embraced has failed to provide an adequate alternative to the old capitalist economic system and—can you believe this, Harry!—the ugly rhetoric of fascism is once again sounding even in America, once hailed as the "beacon of democracy."

Enough of that! Let's end up by wishing them well, Harry, our children, grandchildren, great-grandchildren. May they find the love in their hearts that they will need to see them through.

With love, always,
Peter

December 2021
Sarah's birthday!

Dear Harry,

So, yes, it's time to say goodbye. Strangely, Sarah's birthday, a propitious day.

Before I sign off for the last time, I want you to know how much it has meant to me to be in touch this way. I only wish I had thought about these letters sooner. Before you died! But everything happens, I suppose, in its own good time. I feel I know you better now than I ever did before. It has been good to watch my heart opening surprisingly to receive the love from you that I was never able to feel before. I hope, too, that I've been able to show you some of the love I always had in my heart for you but was never able to share while you were still alive.

I have discovered much in common between us, you and me, not least is the fundamental truth that we are both human, and both mortal. It will not be long before I join you and Peggy and my sister Flora on the journey that your daughter welcomed. If we can expect no better than oblivion, so be it. But I hold out some hope, not that we shall be reunited in the afterlife—that's a leap of faith too far for me—but that, as Flora genuinely believed, the journey would continue in some unknowable but adventurous way.

So, Harry, should I say: Rest in peace, as Christians do? Or should I rather say: Keep looking forward to that next new adventure?

Or what if I simply said: I'm dying to know?

With love,
Peter

APPENDIX

MY DEAR PETER

(Note: I was as surprised as you will
be to hear back from my father!
Well, my father's voice . . .)

From out of time . . .

My dear Peter,

It's my turn to write. This may come as a surprise, but I have been reading your many letters over these past few months—though I have to note that time means nothing to me now!—and paying close attention. That I write to you from "another place" does not mean that I'm unable to respond to everything you have to say. Well, perhaps not everything, because you have said so much, and I have enjoyed the memories that your letters inspired. But some of the big questions, some of the main ideas.

First, then, a big thank you for the letters. I don't like to boast but since you yourself suggest it, I think I can take a little bit of credit for your writing skills. One of the good things—and there were many not so good!—that you learned from me. As I think you Americans say these days, you "tell it like it is"! Or maybe this dates me. I have always had trouble keeping up with your American idioms. But you do tell it all so well. Sometimes, your letters left me feeling a bit weepy. Sometimes, remembering those times, I laughed out loud.

Now to more serious matters. I'm glad that you re-read the many letters I wrote to you over the years and that you came to a kinder view of my role as your father. And I'm glad you noticed how often I doubted myself in that role (and you're right, I did always love to act the part!) It's true that I was not always the father I would have wanted to be.

To my mind, the really big question was the one about sending you away to school when you were still so young. Was that really for your sake, you asked, with your best interests in mind? Well, as you yourself will concede, you did get the very best education a young man could wish for, at least in the academic sense. But you make it clear that it came at a cost to you. You had an excellent brain, by the end of it, but you were cut off from your heart. You had learned to "armor" yourself— your word—for fear of being hurt.

I see this now, Peter. I really do. Your letters are clear about the pain you felt at that early age, being separated from your family. You felt "sent away"—as though you were not wanted. As though you were not loved. And I must confess that I found it hard to make a show of the love I felt for you and Flora. It was not the way I was brought up myself. (And you're right, I think, looking that far back, to suggest that my mother's early death left a mark on me). I think it was the same for Peggy. It was just not in the tradition of our generation. More's the pity, I see now. I admire the ability to love more openly as it was learned by your generation and passed on to your children. Hugs are important. I learned that from you!

Your words now have me examining my own heart, my own motivations. I did honestly believe you'd get a better education at those boarding schools than you would have done at the local schools in Aspley Guise and, later, Bedford. Was there some class consciousness that went into that decision? Yes. I'll admit it. There was a bit of just plain snobbery involved. But also, some history: it's the path I followed as a youngster. It's what I knew best, and trusted.

The other part of that question leaves me more uncomfortable. How much was it selfishness on my part to send you far away from home to go to school? Honestly, my illness was a real consideration. The constant pain was real. (I was tickled by the way you turned my "psychosomatic" diagnosis back on me. You're probably right!) Did I want you gone to spare myself further irritation? I like to think not. Did I want you gone so as to have your mother to myself? Oh, God, I hope not. My reflex response is NO, I'd never do such a thing. But there's a tiny itch in the back of my mind that thinks there might be at least a small element of truth in what you are suggesting.

I'm going to take a break here, Peter. I know there are other important questions to address but they will have to wait. As things stand now, I no longer have the energy of youth. I promise I'll write again when I find the time—as though that were a problem in all eternity! I'll end for the time being with this thought: I may not have showed it in the ways I should have or in ways you would have wanted, but I truly, deeply loved my son. My daughter, too, equally; but I loved my son. I loved you as a child and loved you as you grew up and became a man. I loved you for your doubts (like mine!) and faults (like mine!) and loved you for your struggles. I was immeasurably proud of your successes. I believe you know this now. I wish you had known it from the start. Well, from start to finish.

There's much more to say, but that's enough for now. I'll sign off as I always did—and meant it!

Affectionately,
Your Father

My dear Peter,

Sex! Well, you do seem to be a bit preoccupied by it, if I may say. It crops up rather frequently in your letters, so much so that it reawakens my interest in what I learned all those years ago at university from Sigmund Freud. But I like to think that my interest was more theoretical. You seem unduly interested in my own sex life and I have to say you'd find it rather dull. But more of that later.

First, and most importantly, it continues to pain me horribly that I failed to protect you as a child from that man—I can't bring myself to use his name—who abused your innocence. I should not have allowed myself to be taken in by his friendly invitation and—you're right—the prospect of a weekend away with Peggy was appealing. What you describe in your letter about your experience that weekend is simply appalling. Honestly, so too was my behavior. I do remember that time when I came to your room to talk to you about it afterwards; I should have been able to ask you, gently, to tell me more. I should have given you that hug you so much wanted. I was embarrassed, foolishly, and foolishly I assumed it would embarrass you. Is it too late for a father to ask forgiveness from his son?

It pains me, too, now that I know about it, that your early sexual experiences were so guilt-ridden and confusing. (I'd be happy to take back that St. Swithun's prayer book that

I gave you as a confirmation present, with its endless list of sins!) That you only had other boys with whom to share your first, rather clumsy sexual experiences clarifies your lack of confidence in your early relationships with women. It took you a long time to "grow up" in this regard, and what you describe as your "desire"—that libidinous drive for sex—was the cause of a great deal of hurt to those you loved, and those who loved you. You write a lot about falling in love, but often—I'll be honest—it had nothing to do with love and everything to do with sex.

There are several occasions in your letters when you are curious about myself, and my own experience with sex. You're aware, of course, that your mother and I were brought up in a very different world than the one that you grew up in. We were not encouraged to "experiment" with sex. Rather, the opposite. We were taught that it was something that belonged only in the bedroom, after marriage, between a husband and wife; and it was otherwise not mentioned. You write quite freely about masturbation, as though that were something perfectly normal and natural and in retrospect I don't disagree. Perhaps I'm wiser now. You even want to know if I indulged, which have to say I think is rather rude of you! In our day it was called "self-abuse." We were warned that our wickedness would be betrayed to everyone in the world by the warts on our hands—I remember yours!—and the spots on our face.

You ask too, on several occasions, whether I was ever unfaithful to your mother. Another rude question! The only thing I'm going to say about that is that I was tempted—as I suspect is every man with blood running through his veins.

You mention the Bletchley girls who lived in the Rectory, and who wouldn't be tempted by these vivacious and, well, yes, sexy young women? But I was the parish priest! Even so, I couldn't help myself, I loved to flirt with them, in ways that would be considered horribly inappropriate today. But that was all harmless fun, wasn't it? Or does that attitude date me? Did I hurt anyone with my banter? I'll confess I never stopped to ask.

Anyway, Peter, all in all, I'm glad that things are easier today. The "sexual revolution" in the middle of our century came too late for your mother and me to be much more than puzzled bystanders, but I recognize that it brought about greater freedom for both men and women. In many ways, it's a more enlightened time. But I do still wonder: how much freedom is too much, and how much happiness does it bring? And how much unhappiness results? And hurt? I don't want to get preachy, but you have only to look at your own history, as you yourself have described it, to know that freedom exercised without limits or responsibility can cause great harm—to yourself as well as those you claim to love

I'm beginning to feel a bit like Father William in that Lewis Carroll poem. Remember? "Do you think I can listen all day to such stuff? Be off, or I'll kick you downstairs." No, not really! I continue to enjoy reading what you have to say and will have more to add by way of response in a later letter. We haven't talked about religion yet. Nor the afterlife . . .

With love,
Your father, Harry

My dear Peter,

The afterlife? Rebirth? Such questions! You won't be surprised—but maybe a bit disappointed—to know that I can't help you with this. It can't have escaped your notice that there are secrets that the dead can't share. (And besides, you do realize, don't you, that you're talking to yourself?) Still, we can talk about religion. I've always enjoyed doing that.

I never meant to force anything on you. Of course, we were Christians, Peggy and me. That's how we were brought up. We went to church. We passed on our Christian stories to you and Flora—the birth of Christ, the Crucifixion, and the Resurrection, and so on. You remember particularly those marvelous Peter stories, and I'm especially glad you found the hidden treasure in your name! There was just never any question about Christianity in those days. It was our whole history, our heritage. It's only recently that human beings have had the arrogance and the temerity to cast aside the wisdom of their elders without, it seems, a second thought. We were brought up to be more respectful of the past.

You shared that respect, Peter, to judge by the guilt you felt about your loss of the Christian faith we brought you up with. It's to your credit that you did not cast the heritage aside lightly, thoughtlessly, without emotional and spiritual struggle. I wish only that you had shared those questions with me, rather than fear my disapproval. In your letters, you mention your timidity in sexual matters. Yes. But don't you think it was that same timidity that stood between you and me and the conversations that you say you would have wanted? It's true that I have my part in it too. It's not that I was unaware of your loss of the faith I'd embraced as my life's work; I watched your struggle from afar, weighted down with my own doubts and guilts, and chose not to confront it. It was easier for me, as it was for you, to keep up the pretense, and for that I apologize.

And yes, you are right about my doubts. They plagued me from the earliest days of my awakening to the responsibilities of life. You mention my running off to a monastery for fear of making the commitment to your mother and to the temporal life of marriage, children, and so on. I so much *wanted* to believe in God that I mistook His calling. And there was always some part of my rational mind that insisted it was all a fairy tale, that no such "God" existed, even as I was trying to convince others that He did. It was painful. It was a kind of slow torture that lasted many years. All my life, really. And— yes, again you're right—it showed up in the form of physical, body pain. My ulcers. It was perhaps because of this that I resisted death when it approached. I did not want to die. Did not trust that heaven awaited. I hope for you that you're like your sister—ready, when the time comes. Much easier to slip into death without resistance, secure in the knowledge that it will catch up with you anyway. I think you understand this.

As to sin, I must admit that it always seemed to me much more appealing than abstention! I struggled with that, too. There was some devil in me that sorely longed to be the sinner. That I succeeded (mostly!) in resisting temptation might be more attributed to what you call your timidity than any moral or natural restraint!

Ah, yes, Buddhism. I'm glad you found it. Truly. I know next to nothing about it, nor did I as a minister of Christ, but I'm sure I would have found much in common with your "Than Geoff"—as I did, in Judaism, with Mike. The ecumenism I discovered rather late in my life was really no more than a confirmation of what I had always believed: that the spiritual is an essential part of the human experience, no matter what form it takes. Life would be a very shallow thing without it. I'm sure the meditation that you practice takes you deep into that realm where the petty circumstances of "real life" give way to the vast reaches of the unknown. I choose to call it "God," but I'm not sure there's much difference.

I was much moved to be reminded of that last blessing that you asked for as I lay dying in that hospital bed in Cardigan. I don't remember it myself, of course—I was already too dotty at the time to understand what was going on around me! But I'm glad that you insisted. I do believe in the power of blessing—that one human being with a full, loving heart can pass on that fulness and that love to fellow human beings. It need not even come as a formal laying on of hands—though that was my own preferred way of conferring blessing. It can be passed on silently, by the mere fact of common presence in a sacred moment. You may be reluctant to accept it, but I believe that you too have the qualities you need to give blessing, and I would encourage you to exercise that faculty as frequently as possible as you live through your last years. It is a gift, and one that is not given but earned. If I can offer one last piece of advice it is that you look for it in yourself, and value it.

There I go on again as usual with my meanderings. I must get on with my afterlife! But before I do, I'd like to offer you one last time that blessing that I gave you every Sunday as a child, the one I tried to give you, whether you knew it or not, every single day you honored or struggled with the life I gave you, with your mother, the one you had the wisdom to ask for when I died. Bless you, my son, for who you are, for the man you have become.

> With all the love I have to leave
> you with, your father,
> Harry

www.ingramcontent.com/pod-product-compliance
Lightning Source LLC
Chambersburg PA
CBHW070338090426
42733CB00009B/1222